Psychodynamic Psychotherapy of Children

PSYCHODYNAMIC PSYCHOTHERAPY OF CHILDREN

An Introduction to the Art and the Techniques

Henry P. Coppolillo, M.D.

International Universities Press, Inc.

Madison   Connecticut

Third Printing, 1990

Copyright © 1987, Henry P. Coppolillo

Library of Congress Cataloging-in-Publication Data

Coppolillo, Henry P., 1926-
  Psychodynamic psychotherapy of children.
  Includes bibliographies and index.
  1. Child psychotherapy. I. Title. [DNLM: 1. Psycho-
therapy—in infancy & childhood. WS 350.2 C785p]
RJ504.C626 1987   618.92′8914   86-27537
ISBN 0-8236-4455-3

Manufactured in the United States of America

To
Cathy, Pete, and Rob,
who have always given more than
they have taken and have taught us
the poignant joys of parenthood

Contents

Preface

This book is for child therapists in training and young clinicians who find that they wish to devote at least part of their time to the psychotherapy of children. The care of children is an arduous task. At the end of a day of direct care of children, the therapist often has a stack of necessary phone calls to make to mothers, fathers, guardians, teachers, pediatricians, and others involved in the children's welfare. If he is in a psychiatric institution or general hospital, he will frequently find that people who care for children are at the bottom of the pecking order, no matter how hard they work or how vast their experience or sophistication. More and better care for our children is imperative, but the programs of care for children often are the first to lose their support and the last to regain it.

Why then become a child therapist? For some it will be for the joy of seeing the rapid results that can take place in the successful psychotherapy of a child; for some others it will be the far-reaching effects that a timely intervention can have on a developing organism. For many of us it is the singular poignancy of being graced by the child's trust and commitment. Few human transactions are more rewarding.

I have documented suggestions or clinical percepts with case examples. They have had to be disguised at times for obvious reasons. Whenever possible I have stayed as close to the clinical information as was possible.

I would like here, also, to express some grateful acknowl-
edgments. First, to those who taught me. As I look back I must
recognize the great good fortune at having been in the presence
of giants. Roy Grinker was one of these who never failed to
demonstrate to those of us attempting to learn from him that
we could seek and defend truths without *ad hominem* arguments.
Marc Hollander was another to whom I am indebted for demonstrating the joy to be found in cherishing the contributions
of those he taught. R. Hugh Dickinson, one of the first teachers
I had in psychiatry, demonstrated in every encounter how irreplaceable elegance and profundity are in our field.

Raymond W. Waggoner Sr., while Chairman of the Department of Psychiatry at the University of Michigan, once kept
me waiting for about 45 minutes to go over some budget information that we were to present to the dean of the medical
school. Knowing that this presentation was important to him,
I was perplexed when his door opened and he walked out with
a man dressed in the clothes of a derelict or a vagabond. In
apologizing to me he said that the man had been released from
the state hospital that morning and finding himself perplexed
had wandered over to the psychiatry department and asked to
speak to the head man. Dr. Waggoner not only saw him as
quickly as he could, but spent an hour being of help to him.
When I suggested that we could have had any one of fifty
people on our staff see him, Ray answered, "But he asked for
me." To Ray Waggoner there was no human being too humble
to deserve a full measure of attention. He taught this by living
it and I still feel indebted to him for the lesson.

I am grateful to those who taught me what psychotherapy
could offer a child. Included among them are Jean Spurlock,
Harold Balikov, Helen Beiser, James Anthony, John Kenward,
and Bruno Bettelheim, who found ways to confirm psychodynamic principles in every phase of the human condition.
These and others taught not only principles, they taught a way
of life.

Finally, I would thank Dane Prugh and Lou Sander as friends and colleagues whose encouragement and respect banished faltering and discouragement.

Rosemary Heiser, Pat Riddle, and Jan Bertsch were lifesavers in preparing the manuscript and living through periods of obsessive compulsive changes. Irwin Berry was a tireless helper in tracking down literature. To all a thank you and my most heartfelt affection.

Denver, Colorado

Part I

Psychodynamic Psychotherapy: Some Preliminary Considerations

CHAPTER 1

Psychotherapy: An Art and a Discipline

In the preface to *The Nigger of the Narcissus* Joseph Conrad wrote "Art itself may be defined as a single-minded attempt to render the highest kind of justice to the visible universe . . . by bringing to light the truth, manifold and one, underlying its every aspect. . . . The artist, then, like the thinker or the scientist, seeks the truth and makes his appeal" (p. 11). Psychotherapy is an art, and in his single-minded attempt to bring to light the universe as perceived by the child, the practitioner of this art must work with the discipline that all art requires. Discipline is necessary if we are to describe what psychotherapy can and cannot accomplish in a way that will permit patients to avail themselves of our services or to look elsewhere for relief from their pain. Discipline is necessary if we are to document and reproduce techniques that are effective, and if we are to teach our art to those who wish to learn it.

Despite the fact that few would argue against these statements, a condition exists today that erodes a disciplined approach to our art. A shortage of adequately trained child therapists, coupled with increased awareness of children's psychological needs have made public demand for psychological care for children compelling. Virtually every estimate indicates

3

that there are about 10 million children in the United States that require psychotherapeutic care. All know that there are not nearly enough child therapists to do the job. We should insist that our centers provide high quality programs for training students of child psychotherapy. We should continue to remind our society that there are inadequate numbers of trained people to serve our children's psychotherapeutic needs, and that the distribution of these few across the country leaves many children with no psychiatric care at all. The Summary Report of the Graduate Medical Education National Advisory Committee (1980) indicated that these conditions need to be alleviated if we are to continue to develop discipline and rigor in our field and predicate the practice of our art on this discipline rather than on expediency or despair. I hope that this work will contribute in some measure to these ends.

SCIENTIFIC SOURCES OF DATA

Even as we acknowledge our indebtedness to art and the humanities in developing the techniques of psychotherapy, we must turn to science for knowledge and certainty. Neuroanatomical and neurophysiologic studies are disclosing new relationships between structure and function, and the direction of causality from the cell to behavior or emotion, *and vice versa*. Biogenetics is helping to define vulnerable populations and boundaries of behavior within which variations occur. Psychological and educational testing are establishing patterns of competence and vulnerability in fundamental functions such as perception and motor activity, and sociology contributes rich data on family and cultural aspects of adaptation.

We, who are interested in children, will be in a central position in the next few decades to help integrate findings from these various fields in our continuing quest for knowledge in development, pathology, and therapeutics. It would be unfortunate if we assumed the position of passive recipients rather than active contributors to this integrative effort. It should be remembered that most of the descriptions of psychopathological entities and psychosexual development have come from clinical endeavors. Clinicians observed, sought patterns and generalizations, and reported their findings. In this way naturalistic observation in the psychiatric clinic took its place with observations made in anatomy, ethology, phylogenesis and other disciplines in contributing to science. As child therapists we will have many contributions to offer in the future.

In his daily work with patients, the clinician is in the position of the explorer who has seen an animal or plant for which there is no recorded description. The explorer would determine on the spot if the animal were dangerous or vulnerable, take appropriate measures to protect himself or the animal from harm, and then describe the animal as accurately as his observations and talents would permit. The work in taxonomy and comparative anatomy would come later.

In clinical work, as a condition or psychological trait of the patient emerges, the clinician's first consideration is of course for the welfare of his patient. If we are actively to help the field of psychodynamic child therapy to grow in depth and competence, we must then be willing to impose discipline on our observations and descriptions to communicate them to students in our own and other fields. In the privacy of the therapist's office, child and therapist may discover something as wondrous as the explorer saw in his travels. When the discovery is reported there may or may not be methods available to study it under experimental conditions. If methods exist for further study, so much the better, but if they do not, it benefits no one if the finding is not reported. I would urge young therapists to scrutinize clinical experiences carefully, and to use both content and process as a source of data. When there is no possible harm to the patient, and when indicated by the nature of the data, these should be reported in a continuing effort to understand children, their problems, and their treatment.

Much of what I will offer in this book comes from my clinical experiences and that of colleagues. Some of the concepts form a body of already accepted scientific knowledge, many do not. Some techniques and concepts we utilize may one day be proven

to be of value by the scientific method, while for others, experimental validation may never be available. Here, I would
only ask the reader to serve both art and science by participating
in the evolution of our field via active scrutiny of the therapeutic
process.

PROBLEMS AND PITFALLS IN TEACHING AND
LEARNING PSYCHOTHERAPY

Although it would be desirable to have a fairly standardized
program to teach psychotherapy, and one that could be demonstrated to be the most effective for most of the students of
the field, we have not yet been able to devise this kind of program. Cognitive and emotional differences among students
dictate the pace at which they will develop as therapists. This,
as in all other endeavors that require development of individual
skills and styles makes a standardized approach impossible. In
addition, the psychological approaches to the treatment of children have qualities of their own which make them difficult to
teach. Below, I list but a few of these difficulties.

1. Psychoanalysis can be considered one of the basic sciences of psychodynamic psychotherapy. As such, as well as in
its own right, it is more accurate as a tool for understanding
past behavior than it is for predicting future behavior (Horton
and Coppolillo, 1972). In this it is similar to the study of history
and phylogenesis. We are, therefore, often unable to predict
what will happen in the course of a patient's treatment when
we supervise a student therapist. This sometimes leaves the
student to tolerate uncertainties that can cause considerable
discomfort, and the supervisor is left to offer only the suggestion that the student "be creative." In this sense teaching psychotherapy is comparable to teaching someone to play chess.
The moves of each of the pieces can be taught, some basic
strategies can be described, and even some abstractions such as
pace, timing, and dominance of space can be raised; but beyond
this, little more than practice can be recommended. Even an
accomplished chess master could not tell a pupil what the forty-

fifth move of a chess game should be. The best that can be done is to go over the game to see which moves were productive and which were not, and why.

This unpredictability makes it nearly impossible to anticipate how the pathology will unfold during the therapeutic process. In fact, if we are to be quite candid, we frequently cannot tell from the information available at the beginning of treatment which patient's psychopathology will respond favorably to intervention and which will not. In cases that do not improve, the student is sometimes left not knowing if the patient could not heal or if his own skills were wanting.

2. The student's stay in a training institution is determined by factors that most often have little to do with the clinical process. As a result, children are frequently transferred from one therapist to another. In many cases, the second therapist spends much time treating the child's resentment at being abandoned by his first therapist after having invested trust, confidence, and affection in him. The second therapist may never be able to deal with the resentment completely and be deprived of the opportunity to deal with "natural" conflict successfully.

3. Psychotherapy appropriately takes place behind closed doors. For supervision of the therapy to be effective, the therapist must be able to bring a fairly accurate description of what went on between him and the chld to the supervisor. This is not a small burden: Some trainees become so obsessed with bringing an accurate account to their supervisor that they become reporters rather than therapists. The process of supervision thus becomes a distraction to the process of therapy.

The utilization of one-way mirrors and closed circuit televison has alleviated this problem somewhat, but has not dispelled it entirely. There are still problems that arise in scheduling the child and the supervisor at the same time, and in busy training centers the mirror room and the television equipment are not always conveniently available. Also, some trainees find that the one-way mirror and the television camera are a persistent, uncomfortable, and unwelcome intrusion. Thus, the gains that may be made by having a first-hand view of the material for supervision are lost to the trainee's discomfort and reduced spontaneity.

4. Although the student therapist and patient are traditionally alone in the room during psychotherapy sessions, it is not unusual for the supervisor to be brought into the session in the mind of the therapist. I was not too surprised when, in the course of a supervised analysis, my analysand dreamed of my supervisor directing me. He knew at the beginning of his treatment that I was an analytic candidate and would be supervised. I *was* surprised, however, when his associations revealed that he knew the day that I was supervised. He further revealed that during the sessions that immediately followed my supervisory hours there were changes in my demeanor and communications. This intrusion on the therapist's spontaneity and individuality is subtle and almost impossible to reduce to zero. Children may be less articulate than my analysand in referring to these intrusions, but my clinical and supervisory experiences suggest that they are no less sensitive to them. The obstacle to learning psychotherapy is that the student therapist may not be truly spontaneous until after supervision is finished, and unproductive habits may not show themselves for discussion and remediation. Other external pressures that may alter the therapist's spontaneity and sense of self will be raised in subsequent sections.

THE PLACE OF A BOOK IN LEARNING PSYCHOTHERAPY

Cushing (1925) quotes W. S. Thayer's article, "Osler the Teacher" (1919) in which the admonitions, aphorisms, and recommendations William Osler made, while conducting rounds, are summarized. "Observe, record, tabulate, communicate. Use your five senses. The art of the practice of medicine is to be learned only by experience; it's not an inheritance; it cannot be revealed. Learn to see, learn to hear, learn to feel, learn to smell and know that by practice alone you cannot become expert. Medicine is learned at the bedside and not in the classroom. Let not your conceptions of the manifestations of disease come from words heard in the lecture room or read from the book. See and then reason and compare and control. But see first" (Vol. I, p. 440). These words, written about learning the art of general medicine are applicable to learning the art of psychotherapy. It cannot be learned from a book or from didactic lectures. It must be learned "on the job" with guidance from a mentor who has mastered the art. Clinical practice and supervision are critical ingredients in learning the art of psychotherapy.

While a book cannot teach psychotherapy, it has a useful place in the process in that it can outline for the student areas that need to be explored. It can stimulate the student to ask questions of himself and the supervisor, and it can provide frames of reference in which answers to these questions can be sought. The book can also attempt to collect the experiences and errors of those who preceded the student and alert him to the pitfalls that lie ahead.

SOME GENERAL THOUGHTS ON SUPERVISION

Each supervisor and student embarks on an endeavor that will be unique. The child who is being treated, the setting in which treatment occurs, the level of experience of the therapist, and the experiences of the supervisor all ensure that no two endeavors will be alike. It is impossible, therefore, to anticipate and describe what each supervisor–student relationship will be. There are some principles, however, that may make the supervisory situation more profitable for both student and teacher.

The supervisor must bring to the sessions experiences gained by having treated children and a well-conceptualized and describable frame of reference. The frame of reference must be shared with the student so that words and concepts are being used by both persons in the system in approximately the same way. The supervisor must also bring sufficient knowledge about himself to permit him to recognize when he becomes competitive, envious, or angry at the student.

In his turn, the student must be able to bring into the supervisory situation a commitment to describe the transactions with his child patient as honestly and accurately as he can. He should strive to perceive and describe internal reactions to these transactions and be prepared to tolerate uncertainty, embarrassment, and painful self-revelation when it is necessary. The student must be ready to be surprised, and may have to welcome new insights that turn previously held convictions topsy-turvy in the course of learning his skills. The student therapist must not inhibit spontaneous behavior toward the patient for *fear* of having to report it in supervision. If a wish or an impulse occurs in the therapist during treatment, exploration with the supervisor may be of immense value to both patient and therapist, whether or not that wish or impulse is carried into action.

In order to facilitate this effort, the student may wish to recall that no one treats children psychologically without making mistakes. Each of the two lives in the treatment room is filled with complexity. Put them together to undertake a task as difficult as psychotherapy and the complexity becomes enormous. Fortunately, these errors are very seldom so serious that the child's welfare or even the treatment process is compromised, and even more fortunately, most children are very tolerant when it comes to the errors of adults. Children can forgive both their doctors and their parents for almost anything except indifference and exploitation. For this reason I would urge young therapists to avoid becoming so fearful of error that they become guarded, constricted, and unspontaneous. While no one who teaches psychotherapy would advocate a willy-nilly approach to therapy in which discipline totally disappears, I know of no competent, experienced supervisor who condemns or derides a therapist because of error. In addition, careful, candid exploration of that which caused the student to err may reveal important transferences or character styles of the patient and countertransferences of the therapist that may have otherwise passed unnoticed.

THE THEORETICAL AND THE PRACTICAL: TWO QUALITIES OF THIS BOOK

In some sections, the topics addressed in this book are abstract and theoretical, in other places they are strictly practical. Not only is this the way that I have experienced the psychotherapeutic process, it is also the only way that I believe dynamic psychotherapy can be approached. Once treatment has begun, nothing about the therapist or patient and no transaction between therapist, child, or anyone who has contact with the child can be considered "outside of the therapy." Anything from the rug on the floor to the books in the shelf can become the object by which the child expresses aspects of his inner world. Anything in the office, or communicated purposely or inadvertently by the therapist, can be interpreted by the child to be an expression of the therapist's attitudes toward him or his world. Thus, what appears to be commonplace may become quite important in the course of treatment.

One of the basic premises of this book is the assumption that one of the most objective statements that can be made about human beings is that they are endowed with subjective states and subjective convictions. Some of these states and convictions are readily evocable and available to the conscious scrutiny of the possessor, and some are not. Horton and Coppolillo (1972) summarized how both those that are available to consciousness and those that are not can be causal agents in the determination of behavior, judgment, mood, or affect. This is the essential frame of reference of psychoanalysis and the one that will be largely utilized in conceptualizing personality development, pathology, and treatment. Old arguments and concerns about "purists and nonpurists," often raised when contemplating psychoanalysis, seem to me to be fruitless in a setting that concerns itself with the *general* psychological treatment of any or all children. Some children need to be fed; some to be protected; some need to be educated, while others need to be detoxified of the substances or beliefs that they have introduced into their biological and psychological self. In order to achieve this, child therapists need to avail themselves of any safe method that the therapeutic armamentarium makes available. The child's needs and not our theoretical frame of reference should determine what is proferred therapeutically.

In addition, it must be equally obvious to any seasoned practitioner that a "pure" form of any kind of therapy is an ideal construct rather than a practical reality. I do not believe that a behaviorist would maintain that a program of behavior modification is not influenced by his relationship to his patient; the most sophisticated psychopharmacologist would not insist that relationships do not affect therapeutic modifications; and the most gifted educator could not conceive of teaching without recognizing that he affects the motivation of his pupils. By the same token, it is impossible to conceive that in the most classically conducted psychoanalysis imaginable the patient's behavior is not *modified* by the therapist's conscious or unconscious attitudes and behaviors.

Unfortunately, this acknowledgment by many that no therapy can be "pure" has led some to feel that all discipline in this art is an unnecessary encumbrance. I cannot agree with this posture. While acknowledging the monumental complexity of human interactions, and the need for creativity and flexibility in those who would treat the human mind, if our art is to become more effective the therapist must be insatiably curious about the elements which have occasioned healing. This curiosity cannot be gratified unless there is disciplined scrutiny of what is occurring between the two partners in the psychotherapeutic endeavor. Meeting the needs of our young patients is our unalterable responsibility (please note that the word here is *needs*; we do not always meet their "wishes"), and we are obliged to use every safe therapeutic measure available in order to do so. But in order to meet our responsibility to those children who will need us later, to our students, and to our art, we must be able to study what we do, and, whenever possible, scrutinize its effects. To quote the title of a book that every young therapist should read, written by a distinguished educator and teacher, Bruno Bettelheim (1950), "Love is not enough."

CHAPTER 2

The Theory and Practice of Psychodynamics: Contributions and Content

We are living in an era of dazzling technological advances. Renal dialysis, computerized axial tomography, proton emitting tomography, and intrauterine surgical procedures are but a few of the testimonials that could be invoked in declaring this to be an era of technological revolution. The neurosciences have kept pace with this volcanic eruption of information, concepts, techniques, and questions as neurochemists, physiologists, and pharmacologists have established listening posts in the neurosynaptic cleft, and have made us all familiar with the intricacies of the biology of behavior. As a direct result of these explorations, our therapeutic and preventative skills have increased dramatically, and in many areas where there was largely the oppression of despair, there is now the sparkling exuberance of inquiry and hope. This era, when physiologic research promises more than ever before, also provides us, as psychotherapists with an excellent atmosphere in which to review the theory and practice of dynamic psychotherapy.

Knowledge and practice regarding health and disease cannot be considered outside of the context of the human conditions in which they exist. Moreover, the *subjective* convictions prevalent in a human era will contribute to the determination of what *objective* discoveries will be made in that era, how they will be received, and how they will be used. Consider, for example, that knowledge about the effects of deadly nightshade predated recorded medical history. Humanity's attitude about the plant's relationship to the world in which they lived and their knowledge of it can be detected in the names given and the uses made of this extract. When passive acceptance of the laws of nature prevailed as it did in the Middle Ages, this extract was called atropine after the last and most deadly of the three Fates of Greek and Roman mythology. (Clotho spun, Lachesis measured, and *Atropos* cut the thread of life.) Later, when humanity's renewed hunger for knowledge was proclaimed during the Renaissance, its desire to put this knowledge to work for it, the ladies of Venice no longer feared and avoided atropine. They experimented with it, and found just the right dosage that would bring a comely flush to their patrician faces and by dilating their pupils, an enticing profundity to their eyes. Lethal atropine became useful belladonna (beautiful woman).

It is dynamic psychology that contemplates in its frame of reference the subjective states of human beings in any given era and culture, as these states are determined by conscious and unconscious factors, and our era is no exception. That which we seek to discover, the way we will use our discoveries, and the effect the discoveries will have on our perception of our place in the universe will be understood best when accompanied by an understanding of the dynamics of our own psyche.

Understanding and acknowledging our subjective states has not come to us easily, nor do we live with this understanding comfortably. It is almost as if we fear that the very study of subjectivity is fated to be a subjective exercise. An example of this reluctance can be found in recalling that it was not until the early 15th century that the Florentine architect, Brunelleschi, described the mathematical laws of perspective which were then applied to painting by Masaccio around 1425 A.D. (*Encyclopedia Brittanica Micropedia*, 1974). Despite the fact that humanity had long sought to represent its impressions of the universe, it took until the Renaissance to formalize the study of representing objects as they seem to be (subjectively) in addition to representing them as they are known to be (objectively). This discomfort with acknowledging the omnipresent subjective states of human beings, and engaging them as objects of study, coupled with a fascination for the astounding advances made in understanding our physical world, is exerting pressure on many in the field of human services to turn their gaze *exclusively* toward that which is perceived as *objective* and *real* in the physical world. If this trend becomes widespread and continues, the nineteenth century Comtian (1966) principle of physicalism would return to the health care scene dressed in the dazzling new trappings of recent discoveries. This would be an unfortunate step backward in that it would reintroduce reductionist images of the human condition to the field.

There is much that we who are involved in the study of dynamic psychology can offer as partners to our colleagues in the physical fields of health care to counterbalance this trend. Some important issues in which we can be involved follow.

1. Adequate physical functioning of all systems is not by itelf sufficient to produce a sense of wellness in human beings. In order to feel well, a person must perceive himself as being well, and this requires that the sensor of health, the mind, be prepared to perceive health. Chronic anxiety, depression, and other unrecognized subjective states of the patient erode this capacity to perceive his own sense of well-being. When this happens, all of our technical competencies are as nothing in relieving the vague sense of illness that makes its inevitable appearance when a sense of wellness disappears. Active inquiry about a patient's subjective states and active participation of the patient in the inquiry is necessary to uncover the absence of the ability to perceive and enjoy health.

2. It is not in the physician's office or in the hospital that health is enjoyed or illness suffered; most widely, it is in the world of human relationships and human values that these states are experienced. Often it is not the physical pain or fear of the illness that causes the greatest distress to the patient. It

is too often the illness' interference with human relatedness and
the alteration of the patient's values that cause widespread anguish. In our field, by attending to these variables we can help
our colleagues make a chronic condition less destructive and
healing more complete. Our interest in dynamic psychology
puts us in an optimal position to stand as a bridge between the
science on which the physician bases his treatments, and to
which he may retreat when the patient's pain is too great for
the physician to tolerate, and the humanism which permits the
patient's reentry into the world of relationships. In so doing we
can often demonstrate to our colleagues that the *person* of the
physician is the most predictably potent therapeutic tool in his
armamentarium.

3. There is increasing evidence that not only do events at
the cellular and organ level influence psychological states, but
that primary psychological events, according to Miller, Galanter, and Pribram (1960), can influence cells and organs. We are
obliged to demonstrate to our medical colleagues whenever we
can that the patient's psychological condition may participate
in determining the success or failure of a therapeutic regimen.

4. With increasing frequency we find our colleagues in
pediatrics resorting to medication to control children's behavior
or misbehavior. In too many instances this is done without adequate effort being invested in discovering the meanings or
causes of the undesirable behavior. Also, the fact that controlling behavior may not change the child's vulnerability to im-
pulsivity or anger, or alter the environmental conditions which
stimulate the bad behavior, is ignored. In working with pediatricians, we can render an important service when we demonstrate that to truly help the child we must, whenever possible,
make it possible for the child to regulate his behavior from
within. Regulation from an external source in the form of an
adult standing over the child, or in the form of a pill, in many
cases simply serves to cover the symptoms. With methods that
are in the purview of dynamic psychology we can show what
the causes of the unproductive behaviors are, as well as the
manner in which mastery and regulation can once more be
made available to the child.

5. There is one final issue that we can share with our colleagues in putting forth the dynamic point of view. In order to describe it, I would ask the reader to join me in an unlikely fantasy. Let us imagine that we awakened tomorrow to find that all of the genetic, biochemical, and anatomical conditions responsible for affects, mentation, and behavior had been discovered. Furthermore, interventions that could alter and regulate these physical variables had become available. Would we then be authorized to say that dynamic psychology was no longer necessary? I think not, because there would be important questions left to answer that would require knowledge of human psychodynamics. Who would be authorized to use physical or pharmacological interventions? How would these interventions be used? When would it be determined that an attitude or action had moved from being creative to being eccentric, and when would eccentricity be called madness? Would those who were deemed mad have a choice as to whether or not they would be treated with these new techniques? How would this new knowledge change our relationships to our fellow human beings and to our universe? The ability to ask and to answer these questions depends in part on our ability to understand the dynamic forces that operate in human psychological states. Meager as it may be, we cannot surrender the understanding that we have achieved. If we were to do so, we would pay too dear a price for the advances made in knowledge about the physical world.

It must be emphasized again that what our technology has given us is of immense value. It must be understood, cherished, and utilized in the care of suffering human beings whenever it is appropriate to do so. But we must not permit our technologies to lead us to treat our patients without considerations of respect for human dignity and self-determination. We must be ready to recognize that by insisting on keeping dynamic considerations in the forefront when we seek to serve human beings, we introduce issues of great complexity. To those who object to this complexity, I would offer a quote from the eminent philosopher of science, Abraham Kaplan (1968), who, in defending psychoanalysis against the accusation of being "muddle-headed" said that to trade muddle-headedness for simple mindedness is a "worthless exchange."

CHAPTER 3

The Psychotherapeutic Environment: Its Physical Setting and Psychological Atmosphere

Psychotherapy with a child must be conducted in a safe and relatively comfortable environment. Its safety, comfort, and privacy spell predictability to the child, and, as the therapist prepares this setting for clinical work, it will become apparent to him that the environment has meaning for others too. The size of the office and its location in the institution may convey his position in the pecking order. Its location in town may proclaim not only the commitment to certain populations, but also the school of professional thought to which the therapist subscribes. The manner in which the office is furnished or decorated communicates taste in furniture and values in art. Even the number and subject matter of the books that are kept in the office may be the therapist's expression of the image that he carries with him into therapy. This is as it should be since these are the expressions of the therapist's human qualities, and these qualities are the very tools with which he engages his patients. The room in which the therapist works is not then, simply a physical plant in which an operation is conducted that could be carried out anywhere. The office of the therapist serves a function, has meaning for the child and therapist, and consciously or inadvertently conveys messages to those who enter it. In this chapter some of the issues regarding the physical qualities and the psychological atmosphere of the psychotherapeutic environment will be addressed.

The principle functions that a psychotherapy room serves are those of providing comfort, privacy, and containment. The issue of comfort will be touched on later in the section on furniture. The issue of providing privacy for a child and his family is an obvious one. Less obvious is the fact that the privacy of the office serves the therapist as much as the child. It is difficult to imagine that any adult could regress with a child in primitive play, be spontaneous, or permit himself to be profoundly moved by a child's communications without the comfort of privacy.

Containment is used here not only in its physical sense of containing objects and people, but also in the psychological sense as Winnicott (1949) has written about it. In this sense, the child comes to know that he can experience and express love and hate, tranquility or rage, longing, revulsion, tenderness, or sexuality in the environment without fear of things getting out of hand, or fear of the social consequences that would almost inevitably accompany these expressions in any other setting. These considerations also sometimes apply to the therapist as well. With these premises in mind, we can pass to a description of some physical and psychological components of the therapeutic environment.

THE PHYSICAL ENVIRONMENT

Although the environment in which psychotherapy is practiced varies widely, I will, in this section, assume that a waiting room and consultation room are the minimum necessities and speak of these as well as give some thought to what surrounds them.

THE WAITING AREA

Preadolescent children do not often come to their appointments alone. This complicates the use of the child therapist's waiting room. It requires that the therapist consider the comfort not only of the parent or adult who brings the child and who must wait until their appointment is finished, but also the amusement and comfort of a sibling who may have had to come along as well. For this reason, and because a child patient may sometimes have to wait unaccompanied, the child therapist's waiting room needs some special thought. Children need to be both safe and entertained there if they and the therapist are to be tranquil.

In the best of all possible situations, a secretary-receptionist who can keep an eye on the child if he must wait alone is invaluable. When it is possible to have this kind of help, all that remains to be done is to equip the waiting room, keeping in mind the children who will use it as well as the adults. Comfortable chairs and magazines for various tastes, and not only those that have been discarded by the therapist, provide for the adult who waits. For the child, a child-sized table with a couple of matching chairs is useful. Coloring books and washable crayons, some children's reading material, and building blocks or construction equipment usually suffice.

A waiting child who is not entertained puts an unfair burden on the waiting adult. Any of us who have tried to keep a small child contained in a confined space for an hour know how trying that can be. In addition, if the child sibling must repeatedly accompany the patient to his hours because no other provision can be made, he will begin to resent the imposition, and his complaints will complicate the therapy.

There is much debate about whether or not a television set in the waiting room is desirable. Many people feel that children spend altogether too many hours in front of a television set already, and they are not willing to foster more eyestrain and withdrawal. I find it difficult to argue with this. There is, however, one useful bonus in a television set or having music playing in the waiting area. When the waiting area is immediately adjacent to an office or offices in which treatment is going on, it is sometimes virtually impossible to make the treatment rooms soundproof. Even softly played music or a television show is very effective in reducing the amount that can be overheard in the waiting room. If this device is employed one is well advised to render the TV receiver or radio tamperproof.

Unfortunately, optimal conditions are not always possible, especially for the young practitioner, and the help of a secretary-receptionist may not be available. When this is the case, I would recommend that the therapist not take for granted that the child will always be attended in the waiting room. A tactful reminder to the responsible adult that the waiting room is unattended and that there may be danger if a small child wanders away may prevent future problems.

Recently, another consideration has emerged regarding public areas. There is now ample evidence that smoking is not only detrimental to the health of those who smoke, but also to others around them. In addition, if the therapist has a general child practice, he will eventually see children who have respiratory ailments ranging all the way from the Pickwickian Syndrome to chronic asthma. As professional health care providers, we can no longer ignore the evidence that smoking constitutes a hazard for children, and smoking in the waiting room should be curtailed. I have often found that the signs used to request "no smoking" are judgmental, preachy, or precious. If there is an area around the office where smoking would not be injurious to the nonsmokers in the vicinity, it is probably tactful to indicate that smoking is permitted in that area *only*.

THE CONSULTING ROOM

The consulting room is the single place where most of our waking hours are spent. For this reason, the major investment for the consulting room should be directed toward comfort rather than esthetics or luxury. It is not difficult to imagine at this point the cynical grins of trainees and junior staff members at some institutions, where space shortages are chronic, who have just been assigned a broom closet for an office. What can one say other than, "We've all been there," and that "This too shall pass." In this section imagine that we are in a position to choose our surroundings and have things as we wish them to be.

The comfort of the therapist should be considered first. This is not only because the therapist is the one who will occupy the room hour after hour, but also because the kind of attention required to remain alert to psychological nuances and cues is easily eroded by physical distractions and discomforts. At least one, and optimally two chairs that are a "fit" for the therapist are a necessity in the office. I suggest two chairs, because in some office arrangements, it is helpful to have a chair away from the desk and near a table where a youngster can draw or engage in some other activity during the sessions.

The consulting room also requires at least another adult chair, bringing the number to three to make it possible to see parents together when indicated. Adams (1982) offers the considerate suggestion that the therapist sit at the same level as the child. This would then require two child-sized chairs, a child-sized table, and three adult chairs in the office. In smaller offices, I have found that three folding chairs that can be put away when not in use can be helpful when one must meet with an entire family or when a case conference is in order. A desk for personal use with a file drawer that can be locked or a separate lockable file are also a necessity. Finally, a cupboard, cabinet, or file cabinet with small file drawers in which a space can be assigned to a child is desirable. If this is impossible, a ✓ shoe box or cigar box that the child knows is his own and will be touched by no one else can be used. Many children will never make use of this personal space, but it is important that it be there.

The arrangement of the furniture will of course be dictated by the room and the therapist's taste. Some therapists have put aside a corner of their office or even a small room next to their main office that is equipped as a playroom. Rather than a rug, there is linoleum on the floor, an easily cleanable surface on the walls, and formica on the tabletop. This arrangement has the advantage of providing a place where both child and therapist can be relaxed and unworried about a messy activity that may soil a rug or the desk or tabletop, and freer expressions of aggression or pleasure in soiling may ensue. The disadvantages are that this sometimes invites messiness, and the child feels betrayed when this is interpreted. This arrangement also conveys the notion that the activities that take place in this area are isolated from the therapeutic process of discussing conflicts which often is seen by the child as taking place in the "businesslike" part of the consulting room. These disadvantages are, however, not insurmountable with a bit of discussion, and if the therapist is cognizant of the possible invitation to resistance that this arrangement may evoke, and can afford the added expense it requires, it may prove a desirable way to go. I personally prefer to treat the child where I treat adults.

As mentioned earlier, a person's office may convey special messages. Among these may be the wish to have the office reflect one's good taste and refinement. This may lead to putting some especially cherished object in the office. I would advise against this. There is always the possibility that a treasured possession can become the target of a child's aggression, or the victim of the inevitable accidents that occur in the course of treatment. Even if no great harm befalls the possession, the tension that accompanies its protection, or the shudder or flinch of alarm that animates the therapist as the little, chocolate-smeared hand approaches the oil painting may be interpreted by the child as revulsion for him and not horror at the act.

Items of equipment that are peculiar to the child therapist's office are toys. It is virtually impossible to discuss toys as equipment without addressing issues of play as a technique. I will return to play in the sections on technique. Here it must be acknowledged that there is a great diversity in the toys and games, which therapists keep in their consulting room. Simmons (1981), in his book on the diagnostic process discusses this issue in some detail. Sandler, Kennedy, and Tyson (1980) quote Anna Freud, who expresses a somewhat different posture in discussing toys. She states, "The special role of the toy as a therapeutic agent has been greatly overvalued" (p. 39). This was placed in the context of the fact that too much time is spent in worrying about the external trappings of the analytic situation instead of attending to the notion that it is the analyst who is the therapeutic agent. Beiser (1979) has written convincingly of her use of boardgames in a therapeutic manner. This diversity in opinion and preference in regarding toys and games leads me to believe that there is much that is a matter of personal style in the issue. I keep a dollhouse, with dolls and furniture, paper and crayons, and a small ambulance and fire truck on a table in my office. When a child wants other toys or to bring toys from home, we discuss it to see how it will help the therapeutic process, and then more often than not procure what is needed. This practice is based on my convinction that the therapist's office, is just that, an office to conduct psychotherapy. It is not expected to be Santa's workshop or the F.A.O. Schwartz store, and toys are for the purpose of offering vehicles for expression to the child, not dazzling or seducing him. Other than this, the preference and the style of the therapist should be the determinants in choosing which toys are useful in the office, and where they are kept.

THE ENVIRONMENT AROUND THE OFFICE

Some considerations regarding the location of the child therapist's office are important to the treatment of children, but are sometimes not anticipated. For example, when children become anxious or feel pressured, they may respond by developing a compelling need to get a drink or go to the bathroom. Recognizing this, it is helpful when possible to have a bathroom and a drinking fountain readily accessible to young patients. The bathroom should have doors that can be locked from the inside, but also opened from the outside when necessary. I have spent the better part of a therapeutic hour trying instruction, persuasion, and even interpretation through a locked bathroom door, and am convinced that there are more productive ways to conduct a session.

Readers who have cared for either their own or other children can recall physical settings that are unremarkable when only adults are present, but can become formidable sources of concern when children are around. This is especially true if the children are impulsive, or if their judgment is impaired. Busy streets, stairwells in which long falls are possible, and unattended elevators may become a source of grave danger to the child. When establishing his place of work, the therapist may be able to anticipate and avoid these dangers. Sometimes this is not possible, and in those instances, even the most experienced colleagues have found it necessary to count not only on limit-setting, but also on the cooperation of some family member or other responsible adult, if there was a chance that the child would bolt from the office and waiting room and possibly charge into a dangerous situation. In the section on technique, we will return to the considerations of doing this with the least possible contamination of the treatment.

A clinical vignette of a four-year-old in treatment in a clinic, serving both adult and child patients, is an example of an environmental situation that became a concern to the therapist.

> Tommy was four years old when the scary thoughts and feelings that kept him from going to sleep at night began to be expressed in his sessions. On a number of occasions he preferred to bolt from the office and run around the clinic rather than stay and discuss his fears. On one occasion he ran down the hall to an adult psychiatrist's office, dashed past an astonished and only moderately quick receptionist, and upon finding himself trapped between the pursuing therapist and the back wall of the waiting room, did that which he thought was the only thing he could do. He opened the door and darted into the consulting room of the adult psychiatrist whose patient was reclining on the couch. Tommy, who had already learned at age four that charm and sympathy could get one out of some tight spots, marched over to the couch, and in a voice that seemed to proclaim that the patients of the world ought to unite against therapeutic injustices, said, "Does your doctor make you lay down to take a nap? My doctor can't make me do that!"

The general psychiatrists in that clinical setting never did quite get around to talking tar and feathers, but there was a good bit of grumbling that passed for lucid discussion about whether or not child and adult psychiatry should be practiced in the same wing of a building. There will inevitably be more noise and sometimes more disruptions in a setting that treats children than in one that sees only minimally or even moderately disturbed adults. The child therapist would save himself later headaches if he would discuss this with his colleagues in the immediate vicinity before he established his office in a particular locale.

Although it is not really a matter of the locale of the therapy rooms, a situation occurs sufficiently frequently in the course of career development of young persons that it deserves a few words of attention here. In many instances young therapists need an office only a few hours a week. Other, established therapists may have times when their office is not in use, and would be willing to let it be used when they are not occupying it. Most of us are aware of how much more concerned we are with the property of others than we are with our own possessions. For this reason there is the possibility that the use of the office of a colleague may cause more problems for the part-time user than it solves. If a therapist finds that there is no other solution than that of using the office of a professional colleague, he would be well advised to choose the patients he sees there very carefully, and to make sure that the office he is using is equipped in a way that accidents and outbursts do not turn into catastrophies. Even then, however, the therapist will find that he does not feel that he is on his own turf, and whenever possible, I would recommend the use of one's own space, even if it is less desirable than the use of space where one is a guest.

The principle that runs through these recommendations regarding the physical makeup of the office and its surroundings is that offices should be designed to buffer and protect the therapist and the patient from externally generated physical and psychological stimulation. While no physical environment can practically reduce these to zero, it should not contribute to extraneous stimulation by creating conditions that become worries for the therapist. If a therapist is concerned that a child's activities will bother his neighbors, or will destroy an original painting in his own office, or ruin the couch of the colleague who is lending him his office, his concern will interfere with his sensitivity to the psychological material being presented to him by the child. Moreover, if the child is passive and compliant, the therapist's tension and worry will further inhibit his communications and activities; if the child is aggressive and destructive, the therapist's worry about a danger to the child or an object may be telling the child what to do by telling him not to do it. The physical environment in this way involves itself as a contaminant in the psychological transaction.

PSYCHOLOGICAL COMPONENTS OF THE THERAPEUTIC ENVIRONMENT

The cultural and personal values and convictions of the people who occupy a therapeutic environment saturate the space as invisibly as the atmosphere. The notion that any person or setting can be value-free and function as a blank screen is illusory. The best we can do, therefore, is to be aware of the psychological sets that rest on these values and convictions, examine whether they promote the therapeutic process or not, and then see if the ones that do not can be compensated for, or if the therapy must take place elsewhere. The worst that we can do is ignore these values and convictions, and when they interfere with treatment find lack of motivation or some other trait in the patient or his family to account for the failure. The values and convictions that will be addressed in this section are different from those that are later examined as countertransferences because their existence is not a direct result of the treatment process, and they do not occasion the tension states of anxiety, anger, or tenderness so often seen in transferences or countertransferences. The psychological states we speak of here are ways of life and adaptations that serve as givens in any encounter with our world. Some reflect our cultural heritage, some are the result of our cultural prejudices, some the result of our personal prejudices, all influence our style and our ability to treat patients. A few of the most significant of these values and convictions will be discussed in the next section.

STAFF AND CO-WORKERS

Although many therapists will practice alone in an individual office, with no secretary or receptionist, many others will spend at least part of their time teaching or treating in an institution that will have staff engaged in various activities. Although the staff may not be engaged in formal individual psychotherapy with patients, the effects of their contacts, for better or worse, cannot be minimized.

Attitudes toward psychiatric patients and their conditions have become more casual and comfortable in the past two decades. It is also true that people working in a psychiatric setting have additional opportunities to disabuse themselves of their private myths about psychiatric conditions. Despite this, when there is an outburst, threat, or crisis in a psychiatric setting, old fears and anxieties return and with them the behaviors that defended against these anxieties, and which had adaptively become a way of life.

Some of our co-workers attempt to manage their discomforts and anxieties by attempting to be "too nice" to the child patient. "Too nice" in this context means behavior that goes byond the courtesy, respect, and even affection that should be extended to every child patient. This attitude is sometimes revealed by the workers oversympathizing with the child about relatively trivial complaints, often in a voice that is so mellifluous and solicitous that the child is amused or embarrassed rather than engaged. I focus on these "positive" or "protective" staff responses because they are all the more insidious since they are supported by the accepted cultural standard that one should be kind to children.

In this context of "sweetness" and concern for the child,

the co-worker may at times reveal too much about the therapist. This often happens when the child experiences negative feelings about the therapist, and seeks an ally in the clinical setting. Often in their wish to comfort or reassure the child, the worker may reveal how kind the therapist is to his own or other children, or how pleasant he is to work with. While, it is true that no therapist can truly be a "blank screen" to his patients, revelation of the therapist's activities, habits, likes or dislikes, or family affairs may impede the therapy by interfering with the development of transferences in the child, which may be the only sources of data regarding certain conflicts.

A co-worker's kindness may also interfere with the clinical process when children regress inappropriately to avoid conflicts in the therapeutic relationship. The child will then try to coerce the therapist into accepting the regressed state, by acting helpless or inept. At certain times it will be appropriate to let this go unchallenged, while at other times it will be important to avoid taking complimentarity to the regression. In the latter instance it is not unusual to see a youngster turn to someone in the environment to provide the support for the regression that has been withheld for therapeutic reasons by the clinician.

Billy was a nine-year-old boy whose early years had been fraught with a number of physical problems as the result of an inherited vulnerability. His guilty, concerned, and attentive parents had in recent years realized that they had played into Billy using his illnesses to be the center of attention, to be waited on, and to avoid caring for himself in situations when it would have been appropriate and reasonable to expect him to do so. The issue of his competence to fend for himself had begun to emerge in therapy. On one occasion, his mother brought him to the clinic, told him that she was going to run an errand and then return to pick him up. She warned him that she might be a few minutes late, and if she were, he was to wait for her in the waiting rom. During his session, he complained bitterly about the possibility of having to wait for his mother. He sought to have special provisions made for the anticipated ordeal of having to wait five or ten minutes in the waiting room. He asked that he be allowed to remain in the therapist's office until his mother came. Failing to win this concession, he demanded that he be provided with a typewriter to do his homework. Again, he was offered the opportunity to examine his overreaction rather than simply indulge it. He responded by becoming more creative in his demands. The therapist remained firm in his conviction that Billy's best interests would be served by examining rather than indulging his wishes. At the end of the hour, he left the office for the waiting room with some handwringing and advice that the therapist give up child psychiatry, and become a drill sergeant in the Marine Corps. When Billy's mother returned to the clinic, she discovered that he had been driven home by one of the receptionists because the "poor little guy was so worried in the waiting room."

Later, in discussions with the receptionist she could candidly admit that she felt that Billy was a helpless, inept child, who really could do very little for himself and that her heart went out to him. She further felt that we demanded too much of him when he came to the clinic. As may be imagined, Billy did not fail to use the receptionist's validation of his helplessness defensively in his next appointment.

One last situation that needs to be reviewed is one that is more frequently encountered in day treatment or inpatient units than in the ambulatory clinic. The overt manifestations of this transaction are a child, who behaves more and more aggressively or offensively, and a worker whose responses are always more "understanding." The escalation of atrocious behavior on the part of the child, and the rigid, unyielding "understanding" on the part of the worker can take place over a period of an hour or a period of weeks. The time is not important, but what is important is that the child seems to be locked into the position of being the "hound of hell," while the worker seems to be as irrevocably committed to being "the hound of heaven." If one can get by the overt behavior and has the opportunity to explore the attitudes and thoughts that the behaviors are expressing, one most often finds the child saying something like "What do I have to do to get you to treat me as an *individual* whose anger and pain is to be taken seriously and not as the object to which a prewritten, therapeutic script is directed?" The worker seems to be responding by saying, "There is *nothing* that you can do that will reach me emotionally. No matter how you behave, I will respond in this stereotyped way." I would find it far more realistic and productive if the worker's behavior reflected an attitude that said, "Johnny, or Mary, knock off the rock throwing or biting or hair pulling or kicking and *then* we'll try to find out why a boy or girl who *can be* as nice as you acts the way you're acting now." It is far more respectful to believe a person capable of behavior that will elicit attraction and affection from others than it is to believe that they are condemned to a life that will elicit only "understanding." Winnicott (1949) addressed this issue in an article that should be read by every child therapist. Given these and other normal attitudes, training for persons who work in a child psychiatrist's office or in a clinical setting that treats children is indicated. In addition, staff member meetings in which continuing problems and well-managed situations are reviewed, can be of great help in maintaining high morale and achieving a unified clinical philosophy.

PSYCHOLOGICAL SETS IN THE THERAPIST

Just as our co-workers do, we therapists come into the clinical situation with a set of values and convictions that have their impact on the clinical process. These need to be explored with as much honesty and candor as we can muster. I will discuss a few of these sets in this section as examples of aspects of our own inner life that we need to review continually if we wish to be effective as therapeutic agents.

We live in a culture in which appearance has tremendous

value. The kind of clothes a man or woman wears not only proclaims to others one's commitment to cleanliness, attractiveness, good taste, creativity, exuberance, and confidence, but they are also a vehicle by which one's financial and social success is communicated to the world. This is fine in most circumstances. However, many have been surprised to find that the little patient does not let these external manifestations of the therapist's traits stand between his desire to express affection or aggression and the therapist. If the child is moved to reach out to touch his confidant and friend in a gesture of tenderness, or if he wants to push his persecutor away from him in a gesture of anger, he will do so whether or not his hands are dirty, and whether or not the therapist is wearing his best suit or her best dress. As was discussed earlier in connection with the painting in the office, the child may not be able to distinguish the therapist's dodging and drawing back to protect his apparel from a gesture of repugnance or counterhostility. Therapists who see even normally active children would be best advised to wear clothes, which they can tolerate having soiled, during therapeutic hours.

There is another "given" in our culture to which we, who come from the medical discipline, perhaps inadvertently, subscribe to more frequently than others. This is the notion that unless we have worked ourselves into a state of exhaustion we have not put in an honest day's work. The simple fact is that people do their best work when they are well rested. This is true in all fields. Our field has a special aspect to it that makes this issue more important. When an emergency occurs that is intense and even frightening, reserve energies are mobilized and the person involved in the helping process can deploy his attention as needed. After the emergency has passed, the fatigue may become profound, but during the emergency the person has mobilized the energy available to meet the requisites of the situation. In the course of routine daily work, these reserves of energy are rarely available to the individual. Add to this the fact that some of our patients have protected themselves from interpersonal strife by unconsciously becoming dull, boring, or tediously passive, and it becomes clear how vulnerable the therapist's creative understanding can be to being dulled during periods of tedium or fatigue. Adequate rest and reasonable working hours are a necessity if the therapist is to offer the patient the alert responsivity required to detect and articulate subtle patterns of unproductive behavior.

While on the subject of the therapist's well-being, it is worth remembering that a number of other wishes and requisites need to be met if the therapist is to perform as competently as possible. Those therapists who work with late adolescents and adults, especially, should have a full and gratifying sexual life if they are to remain immune from being intellectually seduced by accounts of their patient's sexual exploits. Self-respect and self-appreciation must come from within the therapist lest he be tempted to demand that his patients admire him or get well for the sake of his self-esteem. Most difficult of all for the young therapist, of course, is to attain the financial security that immunizes against the temptation to let financial considerations influence clinical decisions in recommending therapy or terminations. In a word, patients should not be exploited for personal gratifications, and the best therapeutic work is done when the therapist has available and is capable of enjoying a rich and full personal life. The psychological set of wishing to be "unselfish" may interfere with a therapist's attending to these considerations. Being rested, comfortable, and satisfied is no more selfish for a therapist than being in good physical condition is selfish for an athlete.

Our society is quick to avow that we love our children. That this love is not reflected in our social priorities and where our health care dollars go is not the point of this section. The issue here is that the love of children is a social value that is strongly supported in our culture. This cultural approbation finds resonance in the fact that most people who enjoy relatively good psychological health can remember the great benefits they received from having been loved. It is not surprising, therefore, to hear people in the field of child care state that they have chosen their field because they love children. On occasion, we even hear that the essential ingredient in the psychotherapy of children is the element of love. I cannot agree with some of these statements. I certainly have no objection to the love, affection, or fondness that grows for the child in the course of working with him to alleviate his suffering. This is one of the bonuses that makes the field appealing to many. But it is just that, a bonus. I object to the blanket statement because there are too many pitfalls that a therapist faces when motivated to treat out of love for a child. For example, a number of children are brought to therapy because they can neither tolerate nor elicit love from those around them. Often these children are not only not lovable, they are downright alienating or repugnant. What of them? Are they to be denied therapy because they are not appealing, or to be denied their individuality by camouflaging them under the general rubric of "children" and therefore being automatically lovable? I doubt that many of us could feel comfortable as therapists with either alternative. Another pitfall is the possibility that persons who wish to treat children because they love them, may be tempted to offer love instead of treatment, or love instead of respect. I would find this dangerous because in cases of true psychological illness love would be an inadequate intervention, and also because our job is not to provide an hour or two of love weekly in our office. Our job is to make it possible for these children to love unambivalently and be loved in return by their parents, their peers, and whoever else surrounds them in their daily lives.

In view of the above, and recognizing how powerful the attraction of a child can be to most adults, I have often recommended that those young therapists, who do not have children of their own, find some activity in which they come into contact with children for whom they have no therapeutic responsibility, and let nature take its course. In this way, I think that the children being treated do not have an exclusive on the therapist's affections, and maternal and paternal impulses become more manageable. Thus, the therapy session is less likely to be unconsciously exploited by the therapist to indulge his wish to love a child. Another possible pitfall of too much unex-

amined love will be explored in the section on countertransference.

Finally, we come to the therapist's cultural convictions and
prejudices. While the social and clinical vignettes chosen to describe them reflect wide cultural differences between the people
involved, the therapist must be aware that even slight differences, such as those that might be present when two people
were raised in different parts of the country, can create friction
in an encounter.

The first vignette is drawn from a fishing trip to northwest
Ontario. Our guide was a very competent and experienced
Chippewa Indian, who despite three days of incessant rain, was
able to keep our spirits and enthusiasm high by sharing with
us his knowledge of geography, flora, and fauna of the mag-
nificent wilderness that surrounded us. On the third day of
drenching rain, he announced that there would be sunshine
tomorrow. Without a moment's pause I assumed that he had
seen the wild rice stalks bend in a certain way, or some other
event in nature that foretold the weather. With a bit of awe, I
asked, "How do you know that, Albert?" He looked up at me,
paused for a moment, and with the slightest hint of a smile said
that he had heard a weather forecast on the radio.

Later, I was able to realize that I had unconsciously con-
structed a cultural profile for Albert filled with misconceptions
that had been made possible by my ignorance of his culture.
What I did not know, I filled in with prejudice. If Albert had
not been Indian, I would have immediately assumed that he
had listened to a weather forecast. Since he was Indian, I attempted to dispel my perplexity about his culture by presup-
positions that had little to do with his realities.

Albert acknowledged that he was sometimes as perplexed
about our culture as we were about his when he told of a husband and wife that he had guided. She was the proud owner
of a new rod and reel. She accidentally lost these overboard,
and Albert told us she burst into tears. That evening when they
returned to camp, her husband lost his footing in stepping out
of the boat and fell into the water. Albert told how she could

not stop laughing. When I learned that his culture's values deemphasized investment in material possessions, I could understand his perplexity. (Do you suppose that Albert was also pulling my leg a bit with this anecdote?)

Another bit of cultural enlightenment was made available when I visited a hospital in Arizona and participated in a clinical conference in which a six-year-old boy from the Apache reservation was being discussed. He had a physical problem which required multiple surgical interventions for its correction. After he had sufficiently recovered from his first operation, he arose from bed and with great determination packed his belongings and proceeded to announce that he was going to return home. His mother dutifully followed him, and to the frustration of the people involved in the boy's care, refused to attempt to coerce him to stay in the hospital. The only reason they were able to get him to return to his room was that there was no transportation available to take him back to the reservation. I was given the opportunity to speak to the boy and his mother, and in the course of listening to the shy, but very candid and devoted mother, I became aware that the notion of forcing children to do something simply did not exist in her mental repertoire. I must admit that I had, at first, felt irritation at the mother's passivity. With a bit of reflection, however, I realized that my frustration had more to do with my ignorance of the Apache culture and the rigidity of my own value system. As I realized this and indicated to the mother that I was willing to listen instead of recommend, she herself suggested a solution. There were several people on the reservation that her son admired, and had chosen as his mentors. She was sure that if any one of them were to be brought to the hospital and were to indicate to the boy that it was a desirable and manly thing to be operated on and cured, he would permit treatment. I later learned that the hospital personnel had made these arrangements and were successful in treating the child.

I hope with these examples to urge aspiring therapists to recognize that human beings cannot be understood only in terms of their impulses, conflicts, defenses, or styles of sublimation. They must also be understood in the context of *their values* and *their perception of the world*. Whether or not they will reveal these or the way in which they reveal these may depend on whether or not the therapist is able to suspend the conviction that his cultural values are the only ones that exist. If they can, most patients are willing to show us the world they see through their eyes. I believe this is what Castaneda was referring to in his book *Journey to Ixtlan* when Don Juan told his pupil, "to forget his personal history" if he wanted to learn to see the world of magic.

If the therapist cannot free himself from being bound to these psychological sets, he runs the risk of having two distorted categories of human activities; those that are congruent with his own cultural values and labeled "normal," and those that are alien and labeled "pathological." Of course, there is health and pathology in the psychology of human beings. But these must be determined in the context of the biology, psychology, and *culture* of the person being evaluated and not according to their congruence to the values of the evaluator.

Katz, Carrathers, and Forrest (1979) and Katz (1981) demonstrate beautifully how cultural values of Saulteauz-Ojibway youngsters, who leave the reservations to work or study in the white world, are sometimes misinterpreted as psychopathology. These misinterpretations can have disastrous social and therapeutic consequences. I cannot subscribe to the suggestion that *only* a woman treat a girl child, or that *only* a black therapist can treat a black child, or that only a Native American treat an Indian child. As Katz pointed out in a recent conference, a black child from Jackson, Mississippi may be more like a white child from Jackson than he is like a black child from Chicago or Philadelphia. An Ojibway girl may be more unlike a Navajo counterpart than she is like a girl from Winnipeg. Most of us subscribe to the view that the therapist must be ready to be taught by his patient, and if he finds that he cannot learn, understand, or respect the cultural values of that patient, he should disqualify himself as the therapist.

CULTURAL BIASES AFFECTING CHILD PSYCHIATRY

There are some psychological sets that are so widespread in our culture that it would be unfair and inaccurate to lay them at our own doorstep or that of our co-workers. I will mention only briefly several of them that are relatively widespread in our culture and describe one of them, the issue of privacy, in more detail. The attitudes and convictions I mention here are ones that I feel are detrimental to the welfare of our children and to their health care.

One of the most dangerous myths of all is the cultural attitude that children do not suffer psychological illness. Their woes are due only to environmental influences or bad habits. They can be moved into a new environment or taught to be healthy. This attitude is often bolstered by the culture's conviction that children "will grow out of" most things that trouble them. Repeated demonstrations that there are *causal* connections between early psychological problems and subsequent maladjustment in adulthood or childhood seem not to weaken these convictions.

Children are thought to be relatively insensitive to many environmental tensions. It is still difficult to convince many that children are hurt by chronic parental strife, parental illnesses, community insensitivity to their unhappiness, or the threat of nuclear war, even though evidence continues to accumulate that they are sensitive and in many instances hurt by these conditions. Our culture persists in seeing children as "less than" rather than "different from" adults, and this conviction that they are less perceptive than adults allows us to be complacent about the world we provide in which they must live.

Finally, I would ask the reader to notice the surprise that occurs if anyone mentions privacy in connection with a preadolescent child. Why should this surprise occur? Would any of us deny that a school-age child could be embarrassed if some of the things that they confide to us or to each other were to become generally known? I think it fair to say that this failure to extend the privilege of privacy to children has more to do with adult insensitivity than being an accurate assessment of what is important to the child. Unfortunately, it appears that this insensitivity has not spared institutions in which the psychotherapy of children takes place or some of our practitioners. I have seen three situations, in which children's privacy is violated, occur frequently enough to warrant inviting attention to them.

1. If one lurks about the waiting room of a clinic long enough, one is sure to hear a therapist refer to an event that happened in the treatment, or make an interpretation to the child, while they are in the waiting room or as they are walking down the hall. Sometimes this happens because the child is dragging his feet about starting the hour or sometimes because he is reluctant to end the engagement with the therapist. Other times it happens when the therapist has been embarrassed or stymied by something the child has said or done, and still other times it happens when the therapist is showing other people in the waiting room or in the hall how smart he is. Whatever the reason, the therapist needs to ask himself if he would have done the same thing if his patient had been an adult. If the answer is no, the therapist needs to do a thorough review of his attitudes toward children.

2. The second instance in which there is danger of revealing too much about the child is when the therapist is engaging parents who are distrustful or ambivalent about the importance of psychotherapy for the child. The temptation may be very great to reveal something that the child may not want to have revealed for the sake of demonstrating the importance of treatment, but it should be avoided.

3. Finally, too much may be revealed in those instances when the therapist is defending himself or the process of psychotherapy against the accusations of a parent. Most frequently this occurs when the parent is complaining that there has been little or no improvement, and the therapist protests this by citing the improvement or disappearance or symptoms or conditions that the child had wanted kept secret. In each of these three situations the privacy of the child was quickly surrendered when the therapist felt some stress.

I believe that parents, teachers, pediatricians, and others who in some way are responsible for the child need to be kept informed about the progress the child is making, when the therapist has the permission of the parents *and the child* to keep them informed. I think that this can be done without compromising the privacy of the child. In addition, the child has a right to know what will be told about him before it is revealed to the caretakers, with the added right to object to a revelation if he sees fit. Therapists would be well advised to take these rights of the child very seriously. It is to be hoped that whatever else happens or does not happen in a therapeutic encounter, the child can come away from it having had reaffirmed for him the idea that respect and dignity are paramount values in the human condition.

Part II

The Evaluation Process

CHAPTER 4

The Father in Development and the Clinical Process: An Overview

While the role of fathers has been described, and has even been a dominant theme in Freud's psychiatric writings such as "The Schreber Case" (1911) and "Little Hans" (1909), until recently it has not received the systematic attention that mother–child interaction has received in contemplating development and psychopathology. This neglect has spilled over into our clinical practice, and even today, it is not rare to read or hear a case report that is splendidly detailed in virtually every aspect except for information about the father or his role in the family.*

Recently, authors have included the father's presence with increasing frequency to produce a more rounded picture of the family system. Other social trends have also served to sharpen our focus on the father's role. For example, according to Newman and Schwam (1979) the statistics that describe the number of children in the United States that are being raised without inhouse fathers is astonishing. There are approximately 30 million families with children under 18 years of age in the United States; there are roughly 63 million children under 18

---

* However, it should be noted that there is an excellent book on the father edited by Stanley Cath (1982).

years of age distributed among these 30 million families. Approximately 4.5 million or 15 percent of these families have a female head of the family. This means that there are about 9 million children who are being raised in a household in which a woman is alone as head of the family (p. 357). The sheer weight of these numbers stimulates our curiosity about children being raised without a father.

Conversely, in the past decade there has been a greater tendency in cases of divorce to consider the father the possible custodial parent. This, too, has focused our attention on the father as single parent, and his role in raising children.

Other social conditions that have influenced this scrutiny have included more women in the marketplace and men in the home, the increase in child kidnappings by estranged parents, and an increase in the number of couples in homosexual liaisons who claimed their right to raise their child or to adopt a child. Thus investigative curiosity, as well as clinical problems brought to our consulting rooms, have placed the figure of the father in greater prominence in considering development and pathology.

In this chapter, I will address some ways that are particularly germane to healthy and pathological development as the father interacts with the mother, his sons, and his daughters. I will use them to make a few suggestions about the interview with the father and close with examples of pathology that involve the father in particular ways.

While attempting to describe the father and his influence as an individual, it must be remembered that he is also an element in a family system. As such the father is influenced by other family members even as he influences them. Any change in one member of the family is accompanied by changes in the whole system. The nature and extent of these changes is further influenced by cultural values and intrapsychic states. Even the most ambitious descriptions of conditions or processes in a family pale before the complexity of the living family and this must be borne in mind while attempting to picture the father and his role.

THE FATHER IN RELATIONSHIP TO THE MOTHER

In successful courtships, each individual maintains and cherishes his or her own set of traits, values, activities, and interests even as they develop a union in which other traits, values, activities, and interests are shared. With time the contribution of one partner to this union cannot be distinguished from the contribution of the other. The image to be conveyed is not that of Bill and his wife or Mary and her husband. The image is of an individual, Bill, and an individual, Mary, *plus* unity composed of contributions from each. In their home, for example, an observer can see an area that clearly expresses the tastes, preferences, and even the activities of Mary. Somewhere else Bill's presence and influence are obvious. In other places in the home the ambience is an expression of both partners. There is no way of knowing whose tastes or ideas are represented by the colors or the furniture or the decor because they come from the merger of both individuals.

In behavior we can see the same phenomenon. Some activities Mary clearly undertakes as a separate individual. Other activities are initiated, undertaken, or guided by Bill. Yet if, for instance, we were to watch the hello or good-bye kiss when one or the other was leaving on a trip or returning from it, it would be impossible to say who initiated the action. One person is not totally absorbed, overshadowed, or dominated by the other. Rather, each, while maintaining a firm and discrete sense of self, voluntarily merges part of this self with another separate human being, producing an entity (the couple) that becomes more than the sum of its parts.

When the decision to have children is reached, it is ideally when biological and psychological unity is achieved. The child then is a *product* of this psychological unity, and there are many of us in the field who can attest to the unhappiness and disappointment that may be found in instances when having a child was in the service of attempting to *produce* this unity rather than a result of it. The achievement of this union, and the child's perception of this achievement is revealed clinically when the child refers to his parents repeatedly as my "Momanddad" as if it were all one word. The breakdown of this integration is evidenced by a number of manifestations, among them the child always referring to "Mom" or "Dad" separately and as if they operated only in separate spheres of influence.

Observations and experiments by a number of investigators indicate that during the latter stages of pregnancy, expectant fathers begin to exhibit traits which have been thought of as motherly in our culture. They become nurturant, comforting, indulgent, and offer their wives a gentleness that may not have been comfortably available to them before. These qualities are proffered to the expectant mother, even as the expectant father begins to forego personal demands and satisfactions. This phenomenon finds popular representation in the oft-depicted scenario in which the pregnant mother awakens at two in the morning with an irresistible yearning for pistachio ice cream or a dill pickle. The expectant father then dutifully makes the trek to the refrigerator, or even the all-night grocery store for the "needed" supplies. Imagine the response to a similar request if the woman were not pregnant. This psychological shift on the father's part enables him to play a role in maintaining the mother's equanimity and emotional homeostasis and thus involves him deeply in the process of the pregnancy.

THE FATHER AND HIS CHILDREN

In some quarters, there is a subtle accepted but seldom examined notion that the father's presence in the family is more important to sons than it is to daughters. Clinical experience indicates that the father is important to both in similar ways, and to each in particular ways. Active exploration of his influence and significance must be investigated if a clinician is to understand both his male and female child patients.

THE FATHER AND HIS SONS

As Mahler, Pine, and Bergman (1975) have described, the father is an invaluable ally to the child during the separation–individuation phase. This is true for both boys and girls as the pull of excitedly conquering the world vies with the comfort and safety of mother's arms and lap. For the boy, however, the presence of the father has an added function. From before the time that he becomes aware that there is an environment in which he will grow and live, that environment has communicated what is culturally acceptable masculinity. Messages like the geometric patterns in primary colors, rather than the floral patterns in pastel shades of the bedroom wallpaper in boys' rooms, the hard metal trucks and trains rather than soft dolls that predominate boys' toy boxes, the mock rough handling accompanied by the pseudobass voice saying, "Oh, oh, big fellow" are manifold and incessant in telling the child that he is a boy. The boy then, long before he has the concept of triadic relationships left him by the resolution of oedipal conflicts, must begin integrating processes of identifications with environmental expectations. In order to live in harmony with the environment, he cannot, like his sister say, "I will tolerate separating from mother, but ease the discomfort of it by becoming just like her and in that way carry her with me always." In this period of separation from the mother, the father offers the boy child opportunities for identifications that will allow him to feel like a boy in the world he is beginning to know, without denying or denigrating the identifications he has already made or that he will make with the beloved traits of his mother.

It is as though the father convinces his son that, despite the fact that he can never bear children or nurture them as his mother has, he need not envy or compete with her, or feel minimized in separating from her because he will one day have traits of his own that will individuate him and that will be cherished by another woman. She, in her turn, will have traits like his mother that she will share with him.

Thus, the father helps the child preserve the identifications he has already made with his mother, and offers him new adaptive identifications with which to live in the world that he is beginning to know. Both functions help the young male achieve the separation necessary in order to venture into this world. By cherishing the traits of the mother with which the boy has already identified, the father participates in immunizing him psychologically against later depression. This depression can occur when identifications which have become part of the self-system become targets of self-denigration and self-hate.

To many, the mental images the boy has of his father during the oedipal phase are imagined as prohibitive, punitive, and threatening. Clinical examination of five- or six-year-old boys would reveal that there are images of the father that are infinitely more benign and at least as important as the threatening and prohibitive ones. To be sure, the examiner finds images that, had they words, would say "You cannot be the center of the universe and have your mother all to yourself because I will not be bested by you. And anyway even if she would, you couldn't because you are still small and incompetent." But other themes that the paternal image conveys seem to say, "You are my son, and this fills me with joy. One day you will be great and strong and competent, and then I will be deferential to you. Your mistakes will not diminish you for you are human and forgivable, and when you are grown, I will depend on you to forgive me my mistakes, for then you will be secure and your love will overshadow the small hurts we have inflicted on each other during these years of your growth." The tolerant and available father spreads the balm of firmness, gentleness, and understanding on the scars of the oedipal conflict and helps to turn fantasy into aspiration and hope of actualization at a later date.

In play, the young often rehearse activities that they will have to undertake in their adult lives. In playing with their sons, fathers often guide these preparatory activities. This can happen whether the play is in the area of athletics, or in hunting and fishing, or in model building. In addition, because the father must be away from his sons for many hours of the day, time is left for the child to practice on his own the skills he has learned from his father. In his self-initiated play or in small assigned tasks, the opportunity for spreading his wings is thus afforded the child. In these transactions, not only are talents developed, but also initiative, which is so necessary to utilize those talents, is supported.

Let us consider one last function of the father, which is useful to both boys and girls in development, but may have more far-reaching effects in preventing erosion of self-esteem for boys. Idealization is a common ingredient when children construct an internal picture of their world and the people in it. "My father is the smartest or the strongest man in the world" is not an uncommon thought for the preschool child. Perhaps as an expression of reluctance to completeley abandon the enchantment of childhood, our culture has maintained an image of masculinity which is a combination of John Wayne, Albert Einstein, O. J. Simpson, and Abraham Lincoln. How can the child possibly aspire to live up to these standards of masculinity as he begins to notice that when he scrapes his knee he cries rather than simply trotting back to the huddle like O. J. would. How remote is manliness when six heavies from the first grade gang up on him, and he runs home rather than institute the sytematic annihilation that John Wayne would have put into action. How unattainable maturity is when he cannot even understand easy mathematics and social studies, let alone spell Einstein or Emancipation Proclamation. The child takes the idealizations literally and concretely, and as he grows, he is left with fewer defenses against his inability to meet what he perceives are the demands of the environment. He feels he must live up to the ideal rather than a more realistic image of masculinity. It is at this time that the father by saying, "Ouch," when hitting his thumb with a hammer, or by conceding that he needs to call the plumber after attempting to change the faucet washer himself, or by allowing his moist eyes to be seen by his son on learning of the death of a family friend, or by assuming that the capital of Kentucky is Louisville, permits his son to experience, somewhat sadly perhaps, that a conceptual distance separates the ideal from that which is real and attainable by most humans. Without ever having to say it, the father can demonstrate that a person need not be perfect to be competent, lovable, and reliable. It is sad when Puff, the Magic Dragon, comes to visit no more. But the compensation is that dreams become attainable, the world's treasures come within reach, and the child begins to see the place he will occupy among men.

THE FATHER AND HIS DAUGHTERS

As with sons, some aspects of the daughter's relationship with her father is unique. After a daughter has mastered the separation–individuation phase with the help of her father, there are times when she must return to the nest to learn from, or to identify with her mother before she again ventures out into the world. There is less overt social pressure on a girl to abandon the safe haven of her mother's care than for a boy. At these times, the father's influence is renewed as a facilitator of separation. Through his activities that are independent of the mother and his continuing pleasure in the relationship to his daughter, he gently invites her to partake of the world at large, wooing her away from the comfort of the regression that was temporarily necessary.

It is largely from her father that the girl child learns that there can be gratifying tenderness without sexual activity or sexual intent. This expectation of tenderness from men, once established firmly, remains with the child into womanhood. Later in life it will be reintegrated with sexual wishes that will give the relationship with her mate a multifaceted and multi-dimensional quality. Tenderness experienced from father is far more effective than finger-shaking admonitions in convincing a young woman that if sexual activity is to have any edifying meaning for her it must be accompanied by loving relatedness.

An important step toward maturity is taken by the young female when she accepts without envy, self-denigration or fear that biology has endowed males with more physical strength than females. A father, working with his daughter to build a doll house or book shelves for her room, may, by holding or lifting a heavy board without shaming her, help her to achieve this aspect of reality acceptance without sacrificing her dignity or self-esteem. Just as the mother, in talking to her son about his birth or his early care, conveys the joy she experienced in nurturing and bearing him and thus minimizes any feelings of envy or helplessness he may have about that which he may never be able to do, so the father expresses joy at putting his strength at the service of his daughter. When biological differences are used to denigrate, they can be destructive. When they are used to individuate and unite, they can be a source of joy. Perhaps even more importantly, it is from the temperate and gentle father that a girl learns to differentiate strength from brutality. Thus, later in life, even as she enjoys her mate's strength, the woman who has had a loving and gentle father would probably never tolerate his brutality.

Unceasing curiosity and innumerable observations allow a daughter to watch her father cherish her mother. Idealization of these observations and optimism then endow the daughter's dream for her own future with promises of bliss and fulfillment. Hers will be an ecstatic marriage and her children the most secure ever to live. We assume that these views of the future are ubiquitous, and we are aggrieved and moved when we are confronted with a woman or a girl who has never entertained them.

Lynn (1974), in his book on fatherhood, quotes a passage from *The Diary of Anaïs Nin* that speaks so eloquently about the void that is left by an absent father that it is reproduced here. Anaïs, an American novelist and diarist, lived in Paris for a good part of her adult life. Her father, a talented musician, had abandoned the family in her infancy to pursue his musical career, and Anaïs was left with her harsh and unaffectionate mother. In her diary she describes the search for her father in fantasy and in reality. She wrote the following passage after marrying a man that she imagined to be like her father in many ways and during the time she was pregnant with her first child.

> I sit in the dark studio and talk to the child. You can see by what is happening in the world that there is no father taking care of us. We are all orphans. You will be a child without a father as I was a child without a father. That is

why I did all the caring; I nursed the whole world. When there was war and persecution I wept for all the wounds inflicted; and where there were injustices, I struggled to return life, to recreate hope. The woman loved and cared too much.

But inside of this woman there is still a child; there is still the ghost of a little girl forever wailing inside, wailing the loss of a father. Will you go about, as I did, knocking on windows, watching every caress and protective love given to other children? For as soon as you will be born, just as soon as I was born, man the husband, lover, friend, will leave as my father did.

Man is a child, afraid of fatherhood; man is a child, and not a father. Man is an artist, who needs all the care, all the warmth for himself, as my father did. There is no end to his needs. He needs faith, indulgence, humor, he needs worship, good cooking, mended socks, errands, a hostess, a mistress, a mother, a sister, a secretary, a friend. He needs to be the only one in the world.

"He will hate your wailing and your slobbering, and your sickness, and my feeding you rather than his work, his creation. He might cast you aside for this love of his work, which brings him praise and power. He might run away, as my father ran away from his wife and children, and you would be abandoned as I was.

It would be better to die than to be abandoned for you would spend your life haunting the world for this lost father, this fragment of your body and soul, this lost fragment of your very self. . . . [339].*

THE DIAGNOSTIC INTERVIEW WITH THE FATHER

When the diagnostician is convinced that the father will be a valuable contributor to the diagnostic process and conveys this conviction, it is far more likely that the father will respond positively to the invitation to come to a diagnostic session. The

* From THE DIARY OF ANAIS NIN: 1931-1934, copyright © 1966 by Anais Nin. Reprinted by permission of Harcourt Brace Jovanovich, Inc.

clinician will then find that there are a number of ways in which the information learned from him will supplement that which is already available. Bearing in mind the transactions between father and children described earlier in this section as examples, information regarding identifications, time spent together, the nature of mutual activities, exchanges of affection of father to child and vice versa can be explicitly elicited.

Another contribution that the father can make to the diagnostic process is that of presenting the chief complaints and the developmental history from *his* point of view. Even in the closest and most harmonious of families there will be differences in the way a mother experienced an event or a developmental step and the way a father remembers it. There will be some innocent and some potentially meaningful discrepancies in the history that is gathered from the father. The diagnostician should be alert for these, seeking constantly to understand the reason for them, and if the cause of their existence is not clear, to carry them in the back of his mind as a kind of foreign body that is awaiting an explanation.

While consistently vigilant for points of view that differ between mother and father about the child or the family, the interviewer must observe himself closely to ensure that he is not fostering or seducing differences between the parents. There are bound to be conflicts in families, especially if one of the children is having physical or psychological difficulties. If the interviewer is more attracted to one parent than the other, or finds himself harboring an aversion for one of them, he may find himself spending too much time focusing on areas of conflict between the parents and implying that one or the other aspect of the conflict is causing more of the child's problem than it is warranted to assume.

Impulses or activities which are considered "maternal" are not readily or comfortably acknowledged by men in our culture. These tendencies therefore can remain unconscious and unavailable for self-regulation. Because these "maternal" tendencies have escaped regulation, there are fathers who are quite unconsciously, but nevertheless, actively competitive with the mother. This unconscious attitude is sometimes revealed in interviews by the father's denigration of anything the child achieved under the tutelage of the mother, while seeing as important and significant all that he fostered or stimulated in the child. Even though the clinician may not confront this parental conflict for a long time, its detection may help explain much about what brings the family for an evaluation.

When interviewing fathers of children with chronic illnesses or those who have in some way been chronically handicapped by an accident, the clinician needs to be alerted to the possibility of a special problem that may be torturing the marriage with unspoken stresses. The father may without awareness, and irrationally, hold the mother responsible for the child's difficulties. This may not be expressed in direct terms but made manifest in the father's repeated expressions of disappointment and irritation at what he perceives as his wife's failures.

The psychodynamics of this condition are suggested from several sources. Interviews with divorced parents of chronically sick or injured children are revealing. There is a disproportionately high divorce rate in this group of parents. Care of the chronically ill or injured child gives us further information, and most available of all are the insights we can get from self-observation and the reports of parents whose children have suffered a minor crisis. We can use this latter group to describe the psychological forces involved. Let me create a vignette to describe the scene.

A father is at work and learns that his child has suffered one of those bumps or bruises that are inevitable in childhood and which occurred in a potentially dangerous mishap. For a brief moment, many fathers have a flash of anger at the wife for allowing this to happen. This anger is quickly mastered, and if questioned about it, the father would shamefacedly say that he was being unreasonable and unfair to his wife in blaming her. He had, after all, cared for the child when the child had an accident and knew that they were unavoidable. Moreover, his wife had not only held him blameless, she even sought to make him feel better. Recognizing this, he deplores his anger and repudiates it.

In fact, if fathers are asked tactfully and with an acknowledgment that they themselves recognize the irrationality of this momentary response to a child's accident or illness, a large number of them will admit that they have experienced it. Virtually no woman has this response.

To account for this irrational anger and its distribution predominately among fathers, it can be hypothesized that men begin to repress identifications with their mothers early in life, at a time when mothers were thought to be omnipotent and omniscient. Women do not repress these maternal identifications. They continue to modify and adjust them throughout their lives and this exposure to consciousness and reality leavens the unrealistic connection between omnipotence and maternal care. The father of a chronically ill child may, when pressed by the anguish of his child's suffering, *consciously* repudiate his wish that his wife be omnipotent and omniscient, protecting his child as if he were still in the womb, but *unconsciously* displace his disappointment and anger to the inevitable minor frustrations of his everyday relationship with her.

If this condition exists, evidence for it in the interview may be found by exploring the temporal relationship between the onset of his irritation and disappointment and the onset of the child's difficulties. A microscopic exploration of the thoughts that accompany the irritation or anger toward his wife will also be productive.

The personal history of the father can contribute as much to the evaluation as that of the mother. The format of this component of the history can be similar to that, which will be described for the mother's interview. Information about father's growth and development, position and relationships in his own family, major identifications, major achievements, strengths and weaknesses, and health history, should be sought. It is well to remember that in our society masculine identifications in women are much better tolerated than feminine identifications in boys. Tomboys are often seen as "cute" while "sissies" elicit repugnance. For this reason it may be necessary to make inferences about a man's identifications with his mother, while

almost all women describe their identifications with their father
with pride and fondness.

In investigating the father's work history and military record, the diagnostician should bear in mind that while these
issues have become less important in differentiating the sexes
in the upper-middle and upper socioeconomic groups, they
may still have enormous significance to families in the middle
and lower socioeconomic groups. Joblessness, poverty, or an
unsuccessful military record may, among some groups of people, represent a direct and devastating assault on a father's
manliness and sense of worth.

PATHOLOGY PERTAINING TO THE FATHER

ABSENCE OF THE FATHER

We who worked in the field of child psychiatry during the
Vietnam War must be especially sensitive to the suffering that
can be wrought by the absence of the father. The Vietnam War
was particularly destructive (although after one reaches certain
stages of mindless inhumanity, as exemplified by wars, comparisons are futile) because of the number of fathers that were
reported to be missing in action, and because wives and children
were forced all too often to hear their fathers or husbands
labeled brutes and monsters. The missing in action issue sometimes went on for years, and children and wives could not grieve
for their missing loved one, and thereby get on with the business
of living, nor could they ever really entertain much hope that
he would be returned to them. The sad, drawn faces, the dull,
joyless eyes and the weary, empty hopes of some of these wives
and children were a heartrending testimonial to the suffering
they endured. The labeling of their men as brutes by the mischievous, the insensitive, or the inept who were so busy posing
as the intelligentsia that they could not distinguish between
victim and perpetrator, robbed these wives and children of even
the small comfort of publicly idealizing their men in order to
make their loss tolerable.

In the early 1970s, the juvenile court of the county
in which I was working asked me to evaluate a fifteen-
year-old boy who had come under their jurisdiction.
The boy had been caught stealing bullets from a police
vehicle, and the juvenile authorities, after interviewing
the boy, felt that a psychiatric evaluation was indicated.
Since I was asked to be an agent of the court, I told
the judge that in order to be fair and honest with the
boy I would have to tell him that anything he told me
could be repeated to the authorities. I first thought
that this might compromise my ability to learn much
from him, but the judge felt that an evaluation would
be worthwhile in any event. I was surprised to find
that even after warning the boy that I was an agent of
the court, he was not only willing to talk to me, he was
eager and revealing. The circumstances surrounding
the theft of the bullets were not unusual for the neighborhood in which he lived. There had been a fight in
the neighborhood tavern. A small crowd had gathered
in front of the tavern to watch the festivities and the
youth had joined them. As they watched, a police car
sent in to quell the disturbance drove up, and the two
officers dashed out of the car and into the tavern. In
his haste, one of the policemen failed to slam the door
of the car, and it swung open again. There on the front
seat in plain view was a box of .38 caliber cartridges.
The boy spotted these and without knowing why,
reached into the car, took a handful of them and ran.
After the police had quelled the disturbance, someone
in the crowd who had seen the boy told the police and
they were able to find and arrest him. The boy did not
own a gun, nor did he know anyone who owned one.
He did not intend to sell the cartridges and there were
no friends around for whom he may have been showing off. The motive, therefore, for stealing cartridges
was as obscure to the youngster as it was to the authorities and to me. When asked what he had intended

to do with the bullets, he said he was going to throw them into the fire at home. Gradually, however, his motivation became a bit more understandable as I gathered his developmental and personal history. When he was twelve, his father, who was in the Army, was sent to Vietnam. About one year later he was reported missing in action. While anguished and pained, the family did not permit itself to grieve for the father because to do so would have meant to give up hope. The loss, however, was deeply felt by all. Even by the end of the first interview, I could sense a strong wish in the boy to engage me and talk more. This coincided with the arresting officer's statement that he could not understand how "such a nice kid could do such a thing." He added, "I wanted to take him home with me instead of taking him to juvenile hall." For this reason I saw him several more times before I gave my report to the judge. In the fourth interview, things began to make psychological sense when he revealed to me that since the father's disappearance he would have the horrible vision of his father dying in Vietnam by being riddled with bullets "coming from all over." I thought to myself, like bullets exploding in a fire. Although the act had many meanings, one of the most important of them was that the boy, no longer able to tolerate his grief and anxiety, felt that a fatal identification with his father was better than no identification at all.

The second example of the suffering that may be caused by father loss is that of a twenty-year-old woman who was referred to me following a suicide attempt. I discovered that she had been a prostitute since the age of seventeen, and had gone from being a high-priced call girl with a very affluent clientele to working in a brothel in one of the worst sections of the city. Her history revealed that her father had abandoned the family when she was twelve. She did well outwardly, taking over the care of a younger brother and sister while her mother worked. She maintained good grades in school, and progressed well, when, ostensibly at the urging of a schoolmate she began to sell herself once or twice a week "for a little extra money." She did not keep the money herself, but gave it to her mother. The money was accepted without question in the needy family. Before graduation she left school and began "working full time." After about a year of very lucrative private practice as a call girl, she decided she could make more money in more organized prostitution, and went to work in a nightclub-cum-brothel that catered largely to businessmen who entertained out-of-town guests. She did not make more money there, and despite her good looks and a number of offers of marriage that came from both customers and noncommercial acquaintances, she moved her professional activities to the slum area brothel where she was sometimes physically hurt and always more profoundly denigrated. We came to understand her peripatetic promiscuity and her pain when we were able to put two of her frequent fantasies together. The first was that her father had probably deteriorated since he had left the family, and she now imagined him as a day laborer. The second was in the form of a question as she wondered if he would recognize her if he came into the bordello where she worked. The suicide attempt occurred when she began to have the recurring thought that an older customer looked as she thought her father might have looked in his degenerated and more aged state. Gradually, I began to see before me not a tough and hardened whore of twenty, but a sad, guilty, lost child of twelve looking for a father who would make up for having denigrated her and the family, and who would save her from the denigration she felt for herself.

The father, who is psychologically absent, may be even

more devastating to the well-being of the family than the physically absent father. Stoller (1975) traces the problem of transsexualism to psychologically as well as physically absent fathers. Others have linked homosexuality in men and frigidity in women to fathers who were physically present but psychologically absent. Passivity in boys and hostility toward men by girls can frequently be connected clinically to fathers who are present in body but unreachable emotionally.

Of course, not all children who have had a physically or psychologically absent father succumb to psychopathology. Uncles, grandfathers, and family friends can often, to some extent, fill in for the missing father. At other times the mother compensates for the missing father by creating a palpable and treasured presence of the father in the home through her tales and memories and her expressions of admiration included in her memories of him. While rarely comfortable, a father absence is *not* inevitably pathological.

THE DEPRECIATED FATHER

Men who manage to become depreciated in their own homes also create a situation of high risk for their children's serenity. The daughter suffers a twofold insult. She identifies with a mother, who is inevitably unhappy with her husband, and also suffers the disappointment and sense of loss in not having a revered and slightly idealized model of what she may aspire to one day in her own marriage. This identification and disappointment leave her at risk to constantly gravitate toward the underdog as she begins to pick her boyfriends in adolescence or to repeat the only pattern for adult relationships she knows, and constantly cut the men she meets down to size.

Depreciated fathers also frequently leave their sons vulnerable to two possible outcomes. One is that their sons become so frightened and depressed around their depreciated identifications that they overcompensate by becoming overly aggressive, bullying pseudomasculine shells that are condemned to prove their masculinity again and again to anyone who will watch.

The other outcome that may occur is the passive, with-holding boy who feels that he has gotten nothing and, therefore, gives nothing. The sad part of this situation is that as these youngsters grow up they disappoint their own women and children. Wives and children in turn show their own sadness and anger, and this very anger, sadness, and disappointment justifies further withdrawal and withholding.

THE ABUSIVE AND COLLUSIVE FATHER

A clinical vignette can demonstrate this form of difficulty most clearly.

> A family requested evaluation and treatment after a court had dealt with the legal aspects of the problems some months before. These troubles had come to light when the sixteen-year-old daughter, miffed because her father would not permit her to go out on a date told her best friend and neighbor that her father would not let her date because he was jealous of her boy-friends and wanted to "save me all for himself." The girlfriend chided her by saying that she should "not even say that as a joke." The patient tearfully said that she was not joking, and revealed that her father had had an incestuous relationship with her since she was nine or ten. The girl friend, horrified and frightened by the revelation, told her own parents who, after much soul searching and guilt, reported the abuse to the protective services division of the welfare depart-ment. In the course of the evaluation, I found the father to be an intelligent, middle-class man who was enormously passive, and had had a steady, dreary, mediocre career despite excellent training in his cho-sen field. He, as the rest of the family, had counted on the mother for most of the important decisions and activities that had guided their social and educational lives. Since the birth of the children the father and mother had grown increasingly more distant, and were

at the time of the evaluation barely speaking to each other, let alone sharing any joy or intimacy. He freely acknowledged that he had had incest with his daughter and spoke of great guilt and embarrassment. His guilt and shame, however, seemed much more directed at the revelation and condemnation that followed rather than at any possible harm that he may have caused his daughter.

The mother claimed that she had not had the slightest hint that an incestuous situation existed. She, in describing how physically and psychologically precocious her daughter was, told of an incident when her daughter was about thirteen years of age. She was cleaning her husband's study and while dusting, knocked one of his books off of the desk. As the book fell, out spilled several pictures of her daughter nude and in lewd poses. She went on to describe how surprised she was to see how well developed her daughter was, and moved on to another topic. When asked if she had had any other reactions to finding nude pictures of her daughter in her husband's study, she first looked surprised, and then said, "Oh! I must have thought that my husband had confiscated them from one of her boyfriends. She always was such a wild little vixen."

With clinical evidence like that presented in this vignette, the description of the father as collusive as well as abusive is jutified. A review of cases of physical and sexual abuse and many cases of neglect will reveal that a conspiracy of silence exists in these families that is directly responsible for making the abuse possible. This conspiracy of silence can only be achieved if there is an unconscious (and sometimes conscious) collusion involving both parents. The ability of the mother in this clinical example to avoid giving significance to finding those pictures in the father's study, was denial of almost psychotic proportions. When the diagnostician challenged this denial, distortion and displacement of blame were called in as substitute defenses. That the collusion was a firm one is evidenced by the father's leaving the pictures in a place to which his wife had access.

The issue of collusion is addressed here to highlight the complexity of this kind of pathology. In facing this complexity the clinician must look not only at the father's aggression, self-indulgence, and lack of tenderness for his child. He must also see how the father created, or participated in creating the psychological ambience in which these traits found expression. The child is then hurt from several sources. The psychological hurt that comes from living in a family system in which a child is used and exploited, without the possibility of voicing complaint, due to the conspiracy of silence, cannot be overestimated. The disconsolate state of knowing that her mother will not protect her is poignant and pervasive in the victim's view of the world.

The hurt that resulted from the father's pathology and with which we are most concerned in this section, is complex and needs to be understood from two points of view. The first of these is that there was *active* psychological damage inflicted. This is sometimes accompanied by physical injury, but it is most often the denigration, enforced passivity, hyperstimulation, and aggression toward the child that dominate in the theme of active injury.

The second source of damage is in the area of omissions. This is the damage a girl suffers when she is denied the non-erotic tenderness and affection that fathers ecstatically shower on their daughters. This tenderness and affection that make it impossible for a father to intentionally hurt or exploit his child endows her with a sense of worth that should remain with her throughout her life.

To omit the communication of these paternal affects is in my estimation more injurious to the child and future woman than the committed acts. It is this omission that has accounted for the feeling in incest and abuse victims that they are *nothing*, unless they can cater to even the most unreasonable demands of their men; that they have no right to initiate or perform any act for their own gratification, and that they must constantly seek acceptance in self-denigration. I do not believe these psy-chodynamics are readily observable or can be discovered by simple questionnaires or statistical surveys. They emerge grad-ually as transferences are developed, and the patients become more comfortable and less defensive about revealing these is-sues to their therapists. It is perhaps in noting the devastation wrought by the omission of his love that we can most plainly see the vast importance of the father to his daughters and sons.

CHAPTER 5

The Mother: Her Irreplaceable Role

It would be absurd to suggest, even remotely, that justice could be done to the complexity and subtlety of the mother–child relationship in one chapter. To describe a mother's centrality and irreplaceability in the developmental process would require a review of practically all of the psychoanalytic and developmental literature. In this chapter, therefore, I will mention some aspects of the mother–child interaction that demonstrate the immense importance of this first human relationship for the infant, and try to demonstrate its fundamental significance for both development and the clinical process.

With the discovery of each facet of this earliest of all relationships, we can only marvel at its profundity and reliability as a mechanism for ensuring optimal development. We remain astounded at how much there is to be learned about a transaction whose qualities once apeared to be self-evident and simple. Indeed, we begin to appreciate that in the course of human development many of these qualities of the mother–child transaction form a template which will give shape to all future human relationships.

Once clinicians and theoreticians wondered *if* the mother's psychological states could influence the fetus or newborn. Today we no longer ask if there is an influence, but *how and to what extent* these states of the mother influence her offspring.

Prugh (1983, pp. 669–673) was one of the first to develop clinical techniques to evaluate aspects of the early mother–child transactions in routine interviews. In the course of a clinical evaluation he would skillfully weave questions about five areas into the inquiry. He described these five areas formally many years after he began routine use of the questions. The five areas that he covered involved:

1. The mother's perceived state of well-being at the time of the interview and how she remembered feeling at the time of the delivery.

2. Her comfort and readiness to accept her role as a mother; this area is considered especially cogent in the case of primiparous women.

3. Her reaction to the first physical signals from the infant (quickening movements).

4. Her mental images of the infant during pregnancy and her fantasies of how she would behave toward him after birth.

5. Any actual plans she made to care for the new baby.

With these questions Prugh opened to inquiry the mother's emotional responses to her pregnancy and her psychological states during its course. He made it possible for her without undue difficulty to describe her subjective responses to her new role as mother and to the physical reality of the new human being developing in her body. He further sought to learn how the baby's existence altered her relationship with other significant people in her life. Prugh had perceived the clinical importance of these questions well before the scientific findings highlighting them became available.

Even as Prugh and others were devising clinical techniques to understand and experience the psychological ambience in which early mother–child transactions occurred, other investigators were exploring this period experimentally.

Macfarlane (1975) demonstrated that when breast pads of a six-day-old infant's lactating mother are placed on one side of his head and the breast pads of another woman are placed on the opposite side, the child will discriminate between the two by turning his head to the side of his mother's pad with statistical reliability.

De Casper and Fifer (1980) were able to show that three-day-old infants not only could distinguish their mother's voices from those of other women, they would also produce their mother's voices by nonnurturant sucking bursts on a pacifier that was electronically rigged to a taperecorder.

Spence and De Casper (1982) reported that nine-day-old infants would attend to a taperecording of their mother reading a Dr. Seuss story that she had read aloud twice daily during the last trimester of the pregnancy, while they ignored a tape-recording of her reading a Dr. Seuss story that they had never "heard."

These and other findings attest to the already enormously complex physical and psychological organization of the fetus and newborn and how much they bring to the developing mother–child system. Awareness of the sophistication of this system supports the idea that this phase of development is a legitimate and necessary area of inquiry since its very complexity renders it both an important base for health and potentially vulnerable to pathology.

1. THE MOTHER AND THE CHILD'S FIRST YEAR OF LIFE

There can be no adequate appreciation for the mother–child relationship without a basic understanding of the psychodynamic principles of development. I would strongly recommend that the works of Mahler (1975), Fraiberg, (1959), Erickson (1963), Winnicott (1965), and Lidz (1968) be accorded special attention. These authors provide much of the basic information necessary to an understanding of the trajectory that the developmental process follows in the evolution of the mother–child system. In this section I will offer examples of the fine tuning that occurs in this system during the first year of life.

Let us imagine the mother of a two-week-old child at home

during his afternoon nap. A friend has called her on the phone and they are engrossed in conversation. In the midst of their talk the baby awakens and cries out. Although there is still much to discuss, one can easily imagine the mother saying, "Oh Jane! The baby just woke up. I'll call you back when I can." In the midst of even the most interesting conversation the mother will interrupt the exchange to attend to the child. Now, let us revisit the same mother five or six months later. Again she is speaking to Jane when the baby awakens. This time, however, the urgency is absent as the mother says, "The baby just woke up. I'm going to have to go in a moment, but first let me tell you the last thing she said." The mother then comfortably takes a minute or two more before interrupting her talk with Jane or calling out to her baby that she will be there in a moment. There are certainly obvious reasons for the more leisurely pace involved in attending to her child. The child is older, the mother more experienced, and the mother–child couple know each other better. The complex and subtle mechanisms that regulate the pace of communications between mother and child are more clearly revealed, however, a day or two later when we watch the same mother revert to the old pattern of immediately dropping whatever she is doing to rush to the child as soon as he signals need or discomfort. If the mother is questioned about why a day or two earlier she was able to let the child vocalize or even cry for a moment or two, while on this day she rushed to minister to him, she may well be able to tell of having sensed the child's fatigue or recognized that a cold was disturbing his well-being. The lesson in this is that at any given moment there is an intricate system of signs and signals that allow the mother to know how much tolerance for frustration the baby has available. This knowledge permits her to introduce just the amount of reality into the baby's life to permit the mastery of the inevitable frustration that accompanies reality, and to avoid so much frustration that he would be overwhelmed. With each encounter his tolerance for frustration grows until he can, in the context of her patience and care learn that for those internally generated wishes and needs to be gratified he must commit himself to living with the world of reality and its requisites. It is in this context that wishes are directed toward objects, hungers become appetites, and cries become calls.

If the cues between mother and child are accurately perceived most of the time, and the doses of reality that the child must digest are not too massive, the template of relatedness takes a form that promises gratification in time. In the course of obtaining this gratification the relationship will never ask the child to tolerate more than he can endure. The mother–child system thus provides the context in which the child acquires the conviction that the world is a benign place in which to exist and that the next encounter with a human being will be one from which pleasure will ensue. The basic trust acquired at this stage, when the system functions well, or the basic mistrust suffered when the system functions less than optimally, will cast a light or a shadow that will follow the child into all subsequent stages of development. The pace and timing of the interchanges between mother and child approaches what the biologists of the last century called entrainment.

These cycles of transactions which include segments of tolerable frustration and periods of intense gratification also permit the mother to provide the child with an essential ingredient for his inner world that will last throughout his life unless it is destroyed by subsequent events. As she seasons her attentions and caretaking activities with that exquisite tenderness that her investment, familiarity, and intimacy with the child make possible, he begins to experience himself as a cherished and lovable being. As his sense of self evolves it becomes inextricably integrated with self-esteem, a conviction of self-worth, and a feeling of being loved and lovable. This integration makes possible a self-image that in subsequent years provides the person with a potent antidote to fear, self-doubt, or despair in tackling new tasks or taking new developmental steps.

In the course of these transactional processes, the mother is in a powerful position to guide another essential developmental step. She can now introduce the other trustworthy people in the world to her child. When she is alerted that the child

has begun to distinguish one person from another in his environment and receive them with various reactions of comfort
or discomfort, she shifts her efforts from helping the child to
be competent to seek and receive care from her, to helping him
become competent to elicit and benefit from attention and care
from others. This step, which requires preparation and effort
from both mother and child, is undertaken at different times
in different children's lives. Some of the factors that influence
its timing are, of course, related to the number of people surrounding the child in the early weeks and months of his life
and the quality of his experiences with them. However, no
matter how many people hovered around the child, it is from
the psychological organization that developed from his relationship with a primary caretaker, most often his mother, that
he achieves the ability to relate to the rest of the world of human
objects.

This consideration brings the clinician face to face with a
movement that is occurring in our culture that is central to the
issue of mother–child relatedness, and which has clinical, philosophical, and political aspects to it. More than ever before in
our history we encounter mothers who must work and mothers
who wish to work outside of the home relatively early in the
child's life. At times the task of introducing the child to new
caretakers is well underway by the time the mother must or
wishes to return to work. In other instances the child *or the
mother* is not yet ready to take this step. When the pain in the
separation is too great for one or the other, significant disturbances can occur in the mother–child system. The clinical
cues that indicate that the disturbances are due to the separation
are sometimes so compelling that they cannot be ignored or
denied. When the clinician finds it necessary to reveal the causal
connection between the separation and the disturbance the
child or mother may be having, he will find that there are
instances in which his formulation will be vigorously contested
or even attacked. Naturally we must always consider the possibility that the formulation we offer a patient is inaccurate and
their response is due to this inaccuracy. But I have found two

other reasons why a mother may reject the connection between her having gone to work and a disruption either in the smooth interchange between her and her baby, or in her own or the baby's well-being. One reason for the vigor and intensity of the rejection may be guilt on the part of the mother for having had to go to work, and the other reason may be that there was a conflict between her acceptance of her role as mother and another role or activity that may have a high priority in her value system. Some mothers attempt to resolve this conflict by denying those aspects of motherhood that are involved in the conflict. Thus, if the work they wish to do requires that they spend significant amounts of time away from their child, they may claim that it is the quality rather than the amount of time spent with the child that is important.

In those cases in which the clinician becomes aware that the mother is responding with guilt to his connecting her work and the disturbance, he must review his techniques in offering her the clinical insight. Was he sufficiently sensitive to the ways in which she had defended herself from the guilt before he interfered with the defenses? Had a therapeutic alliance at least begun before he made his clarification? Was he in a position to be of some support to her as he told her of the connection between the pathology and a behavior of hers? The clinician may find it necessary to see a guilt-plagued mother a number of times before proceeding with the process, if the process itself produced a disruption of her comfort and feelings of competence. In any case, it is well to remember that mothers may have cause to feel uneasy during evaluations since in many instances they have felt blamed rather than understood when their children had problems, and often have been seen as an encumbrance during the course of a child's psychotherapy. In some cases, when a mother has felt bereft or guilty about the effect her having to work has had on her child, I have found it useful to remind her that no child was ever raised in heaven—even developmental heaven—and that our job was not to change every environment to meet her child's demands. Rather, we must provide the child with the strength and flexibility to adapt to the inevitable requisites of the different, imperfect environments in which he will eventually have to live.

There is a more difficult problem posed by the case of women who reject evidence of the child's difficulties being due to separation from them because they wish to be somewhere other than near their children. They will sometimes come armed with data from "experts" to demonstrate that separation from the mother at their child's age should not really constitute a problem. Or they may attack psychodynamic theory and challenge the objectivity of the clinician. Virtually every therapist who has been drawn into a debate on these issues has found that it is a losing proposition. The best that the clinician can do is to look into his own attitudes as honestly as he can to see if he is bringing issues into the clinical process that are his own and do not belong in the evaluation of the case that is before him. If these clinician-related issues do exist, or if he detects in himself feelings of antagonism or condemnation toward the mother or her ideas, he must dispel them or disqualify himself from further clinical involvement. Social attitudes and values that are the clinician's cannot be imposed on others without doing violence to the clinical process.

When the clinician is satisfied that he has carried out his self-scrutiny, he can begin to look at the possible causes for the mother's inability to acknowledge or accept responsibility for the intensity of the bond the child has with her. Except for cases in which there is abuse or neglect of the child, all the therapist can offer is a willingness to explore the mother's attitudes toward the child or her role as mother. Once this is offered the therapist can demonstrate, either in meetings with the mother alone, or with the mother and child, that their relationship is unique, and preformed psychological opinions or social convictions do not do its uniqueness justice.

What the clinician must not do is take his or the mother's sociological convictions into the consulting room and use them as a frame of reference to judge psychological health or illness. To the statement that a mother has the right to have a child and at the same time pursue her career, the clinician can only respond that while this is a social statement with which he can agree or disagree, his job is to understand what the status of mother and child is, and the unique system they constitute.

These considerations of a social issue were placed in this section because the clinician's response to it rests on concepts from this period. It also highlights the fact that in some instances, and during some periods of development, the mother's place cannot be filled by another in a totally satisfactory way.

2. EXAMPLES OF THE MOTHER'S UNIQUE CONTRIBUTIONS IN SUBSEQUENT YEARS

With the second year of life come an infinite number of manifestations of the child's desire to try newly acquired functions, to find ways to express and reaffirm his awareness that he is an individual distinct from other persons, and express his autonomy as that individual. In all of these efforts the mother plays a role that is of immense importance and probably never totally replaceable.

As the child ventures into the world from the safety of his mother's side there is much that appears threatening from the outside, and much that seduces impulses and therefore becomes threatening to his inner serenity. The regulatory functions that he has not yet acquired must be supplied by his partner in the system; his mother. These must be supplied with soothing care, rather than terror or anger. Thus, when this regulation facilitates action the child feels encouraged rather than driven. When it inhibits action the child feels containment rather than suppression. It is in this context of an intimate, gentle, loving relationship that these competencies are first proffered by the mother and later accepted by the child as identifications. One has but to watch a toddler in tender interaction with his mother, in a setting familiar to both, to see the variety of glances, vocalizations, movements, games, and other vehicles that the partners use to prepare the child for this phase of development. The child toddles off and glances to see if his foray is permissible or not. The mother may smile reassuringly, or if the expedition has been signaled by the child to be a more formal adventure, wave "bye-bye." The child takes himself off to another room, or around the corner of the garage, and the mother allows him to be there just long enough to feel his autonomy, but not so long that he will be threatened by real dangers, or by impulses that might overwhelm him. At just the right moment a call from her, a few steps to put him in sight, allows him to relax his own vigilance and not become overburdened by the task of regulating his own affairs. On his part he fine tunes his mother's timing by running back to her or getting into some minor trouble if she is too late in reattaching; or he expresses chagrin or runs away if she is too early in checking things out. If she is right on time she will find him playing happily or be offered a warm welcome. Games of peek-a-boo, or ones in which the child threatens playfully to undertake some prohibited action, serve the same purpose. And so the process of acquiring skills that enable or inhibit goes on at a pace that is comfortable for both mother and child.

Another situation in which the mother and her closeness to the child is virtually irreplaceable is in that process we can call validation. If we can recapture the image of the child during that phase of his development when he is an explorer in the world at large, creating new trails in a wilderness never before seen, we can begin to imagine how many questions arise with each new experience. "Can this obstacle be climbed? Can this object be destroyed? Is eating something akin to destroying it or more like loving it? Is there a difference between biting something, like when you're angry or chewing something like when you like it? What is this feeling that I have when I want to be near someone, and the feeling I have when I want to be away from them?" And probably the most important question of all: "Do others experience things as I do and do I experience things as others do?" In organizing these feelings and images of the external environment, some of which are experienced for the first time, the child frequently and avidly seeks cues from his mother regarding the significance and validity of his experiences. With her expressions, her words, and other forms of communication the mother essentially says to her child, "I recognize your exuberance (or fear, or anger) and its relationship to me or to the rest of the world." As far as this process of validation is concerned it matters little whether she approves or disapproves of the affect or the activity, or what she indicates to the child that he may or may not do about them. The important thing in this regard is that the child knows that the mother *recognizes and understands* his feelings or his activities, and that they thus can be validated.

Sorce, Emde, Campos, and Klinnert (1985) carried out an illuminating experiment regarding cues from mother to child that applies to the process of validation. They used a construction called the visual bridge, which consists of two solid platforms joined by a span of transparent material such as glass or clear plastic. Visually then there appears to be a void between the two platforms. With a cohort of one-year-old children they set up the following conditions. With a child on one platform and the mother at the opposite end of the device the child was urged to crawl to the mother. To his eyes this would appear as though the child were being urged to crawl across a void. When the mother conveyed only encouragement and comfort the child proceeded to crawl over the glass and to the mother. When the mother conveyed discomfort or fear with her facial expressions, the child would crawl back to the safety of the platform from which he started. The experiment would suggest not only that the child recognized the cues from the mother, but that he also had an internal organization that allowed him to choose a course of action suggested by these cues. These kinds of interchanges are the vehicles by which validation occurs.

How does this process of validation come into the clinical situation? My clinical experience convinces me that nonvalidation is a more powerful repressive force to a mental process than a threat.

> Trevor was sixteen when he sought treatment for depression and for social difficulties in his peer group. In the course of his treatment chronic anxiety and

debilitating obsessions were revealed. It also became
clear that a cool, somewhat distant but controlling
mother was looked to by Trevor for approval, or for
every important decision he made. As he began to
recall and discuss his childhood, it became obvious to
him and to the therapist that feelings of affection, attachment, or respect for his father were virtually nonexistent. Despite this, he described a number of
instances when his behavior clearly indicated that he
was seeking contact with his father or the opportunity
to exchange warmth and affection with him. The therapist first thought that this repression of the boy's longing for love from his father was due to the father's
passivity and unavailability. Later the therapist had to
alter his assumptions when the boy could tell him that
there were many times that the father was available
and affectionate, but when he attempted to tell his
mother of any positive exchanges between him and his
father, she, because of the silently hostile nature of her
relationship with her husband, would only look blankly
at her son, say nothing, and turn back to whatever she
had been doing before he spoke to her.

Although this is an example of nonvalidation, it was chosen to
underline how profoundly important validation is to an individual's inner responses to the world, and his ability to integrate
these responses into a sense of self and an ability to relate.

This process of validation evolves into another acquisition
that begins with the mother and is later extended into the child's
relationship with many other important adults in his life. During the second and third year of life the child becomes an
explorer and natural scientist *par excellence*. As he involves himself in events and explorations, they must be registered and
catalogued in his mind so that when they occur again, he can
retrieve the image of them from his memory with all the information about the event and his mastery and understanding
of it. In this way, familiarization with his inner and outer world
brings the child economy in adaptation and regulation of effort.

In the process he comes to recognize recurrent patterns of affects, wishes, and reactions. For example, on a given evening at about 6:00 or 6:30, when the child recognizes that it is about time for his mother to start the very pleasant process of feeding him, or that it is time for his father to arrive and begin playing with him, he visualizes the events about to occur with enjoyable anticipation. Just at that moment his mother may say with a lively and pleasant affect, "Oh just look at how hungry my big boy is." Or, in the voice of someone who has just found a treasure, call out, "Daddy's home!" Sander (1982) recognized and described the significance of this interchange. He describes the importance of the child becoming cognizant that someone is aware of his own awareness. This developmental step, that takes validation to a higher level of abstraction, offers powerful flexibility to the child's ever growing dialogue between himself and others. When the mother says to the child, "don't hurt Tabby" as the child approaches the kitchen in an excited or angry mood, she demonstrates to him that she is aware of what he himself is aware of, and at the same time teaches him anticipatory regulation of behavior. When she is correct in her assessment of his intentions she automatically offers him alternative choices of affects, wishes, or actions. When she errs in her assumptions no harm is done because she has confirmed and consolidated his awareness of his own individuality and separateness.

This process that begins in the benign and comfortable ambience of the mother's care, is extended into the interactions with other family members first, and then to teachers and other responsible adults who will enter the child's life. It becomes integrated with the basic trust that was also achieved through the experiences with this first and most treasured person in the child's life. Elements of this mutual recognition process allow the child to learn from others even as he preserves a continuous sense of self. It safeguards autonomy even as it increases his potential for intimacy, and it enriches the child's inner world by adding significance to all human interchanges.

These examples of the interaction between mother and

child were meant to represent only a few of the brush strokes in the immensely subtle and complex portrait of the mother–child relationship. It is a portrait that is as yet far from being fully understood by those who scrutinize it, but one that already proclaims that it is through the portal of the relationship with the mother that the child physiologically and psychologically enters that phase of being we call his life.

CHAPTER 6

Diagnostic Interviews: An Overview

INTRODUCTION

The division of the clinical process into an evaluative phase and a therapeutic phase introduces a distortion that the reader must help to minimize by bearing in mind that many things happen during the evaluation that can be therapeutic (or unfortunately, sometimes antitherapeutic), and that the therapeutic process continually reveals diagnostic insights. From a practical point of view, every person doing an evaluation should constantly remind himself that therapy may have to follow the evaluation, and that what happens during the evaluation may influence the therapeutic process to follow.

There is, of course, a vast body of literature on the development of skills and knowledge that are useful in the evaluation process. I will recommend four works here which I have found particularly helpful in preparing for the evaluation. Dr. J. Simmons (1981) has written a lucid text on the diagnostic process. Greenspan's book (1981) on the clinical interview is of immense help in both diagnostic and therapeutic work. For issues regarding diagnosis and classification, the Group for Advancement of Psychiatry Report (1966) on the diagnostic evaluation of the child offers useful concepts regarding the health and strengths of the child as well as the problems that must be

contemplated in procuring needed help from community resources. Finally, although the *Diagnostic and Statistical Manual,
III* (1980) is written from a descriptive point of view and does
not contemplate the dynamics of internal and external forces
which act on the child, it must be understood and utilized if
the diagnostician is to make his contribution to statistical and
epidemiologic data, and communicate intelligently with insurance companies and other governmental or private institutions.

It would be comforting to imagine that each diagnostic
evaluation found us as unblemished by previous impressions,
and as sensitive as a new photographic plate is before exposure.
We are not, however, and we must take this fact into account.
In the course of the evaluation the diagnostician will likely be
tempted to seek that data which is accommodated most comfortably by the theoretical frame of reference that he espouses.
Yet, no single theory of development or psychopathology has
been formulated that contemplates the child in his entirety as
a biological, social, and psychological being. We in the field may
have become psychobiologists, psychoanalysts, or social learning
theorists, but nature seems not to have complied with our preferences by confining itself to laws that can *all* be explained by
our point of view. Thus, human beings come to us as complex
as always, so the diagnostician must employ whatever framework is needed to observe or explain the phenomena that he
encounters in the course of the evaluation. If there are frames
of reference with which he is not familiar, the help of co-workers or consultants must be sought.

A fourteen-year-old girl was hospitalized for an-
orexia nervosa, after a forty-pound weight loss had
occurred and after bradycardia, skin, and mucosal
changes and hypotonia of the lower extremities were
discovered by a pediatrician. A psychiatric consultation
was requested while she was in the hospital, and history
revealed that the youngster had been undergoing an
outpatient diagnostic evaluation for the past month
during the last week of which outpatient psychotherapy had been recommended. When the outpatient

psychodiagnostician was called and told that his patient had been hospitalized, he wondered if the pediatrician had not jumped the gun on the hospitalization "because he was afraid of psychopathology." When told that the girl had lost almost 50 percent of her body weight, it became clear that he was unaware that irreversible changes would occur with this much weight loss.

In this instance the outpatient diagnostician was ignorant of a significant physiological fact regarding weight loss. He also used his frame of reference to criticize the pediatrician's judgment and vindicate his own. This situation, which posed a physical threat to the young patient, could have been avoided had the psychodiagnostician requested that a pediatrician stay involved with him and the youngster while they were doing the psychiatric evaluation.

INDICATIONS FOR A PSYCHIATRIC EVALUATION

There may be many reasons to start a psychiatric evaluation. Sometimes these reasons are so peculiar to an individual situation that they will probably never recur. I will leave these occasional reasons to be dealt with by the judgment of individual clinicians, and here address those conditions that we are all likely to encounter.

1. A psychiatric evaluation is indicated when a child communicates by his affect or speech that he is suffering. There are times when a child dramatizes a situation and playacts at suffering. These times are usually short lived, and easily alleviated by the adults in the environment. If suffering is prolonged or the posture of suffering is assumed repeatedly by the child, an evaluation is indicated, even if the apparent cause of the suffering appears to be trivial. Causes for suffering may indeed be trivial; suffering itself never is.

2. An evaluation is indicated when a child's social, cognitive, or emotional development is not proceeding at the pace that it should. This requires an evaluation of the biogenetic endow-

ment, the child's freedom to utilize it, and the environment's ability to stimulate the development.

3. Anxiety, sleeplessness, loss of appetite, and irritability are often signs of latent intrapsychic conflict. When these persist for more than a few weeks, an evaluation is indicated.

4. Prolonged interpersonal conflict, especially when this applies to many different people, should be evaluated. At times, normal teenagers will have stormy relationships. When scrutinized more closely, what becomes evident is that the normal adolescent has had a strife-ridden relationship with one person for a long time, or with different persons (usually family members) at various times. Seldom is the teenager without a friend to fall back on. When an adolescent is isolated repeatedly or persistently, a diagnostic evaluation is indicated.

5. If a child or adolescent suffers from recurrent illness or has difficulty in recovering from illnesses, a psychiatric evaluation in *conjunction with ongoing physical care* may be helpful. I do not subscribe to the practice of "turning him over to the psychiatrists" when a puzzling physical symptom or the cause of an illness cannot be found. Psychological illness or psychological problems complicating physical illness must be diagnosed by positive evidence of its presence, and not based on the absence of physical causes.

Other, less frequent reasons for doing an evaluation may include the need to determine the kind of psychiatric treatment needed and when it should start, consultation and advice to a colleague, or the need to offer advice to a school system or social institution located in an area in which child psychiatric services are not available.

There are instances in which anticipatory caution needs to be exercised by the clinician who is asked to do an evaluation. A child should not be evaluated for the purpose of attaching a label to him. A number of institutions in recent years have been put in the position of having to demonstrate that they are serving a quota of emotionally disturbed children in order to receive funding. A diagnostician would be well advised to ensure that if psychopathology is found, there will be an effort made to procure the services a child needs. Hobbs (1975) indicates that a diagnostic label applied to a child who is not treated is not without its harmful consequences, since it may remain with a child for a long time, and may become a self-fulfilling prophecy.

A second situation in which caution is indicated is that in which a physician *refers* a child for treatment when a *consultation* would have been more appropriate. This happens frequently when a child has been worked up for complaints for which no organic cause can be found. As mentioned above, the fact that no organic cause can be found is not a positive sign that psychopathology exists, or that if it exists is a sufficient explanation of the child's complaints. In these cases the diagnostician should request that the referring physician or a suitable alternate stay involved in the evaluation and care of the patient until the evaluation is completed. If it can be demonstrated that psychopathology is present, and there is reasonable evidence to indicate that it played a role in producing the reported symptoms, it may be the appropriate time for the referring physician to bow out of the picture. If this cannot be demonstrated, both consultant and referring physician may have to live with uncertainty and follow the patient until a definitive diagnosis can be made. Uncertainty can be corrosive and humiliating and plague us in the care of patients. We cannot indulge our wish to avoid it by bouncing the patient from one person to another with endless referrals. Consultations should be requested when appropriate, but the person requesting the consultation should stay involved with the patient until he is cured or an appropriate referral is made.

THE REFERRAL

The diagnostic evaluation begins with the first contact that the patient, the family, or the referring person makes with the diagnostician or the clinic. In some settings the diagnostician is the first contact, while in other settings intake workers screen calls, inquiries, and referrals. There are advantages and disadvantages to both methods. An experienced and well-trained intake worker can obtain prodigious amounts of information in relatively brief periods of time. They also develop stores of knowledge about their communities, and are most often in the best position to know what other services the patient needs, and the agencies available to serve them. Experienced intake workers invariably are exquisitely sensitive to the referral that has been made prematurely or inappropriately, and are very competent in recommending the measures necessary to prepare the family for the diagnostic work. For these reasons, the intake worker can in invaluable in saving a diagnostic colleague's time, effort, and frustration.

The advantages to doing one's own intake is that the first exchanges with family or referring agent can be very revealing, and the diagnostician is often alerted to the nature of the problems from the very beginning. An analytic patient referred to me by a senior colleague said when he called, "I called to tell you when you could see me." I am sure that there would have been other cues to alert me to the narcissistic components of his problems, but the phone call prepared me to explore certain elements of his development and human relationships with particular care, and the diagnostic evaluation was more efficient and revealing than it might have been otherwise.

Whether one receives the referral directly or from an intake worker, one of the first questions that must be asked is *who* referred the child. In the case of adults, the patient is very often self-referred. Children, of course, are most often referred by the parents. It is not unusual, however, to see children referred by persons other than their parents, with schools, pediatricians, and law enforcement and service agencies heading the list. As soon as the referral source is known, the next question that must be asked is why one person or agency referred the patient instead of the other? Many times this question can be answered simply. The parents referred the child because they detected the pathology or symptoms. Or, the pediatrician referred the child after a conference with the family. At other times the answer is not simple. One can uncover some valuable information by this scrutiny. For example, a family's motivation for treatment could be questioned if a child, who had been suffering from symptoms since the age of three, was referred for an evaluation at the age of six and then only at the insistence of school authorities.

"Why, now?" is another question that the clinician must ask as he receives the referral. This is often closely related to the question of "who" referred. Again, many times the answer to this question is the most obvious one and the question can be put to rest unless curiosity about it is rekindled by subsequent data. Here, too, however, the true answer to the question may not be obvious, and only revealed by more scrutiny or more data.

> Lori was fourteen when her parents asked that she be reevaluated. She and her parents had adapted well to her mild mental retardation which had been diagnosed when she was about five years of age. She had been a relaxed, comfortable, and attractive girl through her school years, and had utilized the excellent arrangements the school system had made to permit her to function in the regular school program with a minimum of discomfort for her and her peers. Her parents expressed their concern that in the past six months she had become morose, irritable, and querulous. They feared that she might be "deteriorating and require institutionalization at some point." Lori did indeed acknowledge "being nervous and sad" when she was at home, but felt that things at school and with her friends were just fine. With the permission of Lori and her family we made a school visit. Her teachers and counselor confirmed that Lori continued to do well in school. In subsequent interviews with the parents, this discrepancy between Lori at home and Lori in school as well as the question of "Why now?" was explained. During relatively unstructured portions of individual diagnostic interviews, both parents spontaneously associated to situations in which inju-

dicious sexual activity had created painful problems
for them and for people they had known. Lori's blos-
soming womanhood had precipitated their preoccupations and had blunted the tender sensitivity with
which they had customarily treated their daughter.
With gentle and empathic inquiry Lori's parents could
see that they were terrified of what might happen to
their daughter in the next few years. They were afraid
of the sexual implications of adolescence, and the
"Why, now?" question helped to focus the attention of
the clinician and the parents on the real issue, which
had little to do with concerns about deterioration.

The "Why, now?" questions do much to reveal those instances in which the desired therapy may be more for the sake
of the parents or the environment than for the sake of the child.
Prosen, Toews, and Martin (1981) have written a poignant paper on the synergistic effect that the pain of the child going
into adolescence has on the pain of the parent going into middle
age, and vice versa. Another aspect of this mutuality that the
"Why, now?" question reveals is that of the parent who dreads
the child's entry into a developmental phase that the parent
himself had not fully mastered.

In accepting the referral, the diagnostician should, whenever possible, determine the stated and unstated reasons for
which the child is referred. In many instances children are
referred not to make them *well*, but to make them *good*. Many
times these two aims are compatible even if they are not synonomous. At other times to try to only make the child "good,"
or to try to make the child behave in a way that the referring
agents or agency wants him to behave may not be in the best
interests of the child.

Sam was twelve when he was referred by the coun-
selor of an academically demanding private school to
which he had a scholarship. The complaints were that
he was frequently disruptive in some of his classes,
expressed apparently gratuitous hostility to his teach-

ers, and had gotten into a number of fights with his peers. Sam came from a minority family in the lower socioeconomic level of the community. His intelligence fit well with school's sincere wish to help talented minority students, and they had made a scholarship available to him, which his parents had readily and gratefully accepted. What could not have been anticipated was that Sam perceived some of his lessons and school activities as denigrating to his ethnic background. The accomplishments of his culture were never mentioned. His people's heroes were never idolized. Every history lesson successfully learned seemed to Sam to be a betrayal of his father and uncles whom he loved and admired. Sam himself made an excellent case for this during the evaluation when he said of his teachers, "They're always telling me about *their* cool guys and what they did. They never tell about *our* cool guys."

If we had set about to make Sam behave and comply with the standards of behavior prescribed by the school, we might well have succeeded because Sam's parents were so grateful and deferential to the school that they would have gone to almost any length to keep their son there. But if we had done so, we would have done Sam a disservice. His legitimate wish was to comfortably integrate his home background with the world in which he aspired to live outside the home. He was asking himself if it was possible for a person like him to live in the world of his school without having to be disloyal to someone he loved.

When we, with Sam's permission, met with the school officials, they, to their credit, devised plans to help Sam see his culture's rightful place in our society through special projects and special readings for which he obtained academic credit. Sam was then required to present a summary of his reading to the class with the support of his teacher. This left us free to acknowledge that Sam's wish for cultural respect was legitimate, and move on to see if Sam's aggression had been provoked by circumstances, or if it came from his own conflicts and convictions. To have simply forced him to be "good" would not have ensured that we were helping him to develop as "well" as possible.

A question that is sometimes overlooked, but is nonetheless important, even as the diagnostic evaluation is started is simply, "Whose agent am I?" This question is important to ask in any event, but particularly so if the referral comes from an institution like the school, the juvenile or divorce court, or a welfare agency. It becomes even more central if one of these agencies is paying for the services. If the answer to this question is that the diagnostician is the child's agent, the diagnostician should be ready to explain that some of the things that the child may reveal must, in the child's best interests, remain confidential. If, on the other hand, the school, court, or welfare department expects the clinician to be their agent, the child and his family must know, *before they walk through the door of the consulting room,* that the diagnostician is the agent of the referring agency, and may in the future be required to reveal any part of the diagnostic or treatment process to that agency. To omit this clarification in roles at the very beginning of the process would be eminently unfair to the patient and his family and could create ambiguities that could be difficult for the therapist later. To clarify the situation allows the responsible adults to know what the therapist considers his responsibilities and what can be expected of him in the course of the evaluation or treatment.

A medical student with a splendid academic record became convinced at the end of her first year of medical school that she was suffering from malignant melanoma. She had worn out the patience of a number of faculty clinicians with her repeated visits to them and her refusal to be reassured that there was no indication of malignancy. On one of these anxiety-laden visits to the emergency room, she was convinced by senior medical students working there that she should talk to one of the psychiatric residents whom the medical students knew and trusted. She accepted the recommendation and a diagnostic evaluation was performed by the resident who became convinced that the stress of medical school, some concurrent personal conflicts, and an earlier sheltered lifestyle had conspired to produce a conversion symptom rather than a delusion. He further felt that this was eminently amenable to psychotherapeutic intervention. The medical school administration had heard of the student's difficulties, and had invited the young woman to drop out of medical school. She refused to do so, and in the course of her "counseling session" with an administrator revealed that she had started psychotherapy. She told him that she was convinced that neither her problem nor her therapy would interfere with her performance as a student and a physician. The medical school administration contacted her therapist, and with the well-intentioned, but ill-advised help of one of the psychiatry faculty sought to convince the therapist to reveal details of the medical student's difficulties, and to counsel her to leave medical school. Great pressure was put on the resident by reminding him of his responsibility to the medical school and the medical profession. The faculty member stressed the therapist's lack of experience, and was convinced that the student was suffering from "somatic-delusions" and was probably a "frozen paranoid." It was only with the support of his fellow residents and a couple of faculty members that the resident could successfully maintain his position that he was the agent of his patient, and obliged to respect her wishes and privilege of confidentiality.

Had the question of whose agent he was not been clearly defined for the therapist, he would have had a more difficult time in defining his responsibilities to his young patient.

DIAGNOSTIC INTERVIEWS

At times intake information will suggest if one or another family member or the whole family should be scheduled for the first diagnostic interview. I know of no data that has established that any particular sequence of interviewing is more productive than another. Unless there is some indication that it would be clinically more productive to do otherwise, I will invite the mother to come in first to describe the problem and offer a developmental history of the child. Simmons (1981) offers the suggestion that a family meeting is productive as a first interview. Both methods may have their advantages and drawbacks, and I can only suggest that the clinical judgment and the preference of the clinician determine the mode of proceeding. For no other reason than my familiarity, I will describe the process of the diagnostic evaluation, as I have done it, with an appointment for the child's mother first. Whether the clinician sees the mother, father, both parents, or the whole family first, a few considerations are in order at this point.

Parents of the child patient may come to the diagnostic evaluation anxious or depressed. In noting this, we must remember that from the time that we discovered that environmental factors played an important role in the development of the child, and linked development with psychopathology, we have often allowed the blame for the child's problems to fall entirely on the mother's shoulders; in fact, we have sometimes put it there. Phrases such as "icebox mother," "depriving mother," "castrating mother" or the more sophisticated "schizophrenogenic mother" glibly rolled off of our tongues with little evidence that they served the cause of accuracy, and little consideration of the pain and guilt these phrases could cause. We have thus contributed to the fear of humiliation and blame that parents feel when they tell us of their children's emotional problems. There are also unrealistic reasons for the parents to feel sadness and guilt in the revelation of these problems. Virtually every parent wishes their child a joyous and carefree life. Virtually everyone started their careers as parents with the aspiration that they would be the ideal parent, living out a scenario of ministering to an ideal child who would enjoy nothing less than perfect development. Being in the clinician's office is *de facto* evidence that this wish did not come to pass. Often the grief that the parent feels in abandoning the wish for the ideal child in an ideal relationship is experienced by them as guilt or as a sense of failure.

The therapist, at this stage of the process, must have empathy for the perplexity of the parent. The concept of a diagnostic alliance is an antidote against this parental guilt and perplexity, and conveys the message that the parent's valued participation is as important as the therapist's skills. This empathy and commitment to an alliance can be conveyed to the parent by sincerely felt phrases such as, "Since you know the child better than anyone, did you feel that what his teacher said about him was accurate?" Or, "Did it seem to you that Johnny was as angry as people said he was?" Or perhaps even a judicious and well timed, "How sad you must have felt," may be in order.

> The mother of a nine-year-old boy revealed that she had not escaped unscathed from the wars with the school and the community mental health center regarding her son's misbehaviors. She presented the history of the problem, and the developmental history of the boy in a defensive manner and indicated that every measure that she had tried in an effort to curb her son's destructiveness had been to no avail. She implied without saying it that she expected the current effort to instruct her to do what was "right" was going to have the same result. The diagnostician responded by saying, "It has been a rough time, hasn't it? By this time you must be so discouraged that you second guess yourself on everything you do." The mother immediately availed herself of the therapist's offer to hear the suffering and perplexity that her son's problems created for *her*. The groundwork for a diagnostic alliance began to be laid by both mother and therapist.

It is as unproductive and unempathic to try to make the parent "good" instead of "well," as it is to try this with the child. This empathy should be extended not only to the affects connected with current revelations, but also to the affects that accompanied events when the person being interviewed lived them. The past lives in the present for many of us in the form of feelings.

A PROPOSED MODEL FOR THE DIAGNOSTIC INTERVIEWS

I can only make suggestions about a framework within which the data leading to a diagnosis is gathered and evaluated. There is no substitute for an interviewer's style, clinical judgment, empathy, or even preference. The patient will also have much to do with leading and sometimes inadvertently misleading the interviewer. For this reason, the frame of reference employed must be sufficiently flexible to be adapted to countless situations, and the only constants I could recommend here would be that the diagnostician bring with him to the interviews liberal quantities of *curiosity,* willingness to be *surprised,* willingness to be *taught* by the parents *and the child* without feeling resentful or denigrated, and above all, *humility* and respect for the enormous complexity of human development and mentation.

The proposed model for gathering information about the child borrows heavily from the model that is most frequently used in medical settings. This format has served humanity well for over two millenia, and has been adaptable as new findings emerged which made wider diagnostic exploration possible.

I feel compelled at this point to discuss briefly the term *medical model,* and the criticism leveled at it in the recent past. I have always felt that this was a nonsense term, and the criticism built on its use was uninformed. I would challenge anyone to describe a single "medical model." There have been as many models as the institution of medicine has had to employ to address the variety of problems that confronted it. I suspect that the term grew out of the slogans of the political wars that are being waged to see who is going to dominate the health care industry and who will get a piece of the action. I would ask the reader to join me in putting aside the slogans and clichés that are used in the political arena or the marketplace. Children need more psychological care than all of us put together can possible provide for the next several decades and the task of every professional group that involves itself in health care should be to strive for as much clarity, discipline, and effectiveness as we can achieve, and collect whatever tools we need from each other to achieve that end.

The proposed model begins by contemplating the chief complaint, moves on to the history of the present illness, and then explores the developmental, social, and family history of the child and family.

THE CHIEF COMPLAINT(S)

In exploring this, the diagnostician is essentially reexamining the reasons given for requesting an evaluation. The problem or symptoms presented may be those noted by the family, or they may be problems to which the family has been alerted by school authorities or by their pediatrician. In hearing the chief complaint articulated the interviewer should listen particularly for these "signals": whether or not the problems were crisply articulated, or presented in a vague and ambiguous way; clues that indicate to whom the problem was most annoying; indications that the affects are appropriate to that which is being presented.

A young mother who felt she had plenty of grievances against the community in which she lived as well as the world at large, was proclaiming that she was at her wits' end in trying to curb the aggression and destructiveness of her six-year-old son. As she described the scorched earth policy employed by him in school and in the neighborhood, her voice softened, and her face assumed an adoring look, as she said, "I'm beginning to call him my little terrorist."

By noting the affect and associations that accompanied the recital of the chief complaint, the diagnostician was provided

96 THE EVALUATION PROCESS

with a valuable clue about where to look further. Many examples can be found of insights that are provided by the nonverbal components of the communication when the symptoms that were described on the phone are repeated in person.

Again, it must be stressed that the person reciting the chief complaint may not be the one most disturbed by it; he may be only the messenger. Some parents come to the diagnostic process because a school or a juvenile court has forced them to do so, and when asked, they candidly admit that the child's symptoms do not distress them as much as they do the school. At other times, finding the person pained by the child's disturbance may be a more subtle task.

> A six-year-old boy was being evaluated because he had fears at night, and refused to sleep anywhere other than in the parent's bed. Most of the history had been obtained from the mother, who voiced concern, but seemed not to be too disturbed by the situation. Not until the session in which treatment was recommended for the child was it revealed that the boy's father was the moving force behind the evaluation. He bitterly stated that if it had been up to the mother, she would have let him sleep in their bed forever.

With this added information, the diagnostician was able to pursue the other problems in the family, and appreciate how they kept the boy's phobias alive.

HISTORY OF THE PRESENT PROBLEM(S)

This segment of the inquiry is devoted to an exploration of the onset, course, and evolution of the problem or problems over time. Again here, it is important to note the affects that accompany the parents' account of the course of the illness, as well as the general mood and affect during the interviews. It is also well to reexamine this section after a history of the family's development is noted, to see if changes in the course of the illness coincided with any important changes in the family's living conditions.

DEVELOPMENTAL HISTORY

In conducting this part of the interview, the diagnostician must consciously shift his focus. Until this point in the clinical process, the focus had been on problems and pathology. In exploring the child's development, an active effort must be made by the diagnostician to learn about aspects of the child's life other than those that were labeled pathological. Some parents are convinced that normal events are not worth mentioning to "the doctor," and they must be reminded that the child's health as well as his illnesses are of interest to him. It is also important at this stage of the evaluation to resist the temptation to label developmental acquisitions or events as healthy or pathological until the context in which they occurred is explored, and understood.

> The sixteen-year-old daughter of an alcoholic father and a long-suffering, hard-working masochistic mother ran away from home to try to find work in another city. After being found by juvenile authorities, returned home, and referred for a diagnostic evaluation, the young woman revealed that she had run away only after an incident had occurred at home that had forced her to do so. During one of her father's drunken binges, he had embraced her and rubbed his erect penis against her. When approached for protection, her mother had accused her of being the troublemaker in the family, and berated rather than protected her. Fleeing the family had not been as patently pathological as the diagnostician had originally assumed. He could now see that fleeing was possibly the most adaptive thing the girl could think of doing at the time.

When inquiring about the developmental milestones, the evaluator must be reluctant to accept an answer of "normal" from the parent simply because no overt pathology was attached to them. For example, in exploring "walking," the interviewer will not only want to know that the child walked at thirteen months, but also if the child was openly joyful at being able to walk, or if fearfulness and distress accompanied the acquisition. Did the child use the newfound talent in an adventurous way to explore the environment, or was the walking used to follow his mother around and to cling to her? In this way, not only is the timing of the developmental acquisition explored, its significance to child and family is also scrutinized.

Collecting developmental history has thus, a twofold purpose. The first is to discover if there were developmental phases in which conflicts or traumata occurred which could affect later development by being the sources of transferences, ego distortions, or maturational arrests. The second purpose of this segment of the exploration is to learn of the child's assets, potentials, and adaptive style.

Conception and pregnancy. The interviewer can begin this part of the developmental history by inquiring when the pregnancy occurred in the marriage; if it was a pregnancy wanted by both parents; the health of *both* parents during the pregnancy; the eating, drinking, and smoking habits of both parents and especially the mother; and the significance of the pregnancy to either parent. Prugh (1983) has described how certain questions regarding anticipatory images of the as-yet-unborn child, and the feeling states during the pregnancy can reveal much about the parental attitudes and reactions to the pregnancy and the arrival of the baby. Prugh's questions can be useful in this segment of the interview.

In exploring the nature of the pregnancy with the child in question, it is useful to compare it with other pregnancies that the mother may have had. Changes in the parents' relationship during the pregnancy should be elicited and noted.

Two situations that leave the couple and child vulnerable to future psychopathology occur frequently enough to merit particular mention here. They are mentioned at this point since they can most tactfully be explored when discussing pregnancies.

The first involves those instances in which a pregnancy occurred premaritally. Even in the cases in which a marriage was already contemplated, I have seen latent, residual resentment on the part of one parent or the other in feeling trapped into marriage by the pregnancy. These resentments sometimes affect the marriage and, therefore, inevitably the children. The dates of each pregnancy should be ascertained.

The second situation described by Cain and Cain (1964) is that in which a pregnancy, either when planned or by the significance given to it later becomes a way of replacing a child who was lost. Both parents and child are in jeopardy in these instances, even if none of them is aware of the specters against which they struggle.

Description of labor and delivery. In addition to investigating if any trauma occurred to the child during delivery, or if the child was born with genetic deformities, this section can be useful in giving the diagnostician insights into the emotional climate into which the child was born. Issues which might reveal physical trauma or vulnerabilities include whether the baby was term or preterm, the size of the baby, its appearance, whether or not instruments were used during delivery, and whether or not the baby was physiologically stable after birth (today it is not unusual to find mothers who are sufficiently conversant with medical terms to be able to describe the child's APGAR score). The mother's own description of the delivery may provide useful information about her psychological state and reaction to the birth.

State of the mother and child in the immediate postpartum period. I have found the film produced at Case Western Reserve entitled "The Amazing Newborn" a helpful guide to the inquiry about this period. What the mother remembers about the child's cry, its gaze, and her responses helps to describe the emotional climate. Special attempts should be made to learn if the mother had a period of depression following the birth of the child, and how long the depression lasted. This issue should be followed by inquiry about depressions in subsequent pregnancies. I have seen a couple of instances in which the reactions of a child to the birth of a younger sibling, originally thought to have been sibling rivalry turned out to be fear and sadness around the mother's prolonged, postpartum depression.

The first years of life. The first year of the child's life is a time of such individual variability and of changes that are so momentous that every discovery about its nature leaves us more amazed than before. This is the year during which two of the three events that René Spitz (1959) called the psychic organizers occur. (Spitz described the basic organizers of the psychological apparatus as being the smiling response of the baby, the anxiety that appeared in the presence of strangers and in the absence of the familiar parent, and the ability to communicate no and yes. The first two of these occur during this astounding first year of life.) It is the year in which the entire organization of the family can undergo fundamental and lasting changes, and it is a year in which adaptive events occur which leave us awestruck and humble in the face of their subtlety and power. To attempt to present a checklist of elements to be explored would be to denigrate the complexity of the first year of life with a mantle of pseudosimplicity. The clinician should be ready to be surprised, and to follow the clues that emerge in the history gathering. While encouraging wide reading of the developmental literature, I would warn against cramming the family into molds of development that consist only of concepts that have been researched and written on. Rather, the diagnostician should assume an attitude of inquiry that conceives of each history-gathering session as an exercise in research, using the techniques of naturalistic observation. Below are a few of the developmental transactions whose exploration have often yielded useful information about the child and his family.

In terms of the changes in the family, special attention should be paid to changes in the father's or the mother's work patterns and personal habits. The family's eating and sleeping patterns are sometimes described as if they were routine and of no great import, but on further scrutiny are found to be indicators of important change in their relationships. The nature, pace, and stability of the changes in the child's eating and sleeping patterns, when scrutinized microscopically will be found to be not merely the products of the child's growth and development, but more the results of unspoken behavioral transactions between child and caretaker in the context of a cultural environment. Sander (1980) and his co-workers have opened previously unimagined vistas of developmental trans- actions with their investigation of this area. The physical growth and development of the child during this period should be explored, and how the parent experienced this growth should be registered with equal care. For example, the parent who describes her child's feeding patterns in terms that convey ex- uberance, appetitiveness, and excitement, reflects a very dif- ferent emotional climate than one who describes the child as voracious, demanding, and insatiable.

One special variable to be assessed is that of the plasticity or rigidity of all the components of the family system as they adapt to the baby's first year. How capable are the family mem- bers of changing adaptive strategies if a particular form of adaptation is not producing the desired results? What choices and resources does one member of the family have available to respond to a developmental step or a regression that occurs in another member or the child? Are there external factors, such as poverty, ignorance, or ideational convictions that reduce plasticity and increase rigidity in one or more members of the family? As a rule of thumb, plasticity is virtually synonomous with health and rigidity with vulnerability during development. This determination, however, cannot be made by means of direct questions. Most often the family member or historian simply does not have the perceptions available that would per- mit them to give a response to a direct question. It is the diag- nostician's sensitivity to changes in roles, differences in the way each family member responds to internal or external stimuli, and changes in self-perceptions, that are indicators of plasticity or lack of it. A moving example of plasticity is portrayed in the soliloquy from the musical *Carousel*. In it Billy Bigelow, an ex- pectant father, contemplates the arrival of his child. The de- scriptions of his imagined responses to his child are not only psychologically sound, they are poignant and touching.

Information about the baby's fear of strangers and sepa- ration from familiar figures in the second half of the first year may provide evidence for the child's attachments, growing capacity for discrimination and the responsivity of the environment to his emotional needs. To attempt to communicate the *feeling* of the richness of the process that unfolds during this period, I will once more limit myself to just a few of the issues that may invite exploration.

During the first and second year of life, the observer can see the child move from perceiving the meaning of speech, to imitating speech, to imitating the meaning of speech, and finally to initiating speech. It is probably impossible for us to recapture or imagine the difference this creates in the world of the child. To be able to make changes in one's environment with an uttered sound must to the child have all of the elements of magic! Also, to be able to organize objects, perception of people, one's feelings, and other classes of phenomena by attaching symbolic labels to them must be like discovering a new world every hour. How different for the child to be in an environment that supports and encourages this newfound activity from an environment that treats it with indifference or actively discourages the initiative that comes with speech. (Children should be seen and not heard!)

In much the same way the act of walking represents a new scenario in which a host of physical and psychological attributes are represented. Questions regarding the time that the first steps occurred, the uses to which they were put by the child, how they were received by the environment, and the affects that accompanied the newfound talent can reveal elements of the developmental process that might not be available from other sources.

In addition then to discovering when the child began to speak, and what the child's first words were, the clinician would want to know how the child's initiative as expressed by speech and motor activity was tolerated, supported, cherished, or inhibited by his environment. In this issue of initiative important in the developmental process? Let me ask the reader to recall the emphasis with which a child proclaims, "I can do it myself!" when a well-intentioned adult tries to help the child by completing a task that the child is attempting to accomplish for himself. Or let me ask that the reader recall the irritation felt when someone requests that he do something that he had already resolved to do on his own initiative.

The hallmarks of the second year are integration, initiative, and mastery. These qualities change the child from a reflexive or passive recipient of the benefits of the environment to an active participant in his ecology. Those basic skills which the child acquires such as walking and talking are integrated into a whole which the child puts into the service of complex transactions with the world. These transactions involve initiative and mastery and it is by seeking to explore their ebb and flow that the diagnostician will feel his way into the child's developmental patterns rather than simply rediscover the dates of walking and talking as listed in the baby book.

For those children, who are the first or second in the family, this period is the time when the child's parents may be thinking of having another baby. In some families there is open communication to the child about the wish that he have a "little brother or sister." Sometimes the two-year-old is quite competent to convey the notion that his parents should not go to all that trouble on his account. Other times, the child may pretend to be caught up in the excitement of the proposal or actually find the idea an appealing one. Most of the time, a two-year-old can react in an adaptive way to the pregnancy and birth of a new sibling. If a pregnancy did occur during this period, the reactions and mode of adapting should be carefully investigated. Children with younger siblings not only needed to adapt to being displaced as the baby in the family, they also had to cope with the normal self-preoccupation of a pregnant mother. Some children interpret the mother's "normal narcissism" during pregnancy as a withdrawal of affection or rejection of their growing competence.

Much of the value can be learned about the family, the child, and the microculture that the family represents in a description of the philosophies and techniques that were used in toilet training the child. Descriptions of the child's competence

to be trained gives the examiner some notion of the intactness
and maturity of the central nervous system. When difficulties
in toilet training are reported, careful inquiry into the patterns
of compliance and resistance to the training process can reveal
whether the child wanted to be trained, but had not yet acquired
the neuromuscular skills, or had the skills but did not want to
use them. Each of these possibilities describes a different picture
of parent–child interaction in this phase.

The process of toilet training has specific contributions to
make to the development of awareness of initiative in the child.
In introducing the child to the process, the parents are simul-
taneously introducing the child to the culture's standards regarding values, such as cleanliness, privacy, shame, and inhibition.
In being trained, the child is showing not only his willingness
to act in a prescribed manner, he is also demonstrating willingness to identify with a group's standards, values, and modes
of *self-regulation*. To regulate one's self requires that the mentor
be relinquished and that activity or inhibition be initiated from
within. This, then is the time when this lifelong process of
identification with values that lead to self-regulation acquires
a pattern, or style by which it is carried out. Certainly there will
be modifications and alterations to these adaptive patterns with
subsequent experiences, but many of the basic qualities and
accompanying affective tones that these patterns of adaptation
acquire during the period when they are established remain
fundamental and virtually immutable. The foundations of
"character" can be found in this period.

Until that period of life during which toilet training and
a whole host of other do's and don'ts were introduced, the child
had lived in a Nirvana in which he was immersed in love, affection, tenderness, and comforting simply by virtue of his existence. With this new phase of development, there are times
when, in order to get adults to behave in that adoring fashion
that was expectable in the past, the child must be careful not
to walk on the cat, nor to enjoy the efficacy of his grasp by
pulling the tablecloth off of the table, and has to even suffer
the indignity of having to sit bare-bottomed on a hard, cold seat

suspended over a cataract that rushes, roars, and gurgles beneath a vulnerable and undefended bottom. It is a difficult and trying period, and one must wonder if the temper tantrums occasionally seen during the "terrible twos" may not be an expression of the grief at having lost the carefree existence of the first undemanding year of life. How the child coped with this cruel new world of the second year, what new talents were developed, the psychological defenses employed, and the characterological styles that began to evolve are parts of the mosaic that will eventually help define the diagnostic picture.

The preschool years. The capacity for identifications, wish for self-regulation, desire for initiative, and recognition of the self as an entity separate from the parents, which began to appear in the second year of life become dominant themes during the rest of the preschool years. Rapidly increasing motor and perceptual competence is put on display for mothers, fathers, grandparents, aunts, uncles, neighbors, and any other person that the child deigns to designate as a worthy admirer. The attention and admiration of this often captive audience is then used by the child to assure them that they are admirable, worthy of note, and capable of mastering what has now become a boundless world. As the child progresses through this period, activity flourishes, demands for attention and admiration increase, and identifications are more flamboyantly displayed. By the time the child is four or four and one half years old, they are ready to portray that which they have perceived in their microcosm to be the quintessence of being a male or being a female.

During the preschool years the child's world has increased enormously. Television programs, visits to the homes of playmates and neighbors, and contacts with preschool teachers all offer new models with which to identify. Playmates and more egalitarian interactions with siblings provide relationships that make increased psychological separation from the parents possible. Four-year-olds, for example, will repeat a nonsense syllable which has meaning only for them in the presence of an adult and break into gales of laughter. It is obvious that the privacy is more important than the probable scatological meaning of the syllable. This is but one example of their efforts to increase psychological separateness from adults.

Mischief during this phase, usually carried out with fellow preschool miscreants, is more often predicated on love of initiative coupled with poor judgment, rather than hostility or aggression. At the same time expressions of attachment and affection begin to be spontaneous and not just produced on demand. It is a time when the healthy child seems to have become convinced that the world needs to be shaken so that it may awaken to the wonders of his presence. It is a time when the child seems to be convinced that with each shake the world will reveal even more to his immense curiosity. It is a time which when properly scrutinized by the investigator can tell much about the budding temperament and character of the child, and the reaction these elicit from his environment.

The tapestry of oedipal themes. Prepared with the communicative capacity of a thespian, and the readiness to absorb of a sponge, the child enters that phase of development in which oedipal strivings and adaptations will take center stage. From the time of Freud's description of psychological development in essentially human rather than mechanical terms the Oedipus complex has been the portal through which students and observers of human psychology have entered the world of the individual's unconscious, his unspoken longings and strivings, and his unique, individual sense of self. To think of this phase of development as one in which the only important event was the conflict involved in the child's wish to experience sexual interaction with the parent of the opposite sex, is to grossly oversimplify the concept. Although it is a pale and lifeless analogy, it would be better to think of the oedipal situation as a loom to which the threads spun in the earlier life experiences of the child are woven into a tapestry that will to a large extent be the stable backdrop from which the rest of his development will evolve. The individual threads of pregenital development will have been integrated into new figures, shadings, and situations that have a significance and an impact of their own. At the same time, new functions emerge which are the products of the maturation that occurs during these years and not the modification of pregenital elements. We, as child workers, differ somewhat from some of our colleagues in adult work, in that we have always been more attentive to the pregenital elements in oedipal organization. The works of Klein, Winnicott, Mahler, Prugh, and Sander are but a few of the examples of this basic interest. The works of Ferenczi, Abraham, and Kohut are examples of some of the adult analysts who have shared this interest.

One of the important changes that occurs during the oedipal period is the further differentiation of the capacity to relate to others. Prior to this phase, the child was perfectly capable of understanding that father, mother, sister, grandfather, and grandmother were different people and had different characteristics. A bit more scrutiny, however, would reveal that despite acknowledgment of these differences, he related to all of them in a strikingly uniform manner. The most important factors in determining how he related to familiar people at any given moment were his mood and the state of his need tensions or wishes. After the battles of the oedipal wars are joined and resolved, the child is not only capable of behaving differently with his mother from the way he behaves with his father, he also demonstrates awareness that the way mother and father interact will influence the way he will behave with them. Parents, who are divided on issues in the home, invariably find that their five- and six-year-old children are quick to sense, and sometimes exploit their differences. In classical terminology, this is the distinction between diadic and triadic modes of relating. This shift is an important acquisition for the child in that it allows him to abandon an essentially self-centered view of human relatedness, and permits empathic understanding of the relationships of others. As we will see later, this broadens the sources of identifications immensely. Graphically, this change can be represented as in Figure 6-1.

Once the clinician has the concept of diadic and triadic modes of relating, it is not difficult to determine which mode

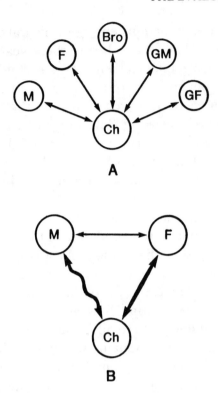

Figure 6-1. The child (ch) perceives his father, mother, brother, and grandparents (Fa, Mo, Br, Gm, Gf) as different persons but relates to them in an identical manner, A. This is the diadic mode. In B, the child not only perceives mother and father as different and relates differently. He is aware that their relatedness will affect the way he relates to them. This is the triadic mode.

the child uses. This determination is one way of evaluating the exent of the child's oedipal resolution.

In struggling with oedipal conflicts and working toward their resolution, the child must find increasingly more acceptable ways of expressing and gratifying wishes and desires. That which had been a relatively frank, sensuous attachment before, now begins to find expression in tenderness. Aggression and destructiveness begin to find outlets in competition, and hungers turn into appetites. The facility and style with which these sublimations take place reveal to the clinician both the talents of the child and the sensitivity of his environment during this period.

As Inhelder and Piaget (1958) have demonstrated, children of five or six have not yet attained the maturity to utilize propositional thinking for trial action. Yet a change has taken place in the way they manage their thoughts. Prior to this period, when wishes and impulses came into conflict with environmental constraints, the child would indulge in open, and even public protest regarding his frustrations. This is no longer true in the oedipal child. It is only through derivatives in play or fantasies that one learns of the oedipal wishes and frustrations that buffet the child. Thoughts and motives have become private and this privacy will affect the way the child relates to his environment. Certainly the diagnostician cannot expect the child to display the unguarded candor characteristic of his preoedipal days. The child's thoughts are his own now, and parent as well as therapist need an alliance with the child in order to learn what these thoughts are. This must be borne in mind both when getting a history from the parent as well as when interviewing the child.

In closing this section, I would recall that we in psychiatry have borrowed unevenly from Sophocles' tragedy. We recall frequently that Oedipus slew his father and married his mother. Only rarely do we recall that the tragedy began when Laius sent his infant son out to the hills to die. We need to bear in mind that while oedipal wishes may start and use as a vehicle *intrapsychic* striving, their vicissitudes and resolution occur in an interpersonal context. How the father resolved his own oedipal conflict will in part determine how he will react to his son's oedipal wishes.

The School-age Child. With the advent of school the youngster enters a new social environment, populated by strangers and, to the outrage of the individual child, by a large number of little people who are just as demanding, noisy, and intrusive as he is. For some children, even though there are elements of frustration in the experience, the overall excitement and stimulation is very welcome. For a few other children it is the beginning of one of the most painful periods in their young lives. For all children it is anything but a neutral experience.

The beginning of school may mean different things to different families. One family may feel that though they are helpless to interfere, beginning school means that their child is facing new dangers and harm. To another family those first trembling, tentative steps that their child takes on his way to the first day of school are the beginning of a pilgrimage that will lead the first of their family away from poverty, ignorance, and degradation. The impact that the beginning of school has on the child is matched by its significance to the family. This too is data that must be elicited, especially from families who are from a minority culture.

In addition to the child's performance in school, the interviewer will want to know what that performance meant to the child and the family.

> Johnny, aged nine, was referred by his school after his formerly excellent school performance precipitously became abysmal. No external events could be found for the deterioration, and all that the evaluator could get from Johnny was that he hated school because his teacher was "boring and a geek." During the third diagnostic session in a fit of anger, Johnny revealed that his teacher, in attempting to encourage some of the more passive students in the class to take more interest in reading, said, "You don't want to be like those dummies who can't read all your life." Johnny's father, who was much loved by his son, was illiterate, and Johnny knew it.

As a rule parent and child cooperate to meet the stress of separation when it is time to start school. In some instances the parents sabotage the child's attempts to find the courage to go to school, and in other cases the child sabotages the parent's attempts to support him in his new endeavor. These are all issues that require exploration when school problems arise. Issues of separation can be difficult for both the family and the child to acknowledge or master. School failure or disruptive behavior may be the disguise behind which the painful intolerance of separation may hide. This is particularly important to remember today because all too often we see a pseudodiagnosis of "learning disability" applied to a child without adequate evaluation of psychodynamic problems. In these cases, even if remedial activities are successful, the problem of separation intolerance may remain.

> Danny was twelve when I began to treat him for a "school phobia." For a number of reasons I was unsuccessful in my attempts to help him, and he returned to school only after he was coerced by the threat of reform school. It was the threat rather than any therapeutic gain that made the symptom disappear, and following his return to school, Danny refused further treatment. I next heard about Danny some six years later from a military psychiatrist, who called me for information. Danny was being tried for being AWOL. He had left high school without graduating as soon as it was legally possible for him to do so, and taken a job. He found that there were days when he simply could not stay at work because of the same kind of anxiety he had suffered in school. After losing several jobs due to his attendance problems, he was convinced to join the armed forces. He was absent without leave twice within the first month, attempting to reach home each time. When imprisoned, he became so anxious that he had to be hospitalized.

Obviously, information about how child and family manage the school years is germane to emotional as well as cognitive development.

The teacher is often the object of the first, intense, adult relationship that the child has outside of his home. It is not surprising, therefore, to see some of the characteristics of the home relationships reflected in the child's interaction with his teacher. The relationship to the teacher not only has a primary importance of its own to the child and his family but in it the child also relives with transference, poignant issues of times gone by.

Puberty. Just about the time that going to school becomes routine, working in school becomes a habit, and even beginning to enjoy school becomes acceptable, puberty comes along to disrupt adaptation. Awareness of feeling awkward, body changes that seem to happen overnight, and an almost constant conviction that someone will ridicule them because of these changes all conspire to make the pubescent child's ability to attend to serene, cognitive pursuits, difficult. If the diagnostician is gentle and the child has sufficient trust, he can sometimes tell of these tribulations quite directly.

Two aspects of puberty that require special attention are the physical changes that occurred in the youngster, and how puberty affected family relationships. Information regarding physical changes should be accompanied, whenever possible, by estimates from the mother of how her son or daughter reacted to these physical changes. Some of the issues that might be included in this section would be descriptions of how growth spurts and new functions affected relationships with peers or altered the youngster's activities in school or at home. For example, menarche and breast development can cause worry and preoccupations that reveal much about psychological sets and relationships that characterize women's roles in the family. Nocturnal emissions may have the same effects on boys. Attitudes toward sexual activities, femininity, masculinity, expectation of the role the child will play in his or her social setting are sometimes quite openly expressed using the physical changes of puberty as a point of departure. Some attempt can be made at this point to elicit information about the child's masturbation and other manifestations of budding sexuality. Despite our system of universal education and the enlightenment that television sets have brought into virtually every home, it is still staggering to see the amount of misinformation and ignorance about human sexuality that characterizes many adults. It is not rare for a diagnostician to detect that a mother has conveyed to her

daughter that her menses were only the overt manifestation of
the pervasive "curse" of being an adult, sexually mature woman.
It is also not unheard of that a father conveys to a male son
that masturbation and sexual activity before marriage will certainly lead to a weakening of the will, loss of cognitive powers,
if not downright softening of the brain, or premature impotence. The converse situation may at times be detected, in which
a mother or father unconsciously stimulates their child and tells
them what to do by telling them not to do it.

> The mother of a depressed and anxiety-ridden
> seventeen-year-old was describing how she had at-
> tempted to help her daughter during puberty. She had
> bought her daughter her first bra and in giving it to
> her admonished her that now that she had breasts all
> the boys would want to touch her. She then went on
> to warn her daughter to stay away from the neigh-
> borhood park with a boy because there were so many
> places there where they could remain hidden, and if
> a boy touched her breasts, the daughter would have
> such ecstatic feelings and such intense sensations that
> she might be tempted to "go all the way." Even as she
> remembered the conversation with her daughter, her
> face was animated by an excitement that was clearly
> conveyed to the interviewer, though she remained un-
> aware of it herself.

The physical changes of puberty are thus the starting points
of far-reaching changes in the relationship between parents and
children. Most of the time, these changes are sensitively
achieved and productive for continued growth and development of both parents and children. For the sake of their child's
privacy, or in the name of allowing their child's judgment to
mature, the sensitive parent becomes less intrusive, less vigilant,
and perhaps even less curious about their child's activities. Even
in unconflicted situations, a bit of parental sadness accompanies
this because the young bear cub or the young swan is about to
begin the journey that will take them away from the den or the

nest, but it is without resentment and without detachment of investment in the child. In fact, the parents stand ready once more to become comforters, mentors, regulators, or confidants if their children stumble or are bruised on the path to independence and need to regress for a while. The following situations are ones that the interviewer may have to spend more time scrutinizing because they are potential sources of problems:

1. Those instances in which the parent or the child cannot tolerate the necessary separation. The attachment in these cases is often manifested as hostility in which the parent undercuts the maturational gains of the child, or the child repeatedly creates crises that the parent must resolve. The end result is constant attention to each other and no progressive maturation.
2. Because of earlier hurt, or current pain, that which should be phase appropriate, flexible, separation–individuation, becomes rigid, distant detachment for the parent or the child.
3. Those instances in which parent, child, or both *experience* rejection instead of age-appropriate separation.
4. Those instances in which childhood modes of expressing affection and attachment are abandoned in puberty, but no new and more mature ways of expressing affection, tenderness, investment, and concern are developed between parent and child.

After a careful inventory of the shifts and changes in family relationships has been made by the diagnostician, the focus of inquiry must move on to an evaluation of the youngster's peer relationships. It may be necessary here to employ active inquiry because many parents will mention peer relationships spontaneously only to express chagrin. They may complain that peer group members are not sufficiently studious or polite, or they may express their concern about drug use in the group, but they seldom worry about a child's inability to develop peer relationships, and seldom acknowledge the maturational value of interactions with peers. The peer group is a helpful waystation on the road to independence, and the youth's success or failure in negotiating it is an important indicator of his mental health.

THE FAMILY HISTORY

By the time that the examiner has completed the developmental history of the child, there will be much about the history of the nuclear family which will already have been revealed. In this section of the diagnostic evaluation the examiner can seek additional information about some unexplained event or situation, or to round out what may be known only in sketchy terms. When the diagnostician finishes this section of the examination, he should have a working knowledge of the following areas.

Family development. A relatively clear, sequential account of the development of the nuclear family from the time of the parent's marriage to the time of the evaluation should be available to the clinician. This should include moves, work patterns, financial history, and separations or disruptions in the family's composition or in the family's customary life-style. The timing and sequence of the births in the family should be accompanied by descriptions of how each family member reacted to the birth. The family's reaction to any other important event should be sought and evaluated.

Financial history and fee setting. The financial history of the family has practical and immediate significance in addition to its historical relevance. At some point during the diagnostic evaluation, the therapist must discuss the question of fees with responsible members of the family. Many times setting a fee will pose no particular problem, and occur almost automatically. At other times, it will become an important issue to manage and more will be said about it later in a section on management. During the evaluative phase of the treatment, it can be a delicate issue of remarkable complexity. From the point of view of assessing the family's resources, it is not enough to know only how much money the family has available to them. Equally important is the family's attitude toward money and priorities in spending it. It is not rare that a fairly affluent family manages their money so poorly, or has expenses that are so depleting that they cannot afford treatment. At other times, one can find a family that is simply unwilling to spend this money on therapy. The therapist must discover these conditions if therapeutic planning is to foresee and avoid false starts.

The clinician must be aware that his status is also a variable in the fee setting procedure. If he is in a private practice, fees will be a source of his livelihood and have a different significance for him than if he works in an institution that is supported by taxes, grants or other funds. The fee also conveys a covert message of where he is seen on the pecking order or seniority or prestige and this significance may spill over into the clinician's perception of his own worth. Fee setting can be contaminated by punitive or indulgent attitudes toward the parents, and these attitudes may be undetected if the process is not carefully scrutinized.

These are but a few of the issues that may enter into the fee setting component of the transaction with the child's family. The rules of thumb that best safeguard against inadvertent contaminants are that fees should not be set without scrutiny of the content and process of the transaction, and that the concrete issue of the number of dollars not be allowed to detract from the significane of the fee to the patient and therapist.

When to discuss fees becomes a matter of clinical judgment. If the fee is discussed too soon, the clinician may convey an attitude of detachment or crassness. If not done soon enough, the family may feel trapped into a undertaking that seduced them into paying more than they could afford. I have usually found it most convenient to discuss insurance and fees with the mother sometime during the process of gathering the family history when she indicates that she pays a good number of the bills of the household. In case this is not the arrangement in the family, I will hold off the discussion until the completion or reporting interview when the mother and father are together, or make arrangements to speak to the father alone at some other time. If the family cannot afford the therapist's fees, and the therapist feels he cannot or does not wish to accept a low fee patient at this time, a genuinely concerned effort made to find a suitable, competent therapist, who can treat the child for a reduced fee, is usually appreciated by the family.

Medical history. Medical history in regard to any pertinent biogenetic information should be described in this section. Hereditary conditions are, of course, important, but some caution is in order when we remember that genetics have probably been blamed for more neurotic traits than any other medical cause, with the possible exception of dietary deficiencies or excesses. Illnesses of major import and also recurrent less serious illnesses and their effects on each member of the family need to be recorded. The state of the child's grandparents may assume major significance here and especially important may be the child's reaction to a grandparent's death.

In this segment of the history, the diagnostician should include a developmental profile of the mother and father as well as any significant psychological or physical ailment they may have suffered. This is also an opportune time to learn of the way the mother and father met, when and why they decided to marry. Some of this information may have to be obtained in a later interview with the father, but should include a sexual history of both parents and also the current status of their sexual relationship.

While I will reserve the bulk of the discussion on how we can place the history in a useful frame of reference for a later chapter, I would like to mention here that after collecting this much anamnestic material, I have found it useful to begin to look for patterns of behaviors or emotional states that seem to have recurred in the history of the parents, and may now be making an appearance in the life of the child.

An eleven-year-old girl had been referred because she had been having outbursts of anger toward her mother, and had become physically abusive to her five-year-old sister. Her mother was also afraid that she would become aggressive to her two-year-old brother, even though there had been no evidence to suggest this might happen. In the course of presenting the family history, the mother recalled that she was the eldest of five children and when she was about nine years of age her own mother's capacities to manage the household had been eroded by the onset of severe arthritis and alcoholism. As the eldest child, she was burdened with too much responsibility too soon, and recalled bitter quarrels with her mother about having to do all the work while her siblings did little more than add to her load. She sadly added that she had resolved that her relationship with her daughter was going to be nothing like the unhappy relationship she had with her own mother, but ironically she found herself sitting in a psychiatrist's office complaining that the very thing that she had dreaded had come to pass. What this sad and hurt woman was not able to perceive was that a pattern had evolved from her past and was having an effect on her present life. Whenever she needed to request help or to assign a task to her eleven-year-old daughter, she was so convinced that her daughter would feel the same resentment toward her that she had felt toward her own mother that she became inordinately sensitive and saw hostility everywhere. The daughter, in her turn, felt that nothing she could do would ever satisfy her mother and that her younger sister and brother were the favored ones in the family. A dusty, old, unhappy script from the past forced its patterns into the present.

When the diagnostician feels that he has learned as much as is necessary or possible to learn from the mother, the question arises of who will be seen next. At times this question will be answered by some of the data already collected. If there are no clearcut indications it can be left to the family's convenience or the clinician's preference. Mothers will sometimes, for a variety of reasons, declare with great certainty that the child's father will refuse to come in for a diagnostic interview. I would urge that this not be taken at face value, and that the clinician ask that he be given a chance to contact the father directly. It is surprising to see how a father who had been billed as absolutely recalcitrant, can accept and welcome the chance to participate in the care of his child when this is requested by the professional caretaker.

The topics discussed in this chapter are intended as an *overview* of the kinds of issues that require scrutiny if the psychodynamically oriented evaluation is to lead to a dynamic formulation that serves both understanding and planning. Every evaluation will have a pace, profile, and character of its own, and in respecting this the diagnostician may find that one section in the history may be greatly more detailed than another. When not forced into the mold of prejudgment, the history of most families will come alive of its own accord, and guide the diagnostician to understanding.

CHAPTER 7

Meetings with the Child and the Completion Interview

PREPARATION FOR THE CHILD'S INTERVIEW

When the diagnostician is satisfied with the amount of historical information he has available, preparations for meeting with the child patient can begin. The decision to meet with the child should not be an automatic one made simply because there have been meetings with the parents. It should be predicated on adequate information that the child has symptoms that require psychological investigation, that it is a time when a diagnostic interview can reveal something of his inner world, and that there are no current contraindications to a diagnostic interview.

Once it is determined that the child should be seen, the time of the appointment needs to be set. There is a way of doing this that reduces the child's anxiety and increases the opportunity for a productive first session. This technique also illustrates a therapeutic philosophy that should apply to all phases of the treatment, and for this reason I will describe the origin of the principle, the technique, and its significance.

D. W. Winnicott was a pediatrician as well as a psychoanalyst, and continued to teach pediatrics to medical students almost until the end of his life. Part of this teaching was conducted in the well baby clinic of the hospital in which he worked. There, he sat on one side of a table, with the medical students seated behind him. As each mother–child pair came into this consultation room, he would invite the mother to place the baby on a mat on the table, and sit opposite him. Thus, Winnicott would create an assembly of three, as he, mother, and the child contributed to the evaluation, each in his own way. When the evaluation was over, the mother would pick up her child and make for the door at the far end of the room. On occasion, Winnicott would ask the mother to pause for a moment before exiting as he looked at the baby intently. After a few moments he would thank the mother and allow her to leave without further comment. The medical students were convinced that he was observing something, but could not fathom what he scrutinized at the door that he would not have been able to see when the child was on the table. When, finally, they asked him why he was stopping certain mothers at the door, he remarked with some surprise that they must not have noticed that some babies were not ready to terminate the interview yet. They were puzzled, and he was obliged to explain further that some babies after being picked up and safely ensconced in the mother's arms could do something that they had not been able to do when lying on the table. They could *initiate their own observations* of the people who had been observing them. At times, when they reached the door, they were still craning their necks and looking, indicating to Winnicott that their curiosity was not yet appeased. He then would ask the mother to wait until the baby was ready to go.

In addition to the delightful creativity and sensitivity, there is an important therapeutic principle that was exemplified by this practice. That principle was Winnicott's profound *respect* for the child's individuality and *initiative*. Successful psychotherapy requires that this respect be sincerely felt and clearly demonstrated to the child by the therapist. It can begin with the first interview, and for this reason I will attempt to show how this principle can modify technique even as early as the time when the therapist makes the first appointment with the child.

After the parents' interviews, I ask them what they have told their children about their own meetings with me, and the child's future visit. Often they will say that they had not yet mentioned it since they had hoped to get some suggestions about how the child should be prepared. If the parents have discussed the appointment, I ask what the child was told and how he reacted. If they have not mentioned it, I suggest that they tell the child, *in their own words*, that they are concerned about his behavior, or worries, or his unhappiness. For this reason they've talked to a person who *listens* to children (please note that the word is *listens*, not *talks* to children), and who will then try to *help them* make things better for themselves. I will then check my schedule. If I have one hour open, I explain that to the parent and ask how it fits with the child's schedule. Whenever possible, I try to provide several choices. If the parent can bring the child at any of those times, I ask the parent to have the child call me in the next day or two to make his own appointment. The parent may then say, "But Johnny is only four." I remind them that he talks on the telephone to Grandma and seems to enjoy it, and usually the parents are pleased to comply. Occasionally a parent will tell me that they are convinced that the child will not call, or won't talk to me if they call. I ask them to give it a try, and if it is absolutely impossible to get him to talk to me, we will arrange an appointment without the child's participation. My experience has been that it is rare that a child will not call. The conversation that takes place when Johnny calls will, of course, vary with age, but for now let's assume that Johnny is four years old. Then it may go something like this:

> Therapist: Hello, Johnny.
> Johnny: Huwo.
> Therapist: (After a brief pause to see if Johnny has more to say), I'm the person your mom and dad talked to about your worries (or problems, or sad feelings) and I wanted to hear what you thought about these worries to see if you and I could figure out a way to help you feel better. Can you come see me on Monday?

Johnny: What's Monday?

Therapist: Well, you know the day that Dad stays at home and watches the Broncos on television? The day after that is Monday. (By this time the diagnostician should know enough about the family habits to permit him too use recurrent events as markers if time concepts are too abstract for the child.)

Johnny: Oh yea. That's the day I go to widdle cwitters.

Therapist: Oh? What's widdle cwitters?

Johnny: Nooo! Not widdle cwitters. Widdle Cwitters!! That's my pway school. (The mother may have already informed you that Johnny attends Little Critters Nursery School on Monday afternoons.)

Therapist: O.K. How about coming to see me after play school?

Johnny: No. That's when I watch "Giwigan's Island."

Therapist: I see. Then how about coming to see me on Wednesday, that's two days after that?

Johnny: (Almost invariably) O.K. Bye.

I then ask to speak to mother, or if Johnny has hung up on me too quickly, call her to confirm the appointment time.

In examining this transaction closely we can make some inferences about it. Johnny's first contacts with the clinician occurred while he was in a safe and familiar place. In addition, he was in virtually complete control, because if he became too anxious he could simply hang up the phone. While Johnny was in this relatively safe situation, the clinician communicated his responsibility to tell Johnny what the transaction was all about. Also, the clinician assured Johnny that if he did not understand a word, idea, or concept (What's Monday?) the clinician would find a way to make it comprehensible. Finally, by allowing a bit of flexibility in choosing the appointment time, Johnny was assured that what was important to him ("Giwigan's Island") would be respected and that he had something to say about what was going to happen.

Let's contrast this with what can, and sometimes does happen when a child is taken to an appointment that has been arranged without his participation. Mother or Father may or may not have been sufficiently clear about where they were going and why they were going there. Johnny is taken by the hand, put in the car, and *passively* led to a room, where there may be strangers milling around. After a wait, during which he may see other children taken off by unfamiliar adults, and may not see them return, a stranger comes to him and says "Please come with me, Johnny." Again, he is *passively* escorted to another room, and then the stranger says in essence, "Now be *active!*" Tell me about yourself. What a perplexing and perhaps frightening experience that must be for a child.

At a conference in which some of these ideas were discussed, a participant, in an impatient and irritated manner, told me that he had a busy practice, which did not lend itself to scheduling children only when they weren't watching "Gilligan's Island." The cognitive portion of his comment told me that I had not made the principle clear. I am fully aware that sometimes a schedule does not permit the luxury of offering a child two or three different hours from which he can choose. If we are to be fair, we would have to acknowledge that we are more prone to brush aside children's commitments than those of adults; but even granting that no such denigration existed, it is not the specific technique of letting the child pick one of several hours that is essential. It is attending to the principles involved that is the essential part of this recommendation. The principles are as follows:

1. We must respect the child's *sense* of what is important with as much sincerity as we do the adult's, if we are to effect an alliance with the child.
2. We must recognize that many children will feel perplexed and fear the diagnostic process. The relationship with the child should start in a way that invites the child to actively master these fears rather than in a way that expects him to passively tolerate them.
3. Psychotherapy, based on dynamic principles, requires the active participation of the child in the process. Extending the invitation to actively participate in setting the appoint-

ment communicates this requisite to the child from the beginning of the process.
4. In the context of his family, school, and social world the
   child has a right and a need for some autonomy. Allowing
   the child to participate in the setting of his appointment is
   but one way of acknowledging this.

In my practice I've found that engaging the child around
the issue of his first appointments is a timely and productive
way of observing the principles stated. Other therapists may
find that in their daily work there is another more fruitful and
predictably convenient way of establishing these working principles. In this sense the issue that one's schedule cannot be
adapted to "Gilligan's Island" is really a trivial one.

While the conference participant's protest about the scar-
city of his time convinced me that I had not made clear the
principles that I was trying to convey, his affect alerted me to
another problem. It is frequently inconvenient and irritating
for adults to grant children the right to enjoy some degree of
autonomy in their behavior and in establishing their value systems. In order to avoid recognition of this discomfort we often
present rationalizations to ourselves and the child that are
adorned in impeccable logic. If we allow ourselves this indulgence in our psychotherapeutic practice, we may enjoy the
short-term advantage of increased immediate comfort, but at
the expense of a firm and productive working alliance with the
child. Since I have begun the practice of having the child call
me to establish the time of his appointment, I have found the
first diagnostic hour with the child to be more productive, less
anxiety laden, and the resistances to self-revelation less rigid.

Before meeting the child it may be useful to the clinician
to review some attitudes that affect techniques. The first of
these has to do with accepting the idea that children require
confidentiality. When they are comfortable, children will often
reveal that they don't want anyone to know that they are coming
to see a psychiatrist.

My conviction is that the most frequent breaches of sensitivity to the child's wish for confidentiality occur in the waiting

room. This is probably because it is a tense moment for child and clinician, and because many clinicians think of technique as beginning in the consulting room. The child does not make this distinction. If the waiting room is in a clinic and several people are likely to be around, the clinician is well advised to consider techniques and courtesies applicable to that area.

It is probably better in greeting the child in the waiting room, to say something like, "Hi. I'm Dr. Smith (or Mr. Smith). How are you?" rather than "Are you Johnny Jones? I'm Dr. Smith." While most of the time the little patient will not object to his name being used in a public place, there are times when this can add to the discomfort the child may be feeling because he is afraid that someone he knows may overhear his name.

As mentioned earlier, there are times when workers refer to the child's symptoms, or to some other psychological issue in the waiting room. This happens frequently when the child is having trouble leaving a parent and going with the therapist to his office. I have yet to see the instance in which this breach of confidentiality was justified. If a situation occurs in the waiting room that requires discussion, and the clinician simply cannot get the child into his office, the best bet would be to suggest to the child that he call on the phone so that the matter can be discussed privately. An alternative suggestion is to ask the child if inviting the parent into the session *for awhile* would help make him more comfortable.

The forms of expression that *sincerely felt* courtesy for the child will take, depend, of course, on both cultural expression and personal style. This cultural component is sometimes too readily overlooked. To a child from Tennessee, for example, the use of the word *Darlin'* may convey warmth, while it may have a seductive connotation to the youngster from Chicago. It is incumbent on the clinician to ascertain that the mode of expressing courtesy is appropriate in the culture of the child that they are interviewing. This, of course, is as true in the waiting room as it is in the consulting room.

There is a special situation in which courtesy and technique fuse. In order to render its description more affectively meaningful, let me ask the reader to recall a situation in which virtually all of us have found ourselves at one time or another. We are engaged in vigorous conversation with friends when from out of the blue comes a slip of the tongue that is both painfully revealing and excruciatingly embarrassing. Today everyone knows about "Freudian slips." Almost invariably there will be in the group an amateur "parlor psychoanalyst" whose genius cannot be contained by the boundaries of common courtesy and consideration. He will have to call attention to the slip, and sometimes add the obvious interpretation for it. Nearly everyone who has been the unwilling recipient of this kind of interpretation can recall the embarrassment, defensiveness, and irritation with which it was received. There are good reasons for these feelings. Most of us have paid very tidy sums for the privilege of having the door closed and a trained person officiating when we revealed unwelcomed preconscious or unconscious tendencies. More importantly, when a person explores the significances of inadvertently revealed impulses, wishes, or thoughts in a therapeutic setting, there has already been a commitment made by both therapist and patient to undertake these explorations. It is this commitment, made for the ultimate benefit of the patient that makes the pain and embarrassment of these explorations worth tolerating. No such conditions obtain in the parlor situation, and the person who made the slip has good and legitimate reasons for his chagrin.

Imagine now the situation of the child who is struggling with his fears in a waiting room, or who has just become comfortable in chatting with the diagnostician. We can see how the child would feel denuded and betrayed if, out of the blue, a confrontation, interpretation, or even question struck at the heart of something that embarrassed the child. The child's experiences would not be too far removed from what one of us would feel at the hands of that genius, the parlor analyst.

It is poor technique as well as a breach of courtesy to "sneak up" on the child with an insight, before first explaining the nature of the task to the child in the diagnostic interviews, and later in therapy, if indicated.

No amount of technical excellence can be of help if the therapist is disinterested, detached, or emotionally distant from the child and his problems. If the therapist detects disinterest in himself, this should be explored before seeing the patient. This is not the same phenomenon as the occasional boredom, which was mentioned earlier, and to which we will return in a later chapter. The phenomenon referred to here is much closer to an inability to feel curious or otherwise moved by the child or his problems. There are a number of possibilities why the otherwise normally empathic therapist might experience this apathy. The three causes for it that I have encountered most frequently in supervision or in my own case work, and that I would mention here are:

1. The therapist is fatigued or depressed.
2. The current situation is likened by the therapist to one that was previously encountered in which there was a painful therapeutic failure. This often happens with children who have multiple problems (usually of an organic or social nature) in addition to their psychopathology, and we will return to this in a special section later.
3. The cultural background of the child is so different from that of the therapist that the therapist cannot find internal resonance to the family's description of their struggles.

If the therapist's perceived apathy or disinterest cannot be eliminated, he should consider disqualifying himself as diagnostician or therapist and provide for the family's care through a respected colleague. He can then alone or with a colleague discover what internal impediment was triggered by the clinical situation.

THE COURSE OF THE DIAGNOSTIC INTERVIEW

In suggesting the flow of this first diagnostic interview, I will inevitably describe what I have found to be most natural for me. Again, I urge the therapist to develop a style that is his. What will be offered in the next pages and indeed the rest of the book is an effort to describe a process and some techniques. It is not a checklist or a road map. Each therapist–patient system develops its own road map, and together they supply the content to the process.

Having arrived at the consultation room, the child will naturally be both a bit uneasy and also curious. On entering the room, I say to the child "Please sit wherever you're comfortable." From the first I would like him to know that his comfort is a mutual concern. I then note if the child selects a chair close to or distant from the one that is obviously my chair at the desk.

The neutral conversation, which may have been started in the hall may be continued, but now with an added consideration in the mind of the therapist. The child's world may be roughly divided into the world at large (or perhaps since *Star Wars,* the universe), the world of family and intimate friends, the space that surrounds the child and the diagnostician, and the inner world of feelings, wishes, and perceptions of which only the child can be aware. In most instances, unless otherwise indicated by the child or by circumstances, it is best to move, or better yet, to let the child move from the world at large, to the world of his intimates, and only gently and gradually begin to explore issues in the interpersonal sphere of therapist and child, and his intrapsychic world.

Thus, the subject of the ride to the appointment, the location of the child's home, the activities available to the child around his home are often the starting point for the interview. From these topics it is a relatively easy step for the child to begin to describe activities that are a bit more personal and reveal the patterns of his daily life. I will often at this point ask what the child would be doing if he hadn't made an appointment for this hour. Depending on the hour of the appointment, this question will lead to a description of the school, home, or play environment. If it is school that is being talked about, favorite subjects and favorite teachers can be discussed. If it is the home, the after-school activities are discussed, and the people with whom these occur. The area of play allows for exploration of friends, sports, playmates, or how the child copes with being alone.

Here, the art of the therapist must begin to make itself felt in that he must provide an amount of structure that is optimal for each interview. Some children, perplexed as to the significance of the interview, or anxious, or perhaps disorganized, may hop from one topic to the other with such little communicative skill that the diagnostician gets no picture of what the child is trying to tell him. Others are so detailed or so microscopically organized that the child evolves toward telling the clinician more and more about less and less. The therapist should be ready to complement the child's skills by just enough intervention to get the interview into the proper range. He can do this by asking questions that are specific enough to focus the child if the interview is rambling and chaotic, or by asking open-ended questions that require expressions of feeling or preferences if the child has become too detailed or is swamped in anecdotes. Thus, the aim is to help the child avoid an interview that is so rambling that it is chaotic, or so structured that it is a recital.

As the interview progresses, the child will reveal his growing comfort in a number of ways. More animation in speech and other forms of motor expression, more open exploration of the office, requests to look at toys or items on the desk are all familiar communicators of increasing comfort and growing trust. This is an appropriate time to ask the child to describe the activities of a typical day in his life including the "most favorite" and "least favorite" things that he does. This helps the child to see that the diagnostician is interested in both pleasurable and troublesome aspects of the child's life, and opens the door to later explorations of ambivalence.

As the day is explored, the child will frequently move from a description of activities to descriptions of the people with whom these activities are undertaken. This shift provides an excellent opportunity to investigate both the significance of human relationships to the child and the actual status of these relationships. The number of friends the child has and the intensity of the friendships, the length of time that relationships have endured, memories of friends from the past, and other aspects of interactions with peers and adults can provide a detailed description of the child's capacities for human relatedness. An inability or unwillingness of the child to move into this area, even after gentle guidance by the therapist is an indication that there are difficulties that will require further investigation.

It is usually natural to move from an exploration of friendships to an assessment of the child's interactions with family members. In obtaining a description of family members the clinician can, by providing the child an opportunity to describe what he enjoys most and what he enjoys least about each person in his family, achieve two ends. The first is to begin to map out where in the mosaic of family relationship there are conflicts and difficulties and the other is to further the work started earlier on making communication about ambivalence possible. This latter is particularly important since, in younger children, the concept of ambivalence is confusing and the child may not have as yet acquired the verbal skills to express these complex and conflicting feelings. By providing structure in the form of questions the interviewer can provide tools for more sophisticated dialogue even as the interview progresses. Care must be taken, of coourse, to insure that it is tools to explore that are being provided and not suggestions of what will be found on exploration.

Often, at this point, the child will be ready to reveal the difficulties that required evaluation and perhaps treatment. This may come in the context of describing relationships in the family, or while telling of school or play activities. If the child does indicate directly or through his associations that he is ready to discuss the reasons for the evaluation (not necessarily his pleasure or his agreement that an evaluation is necessary), the therapist will find that candor and openness will be served by an acknowledgment that the child's parents were also worried about some of the problems being described. Again, there is no substitute for the clinician's judgment as to the child's readiness to speak about personal problems, but he should remember that we more often underestimate the child's ability and willingness to be candid than we overestimate it.

As the child begins to articulate what he perceives the difficulties to be, the therapist must recognize that this is not the
time to demand truth, accuracy, consistency, or validity of the
child's story. This is also not the time for confrontations or
declarations of the parent's contrasting perceptions. At this time
the therapist should try to be as unintrusive as possible and try
to get the child's *subjective sense* of the situation. The interviewer
is not looking for the "truth" as would be described by twenty
independent observers. The interviewer is looking for what the
child *thinks* is the truth, or what the child would like to convince
the interviewer is the truth. It is these perceptions, often passionately described by the child, that afford the clinician entry
into the subjective world of the child where he can become a
therapeutic agent.

That which the child feels is the essence of the problem,
the words used in telling his story to the clinician, and the affects
that accompany this revelation are all examples of the components of the interview to which the diagnostician should be
attending in addition to the substantive parts of the narration.
If, for example, the child in the midst of telling that the reason
he is being seen is because he fights with his siblings and has
hurt them on occasion, the interviewer must be as curious about
the affects and attitudes that accompanied this revelation as he
is about who started the fights and how badly the siblings were
hurt. These nonverbal components of the communication may
point to the real problem with greater reliability than the words
of the parents or child.

> Sally was a ten-year-old, being evaluated because
> her school performance was far below what it should
> have been, based on her proven abilities. Both mother
> and father were very successful professional persons
> and implicitly expected intellectual excellence and suc-
> cess from their children. As Sally was describing the
> problem of her "mom and dad getting bent all out of
> shape when I goof-up in school" she alternated be-
> tween looking perky and mischievous, occasionally
> defiant, and downright angry for having been dragged

into the evaluation. She continued by stating that her parents expected her to continue to do as well as she had done in first and second grade. As she told of her successes in these earlier grades, her demeanor and affect changed to that of a forlorn and desolate little girl. It took only one or two questions to reveal that her very busy parents never noticed or commented on success. Only "goof up" brought instant attention in her home. The diagnostician's impression that her disappointment in success needed more attention than her investment in failure was confirmed by subsequent data.

If at this point in the diagnostic evaluation, the child does reveal what his perceptions of the chief complaints are, it is probably wise to follow the revelations with a description of the explicit verbal contract regarding the interviews. The clinician should use whatever language is comfortable for him and which he is fairly certain will be understood by the child. The contract should, either explicitly or implicitly, include the following:

1. The child has a right to expect confidentiality, and unless it would constitute a clear and imminent danger to the child to remain silent, the clinician will discuss nothing with any other person without the child's knowledge.
2. The therapist will be the agent of the child and the child's ultimate welfare will be his *main* commitment. Together, they will work to understand the child's problems and to find ways by which the child *may choose* to alleviate these problems.
3. *All* human minds sometimes play tricks on themselves by distorting perceptions, or limiting the number of behavioral options available. In order to discover *if* the child is doing this to himself, the child and his therapist will work together in exploring thoughts, feelings, and events. This will not be for the purpose of coercing or restricting the child in his choices, but for the purpose of increasing the number of choices the child has in thought and behavior.

4. For therapy to be successful the child must be an active participant in the process. This will involve the child not only as he reveals his inner world, but also as he helps to formulate the conclusions that the therapist reaches. The therapist should tell the child, by word, and later by attitude and deed that he will not reach conclusions about the child without the participation of the child, or at least the child's awareness.

5. The child should be convinced that information will not be exchanged behind his back. Information about the child that the therapist receives from sources other than the child will, whenever possible, be revealed to him.

Some may disagree that this contract should be implicitly or explicitly proposed to the child this early in the relationship, and there are valid arguments to support this contention. Most convincing of these arguments is one that maintains that therapist and child have not yet had time to develop a dialogue in which words, expressions, and concepts mean approximately the same thing to both. This is a valid argument, and I would add that it may be premature to expect a child, who barely knows the diagnostician, to enter into such an important agreement with him. But the importance of a fair and honest description of the relationship and the reasons for it speak for an early discussion of the conceptual contract. In deference to the validity of the opposing argument, I would support returning to a discussion of the contract a number of times in the treatment, for the purpose of being sure that the child understands the reasons for the meetings, and because as we shall see later, the therapeutic alliance needs revitalization at times.

Sometimes it is known from the outset that if the child needs treatment the diagnostician cannot be the therapist. Despite the possibility that it may reduce the child's willingness to reveal himself, there are reasons why this should be told to the family and the youngster as soon as possible. The most potent of these reasons is that if the diagnostician waits until after the diagnostic interviews are completed the child may have already formed an attachment to him and feel betrayed by the transfer. Also, the child may feel that a shameful revelation about himself led to his being sent to someone else. Finally, from the point of view of the child, predictability is a powerful source of security. If, therefore, the child must be transferred to another therapist, this information can be introduced at the beginning of the evaluation, and repeated in the context of the contract.

Once the child has begun to disclose problems and worries, and the contract has been described, the clinician must be prepared to supply another facet to the interview. There are times when pathology becomes the compelling focus of the interviews. This can distort the perception of both the clinician and the patient. Besides the demoralizing effects of a person's being defined or defining himself only by his deficits, it deprives both therapist and child of the ability to review the strengths and assets which will be the vehicles for implementing therapeutic or remedial changes. The therapist must, therefore, be ready through attitude, questions, and observations to acknowledge the fun, victories, achievements, and other assets the child and family bring with them. He must also be sure that the child knows that he considers these assets important.

The diagnostician can now explore the life of the child by following his descriptions of himself among his peers, in play, and school, as an individual family member and as he stands alone, unique in the world. Some aspects of his descriptions the child will feel are perfectly normal to reveal, even to a stranger, while other aspects seem private to him and not to be mentioned. Frequently in our culture, a child speaks readily about interpersonal events, but is embarrassed when speaking of intrapsychic phenomena. Thus, a child may tell about his mother and father quarreling about money matters, but be very reluctant to talk about the fear or anger he felt at their fighting. The clinician may, therefore, have to explore these areas with gentle, tactful questions rather than wait for them to emerge spontaneously.

In the course of exploring the child's psyche, dreams can offer important clues regarding preoccupations and desires. The clinician should not ask the child "Do you have dreams?" Rather, in a manner that conveys curiosity, and perhaps a reassuring smile, the clinician can request that a child tell him one of his dreams. Frequently, the child will respond that he does not have *bad* dreams. This is often due to the child's conviction that only his troubles are legitimate topics of conversation. The interviewer can counter this by following the child's disclaimer with "Well, tell me a nice dream you've had, then." If a "nice dream" is recounted and explored, the interview may find that this has broken the ice, and he can go back to nightmares by asking, "And what about a scary or bad dream?" Inquiry about recurrent dreams should not be neglected.

After telling of night dreams, children can frequently tell of daydreams or fantasies. This often requires a bit of preparation and reassurance to the child that daydreaming is not pathological and unique to him. A statement that often suffices may be, "most of us have daydreams, or make up stories inside our heads in which we're heroes or the main characters. Tell me about the stories you make up."

Both Adams (1982) and Simmons (1981) have excellent technical suggestions in their books on how to elicit psychological sets from children. Two that were particularly useful had to do with inquiring about the child's favorite joke, and asking the child to describe how they would ideally like their parents to be.

Winnicott (1953) saw the areas of play, religion, and art as direct extensions of the intermediate area of experience. An exploration of the derivatives of transitional objects, and the intermediate area of experience can produce illuminating information about the child's preferences, preoccupations, and efforts to master stimuli. This area is relatively easily investigated by asking about favorite games or toys, and what the child pretends when playing them or with them. Favorite stories, television programs, and movies should be elicited, and followed by an inquiry about which part of the story appealed to them most. Often a pattern of preferences can be detected that reveals issues with which the child struggles in real life.

I don't often find a formal mental status examination necessary. Most of the time the child has revealed all of the information necessary to answer the questions that might be put to him in a mental status review. There are times, however, when it is desirable to conduct a formal mental status examination to assess a number of personality functions. When necessary, it is recommended that the child be told he is being tested. Whether or not the diagnostician organizes this part of the evaluation in the form of a game or not is less important than making sure that the child does not feel that he is being deceived or lulled into complacency while the diagnostician is extracting information without the child's willing participation.

The mental status examination has no meaning, of course, unless it can be placed in the context of the age and development of the child. A working knowledge of average, expectable developmental achievements is necessary to give the mental status examination meaning. Also, cultural experiences may influence the responses the child gives to the question asked in the formal examination. In some cultures, for example, events are recalled in connection with *where* they occurred rather than in connection with time or *when* they occurred. To a child raised on a farm it is far more important to know that you don't bother a sow who has baby piglets, than it is for him to know the answer to that frequently asked question about what you do with a stamped, addressed letter found on the sidewalk. Many farm children haven't even noticed street corner mailboxes when they visit the city. The component parts of the mental status examination, suggestions on its application, and how to report the results are well reviewed in James Simmons' text (1981) on the psychiatric examination of children.

Toward the end of the first diagnostic interview, I have found it useful to invite the child to draw a person. This has been a long, well-established, and reliable component of psychological testing, explained by F. L. Goodenough (1926) and A. A. Silver (1950), and although most of us cannot interpret as much from it as a tester who is formally trained in its use, enough can be gleaned from it, and it is sufficiently convenient that it has become a routine part of the examination of the children that I see. The examiner can note the child's willingness or reluctance to draw. Motor skills or their absence quickly become evident, and the child often comments on his own work quite spontaneously. He will reveal how he reacted to assigned tasks in his responses to the request to draw, and the task is often an ideal opportunity for obsessional traits to emerge and for the child to demonstrate whether they hinder or help organize his endeavors. The gender of the person being drawn can often be determined by asking the chld to give the person in his drawing a name. Only rarely do children assign names to their drawings that could belong to either sex, such as Toni, Leslie, or Tami. When they do there is usually a reason for it, such as parents who wanted a child of one gender and had another, or a family name. With the gender of the drawing identified, inferences can be made about the traits that the child associates with that gender, familiarity or preoccupations with parts of the body, and even some aspects of the child's own identifications. After the child has drawn and identified one person, he can be asked to draw next to it a person of the opposite sex. A comparison of the two figures can yield important information regarding the child's perceptions of the relationships between the sexes, most often acquired in his own name.

In some evaluations the diagnostician may not have a good estimate of the child's capacity to make psychological connections and use psychological concepts in his thinking. I have found that a tentative, and relatively superficial statement made to the child at this time may be useful to clarify this question. For example, saying to the child, "You told me that you get mad at your little brother when he interrupts you. This seems worse when you're with Mom than when you're with Dad. How come?" may elicit a response that gives good indications of the readiness or willingness to consider psychological issues. Conflicts or concerns that would be frightening or embarrassing for the child to face at this stage of the relationship should be avoided, but readdressing something that the child has already introduced may be useful.

Even the most carefully conducted diagnostic evaluation

can leave the clinician with various unanswered questions. Sometimes the whole situation is confusing, while at other times, more circumscribed, but nonetheless perplexing questions remain unanswered. In many instances clinicians attempt to bring clarity by "ordering psychological testing." This is not the most productive way to do it. Consultation from a psychologist can be helpful, of course. But consultation requires more communication than simply "ordering tests." A conversation with the psychologist which lists the child's problems, the positive findings, the problems the clinician wishes to have clarified and the difficulties the clinician has encountered is essential. This permits the consultant to orient himself regarding what is sought from the testing, and permits him to anticipate and avoid possible pitfalls in evaluating the youngster. His consultative replies are, therefore, more cogent and focused. Some clinicians become uneasy that the "objective evaluation" may detect something obvious that they missed. This is unnecessary! Competent clinical psychologists are aware of the complexity of the psychological apparatus, and that this complexity is compounded by the process of evaluation. The successful consultant knows that his utility will be in a mutual exploration of the clinical situation, not second guessing. Pontificators do not continue to get many referrals.

When the clinician has reached well-defined diagnostic impressions, he must communicate these to the child, the family, and perhaps some community institutions in a way that will cause the least harm and will be of most benefit to the family. Unfortunately, there is still possible harm that can come to a child from having a psychiatric label attached to him. The terms *idiot, imbecile,* and *moron* were originally introduced to protect retarded children against pejorative terms. They have become terms of opprobrium. Laing once stated that our psychiatric jargon had become a "veritable lexicon of denigration" (1965, p. 27). No label can take the place of a compassionate, simple description of the forces involved in the child's problems, and whenever possible, a suggested course of action for relief from these problems.

The child should be the first one told how the clinician proposes that his problems be alleviated. This should be followed by a discussion of what will be told to the parents. The child should then be asked to react to these proposals, and although there can be no promise that the child's wishes will prevail, they must be attentively heard and whenever possible heeded. Frequently, the child will give the clinician *carte blanche* regarding communications with his parents. An effort should be made in any event to learn if anything that the child told the clinician is to be kept secret. If the information can remain confidential without endangering the child's welfare, and without misleading the parents, it should not be mentioned. If possible, the child should be asked if he wishes to be present when the results of the evaluation and the recommendation are presented to the parents. Should the child wish to be at the interview, and the parents not want him there, the therapist should explore with the parents their willingness to take the responsibility for excluding the child.

If the person who did the diagnostic evaluation will not be able to see the child, the child should be reminded of this fact, and the reasons for it should be explained once more. If the diagnostician can follow the child, the child should be told that the names of several therapists will be given to the parents including the diagnostician's, so that parents and child will have a choice of therapist. This becomes particularly important if the parents or child may have a preference for a therapist of a particular race, religion, or gender. This also helps to convince the uneasy parent that the diagnostician's self-interest has been reduced as near to zero as possible in making the recommendation for psychotherapy.

THE COMPLETION INTERVIEW

The interview with the parents that completes the diagnostic evaluation may well be the most delicate and sensitive time of the whole therapeutic process. Virtually all parents dream of the future perfect child and the ideal relationship as they hold their newborn in their arms. Slowly the process of living erodes some of these idealized aspirations. Having to seek psychiatric help explodes these dreams of perfection in a cruel and precipitous way. The completion interview may be for some parents concrete evidence of their failures and futility of their dreams.

On other occasions parents may have undertaken the diagnostic evaluation with the unarticulated, and perhaps even unconscious wish that it would prove there was nothing wrong with their child. When the diagnostician must tell them that there are problems to be dealt with, either in the child or in the family relationships, this revelation may be received with disappointment, doubt, or even open anger.

The converse of this last situation are those instances in which surprisingly the parents wish to find more pathology in the child than is actually there. The child has come to be seen as the repository of all the family psychology, and the reluctance to acknowledge the pain or fear of more widespread family problems sets the child up to act as the scapegoat. E. Berman (1973) has offered profound insights into this problem in his moving book *Scapegoat*.

The diagnostician must, therefore, approach the completion interview with compassion for the family's feelings of vulnerability and understanding for the possible defensive maneuvers he may encounter. Thus readied, he may proceed to discuss the diagnostic findings in terms that are free of jargon and that are comprehensible to all in the room.

Therapists are vulnerable to being fascinated by pathology. Health is so taken for granted that we cease to marvel at the accomplishments of development and adaptation. It is useful to overcome this vulnerability when reviewing the diagnostic evaluation with the family. Reviewing the positive attributes and achievements of the child and family serves the purpose of comforting them. Placing the pathology in a realistic perspective, it also serves to help establish the alliance between the therapist and the healthy portions of the family system. It is this alliance that will constitute the main component of the base

from which child and therapist will venture to explore, understand, and master the pathology which will confront them.
These very attributes realistically reviewed at this time will also
be called upon later to help undo the pathology that is encountered.

As the diagnostician reviews the pathology found in the
evaluation, he must remind himself that it cannot be perceived
in the context of his own cultural and moral values. The family
members have their own value systems and it is these systems
that determine how they will react to the description of the
pathology. The family's value systems will be more likely to be
preserved if the clinician refers back to their own words and
examples in giving the results of the evaluation. To hear their
own words acknowledged and used in explanation conveys to
the family that they have been listened to attentively. It also
reminds them that their participation is essential in understanding the problems they presented.

Often, before therapeutic recommendations can be offered
by the clinician, a parent may begin to ask for recommendations
about how to react to the child in given circumstances, or how
to manage one symptom or the other. If the therapist can avoid
this situation he should. Most of the recommendations that the
clinician can make at this time have already been made by others, or have been instituted by the parents. More often than not
the real problem for which the parent is seeking relief is a
breakdown in empathy between them and the child (Coppolillo,
1965b). Any suggestions that the therapist offers is likely to be
met with "We've tried that and it doesn't work!" Exchanges like
this can quickly evolve into mutual frustration and loss of confidence. The clinician would probably be best advised to make
only those recommendations which are essential at this time,
and reserve other recommendations that must be made for the
process of therapy. As treatment progresses, demands for
quick-fix recommendations will be reduced.

Problems tend to act as catalysts for each other, and in a
later chapter there will be a discussion of the multiple problem
child and family. This is mentioned here to acknowledge that

there are times when the problems that are presented appear to be such a formidable series of Gordian knots that the therapist feels that his wits, knowledge, skill, and patience have all been exhausted to no avail. This is the moment that our frustrations begin to seek a whipping boy. Sometimes in the most subtle of ways we attempt to make the children or their families the target of our disguised frustration. Despite romantic notions that imply the opposite, pathology can sometimes be alienating and ugly. Our revulsion and wish to distance ourselves from this ugliness may be camouflaged by words like *untreatable* or the milder *unmotivated*. Perhaps the insight revealed in Shakespeare's words from *Twelfth Night,* Act III, Scene 4, can be helpful when the therapist feels alienated and hopeless.

> "In Nature there's no blemish but the mind.
> None can be called deformed but the Unkind."

Part III

Some Technical and Organizational Considerations

CHAPTER 8

Organizing Diagnostic Data: Models of the Parents, Ego Psychology, and Topography

In this chapter four models will be reviewed to show how they can be used to organize the data obtained in the diagnostic process. Models are useful in that they provide a way to organize facts and inferences to produce a picture that can then be compared, or can be scrutinized regarding its own integrity, logic, or harmony. The danger in using models is that they are sometimes reified as if they were concrete objects. Replicas of the models I will propose and describe cannot be found by dissecting the brains and exploring the homes of our patients. They do not have the solidity and invariability of the concrete device. They are rough, bare conceptual constructs that become lifelike only when the clinician skillfully adorns them with the joys and woes of people's lives.

The human individual is a system unto himself, composed of an enormous number of subsystems with fluid boundaries. Biochemical pathways interact with anatomical structures, and vice versa. These are constantly influencing psychological states and are in turn influenced by them. The psychological states will participate in determining the nature of the individual's transactions with the world that surrounds him and these will

147

alter his biology and psychology. This constant interaction of open systems which themselves are in ceaseless fluctuation constitute the process called life, and there has been no single model ever devised that can serve as an adequate frame to contain even the small part we know of its intricacies. For this reason, we will need a number of models to convey the concepts in this chapter. These, of course, will also not be adequate, and the clinician must stand ready to modify them or to develop a new model to accommodate the facts he finds in his patients' accounts of their lives.

THE PARENTS

Here I will elaborate on the model of parental unity presented in an earlier chapter. This conceptual model serves to organize the information about the emotional environment into which the child was born and the readiness of that environment to offer the child multiple opportunities for transactions and identifications.

As was described in chapter 4, two individuals are brought together by the way each perceives, and is perceived by the other. These perceptions are an astonishing mixture of unerring accuracy and illusion. Perhaps courtship sharpened the curiosity of philosophers and artists about the interplay of reality and illusion in the human condition.

With time, each partner develops an image of the other composed of these real traits and illusions and each reflects these images back to the other in countless exchanges. These reflected images modify each partner's behavior in that each seeks to fulfill the other's realistic or idealized expectations.

With the growth of communication, understanding, and intimacy some illusions are naturally eroded and disappear while others are cherished and sustained. Some realistic traits of both partners enhance closeness while others foster their individuality and even disparity. In this way the process described earlier of a couple maintaining individuality even as part of their life fuses, proceeds. (See Figure 8-1.)

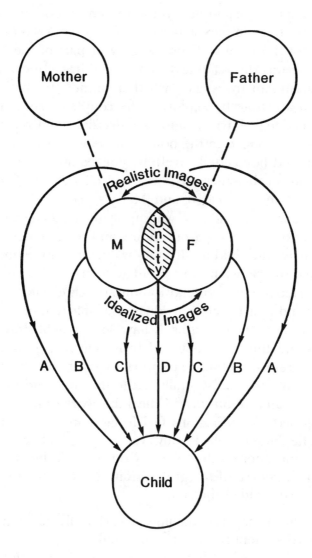

Figure 8-1. As the mother and father grow together to become a couple that shares unity as well as retaining their individuality (M-unity-F), they provide their child with increased sources of identification. The child can identify with: the realistic image each parent has of the other (A); his own perception of a parent's qualities (B); the idealized image each parent has of the other (C); the unity the parents have achieved (D).

In chapter 4, examples and some clinical evidence for the existence of this complex state were offered and it was proposed that one of the results of the merging of part of the couple's mental life was the readiness to have children. In evaluations the clinician can investigate whether or not this process occurred in a couple by exploring the couple's tastes, cultural, and recreational activities, and how decisions and reactions to stress were managed in the home. Subtle modes of communication should be heeded carefully. For example, the number of times one or the other says, "we decided" or "we enjoyed. . . ." as opposed to "I decided and Mary agreed. . . ." or "I enjoyed . . . and Mary did too" will supply the needed evidence.

The extent of the parents' unity and separateness will, of course, affect the child in different ways. One of the important issues that the clinician must evaluate is the way in which this state affected the child's identifications. If a child had two wholly separate and nonrelated individuals available to him as sources of identification, he would likely have some trouble integrating a number of the traits assumed from one person with those obtained from the other. The work of synthesizing and integrating would be almost totally left to the child and this could prove to be an arduous task. Unless this work of integration is accomplished, identifications feel foreign and do not become part of the sense of self. If, however, the two had achieved the intimacy and oneness described by this model, the child has a ready-made source of integrated traits as well as a number of other sources of identifications.

1. The real and separate qualities of each individual parent are a source of identification for the child.
2. The child can identify with each parent's perception of the other parent's qualities. The values that determine how these qualities are appreciated are also a source of identification. For example, the child sees mother reading a book. The book is discussed at dinner and the child hears the father say to the mother, "What you tell me about the book is fascinating. I want to read it too. You're one of the best-informed people I know." The child identifies not only with

mother's ability to read and be informed, but also with the father's admiration of this ability.

3. For the sake of description let us assume now that in addition to the father's unrealistic appreciation of the mother's erudition, he also tends to idealize her ability to write. The child then has this idealized image of the mother and the father's ability to idealize as sources of identification.

4. As has already been said, the unity of the parents offers the child already integrated traits of the parents with which he can identify, as well as the *image of the unity*, which may become the basis for his own ability to tolerate and seek intimacy later in his own life.

Thus, the availability of two parents who have, or have had an intimate relationship to each other, provides the child with soources of identifications that are more than doubled. Data from the diagnostic interviews can be reviewed to see how many of the child's identifications came from this unified mother–father team, which offered images of unity as well as individuality. The frequency of the child's use of "momandad" or "they" as opposed to "she" or "he," or how he describes his external regulators, or how he externalizes his superego are some examples of how this determination is made.

PREGNANCY, INFANCY, AND PARENTHOOD

This model was designed to contemplate the interpersonal role changes and intrapsychic phenomena that occur during the latter stages of pregnancy and during the infancy of the child. This section, too, is an elaboration of the concept presented in chapter 5.

Although the impetus to develop a conceptual model came from work with cases of extreme dysparenting, the model itself emerged from interviews with normal expectant parents, parents of infants, from naturalistic observations of healthy parents and babies, and from the literature on parenthood.

These sources authorize us to believe that in the latter stages of pregnancy and through the child's infancy the process of mothering absorbs an enormous amount of energy and psychological investment. During the pregnancy, the gradual withdrawal of interest in the external world and growing interest in the pregnancy itself can be ascertained by direct observation or through interviews with most women. What appears to be preoccupation with herself and self-protectiveness, on closer examination is revealed to be preoccupation with herself *as a pregnant woman*, with the pregnancy and with images of the unborn child. Later of course, in addition to psychological preoccupation, care of the child demands investment of actual physical energy. In considering the homeostastis of the system (or perhaps homeorhesis, would be more accurate)* questions arose as to the sources of replenishment for the invested energy and the nature of the gratifications that seemed to make these boundless investments possible for the mother. Our answers were to be found in the literature and in family systems that were scrutinized.

Benedek (1956a) was the earliest worker to formally describe one of the ways that expectant mothers find solace, replenishment, and a sense of competence during the pregnancy and early childhood of their offspring. In the psychoanalytic work and clinical interviews with the expectant mothers she studied, she found that during this period they consciously thought of their own mothers more than they had when they were not pregnant. She found evidence that they were unconsciously reliving the gratification they had experienced in being mothered. In addition, we found that expectant mothers reevoked idealized images of motherliness, that they had elaborated as children. Benedek did this work in the late 1930s and early 1940s. It was not until 1965 that experimental evidence was produced by H. F. Harlow and N. K. Harlow (1965) that primates required the experience of being mothered in order to undertake motherhood successfully in their turn. This primate work suggests confirmation of Benedek's findings that having been successfully mothered is a prerequisite for com-

---

* Homeostasis contemplates stability around a point. Homeorhesis involves stability around a trajectory.

fortable and gratifying motherhood. Memories of the gratifying experience of being mothered rekindle in the new mother the confidence and optimism which had its origins in her own infancy and returns now to fortify her as she nurtures and invests in her own child.

The sources already mentioned also led us to hypothesize that there was another source of gratification and replenishment for the pregnant woman. In families in which successful mothering occurs, the father, during the latter stages of his wife's pregnancy and the early months of the child's life, becomes motherly *to the mother*. The father begins to exhibit traits that in our culture, we identify with maternal functions. He becomes actively nurturant, supportive, indulgent, and non-demanding to his wife. He foregoes sexual gratification, and becomes available as a hovering protector and supplier. It is this shift in role that permits the husband to indulge his wife in the way that was described earlier.

Josselyn (1956) has stressed that a capacity for many of the traits that go into motherliness is not confined to women. Rausch, Barry, Hestel, and Swain (1974) have described this maternal tendency of the father toward the mother around the issues of conflict resolution during pregnancy. Findings by B. Liebenberg (1967) indicate that during the wife's pregnancy, men appeared to need their own mothers more as reflected by greater numbers of phone calls, more frequent letter writing, and wanting to spend more time with them. Some men expressed a desire to shop for clothes and other personal items for their wives. This author concluded that the wife's pregnancy may reevoke old forgotten conflicts with his own parents, especially around issues of separation and dependency. An alternative or possibly additional interpretation of Liebenberg's data is that these behaviors are a manifestation of the father's motherly, nurturant tendencies for his wife.

The third source of gratification and replenishment for the mother is to be found in the relationship with her own child. This is an area studied by psychoanalysts from the earliest days of the field, using the reconstructive tool, and later by developmentalists using techniques of direct observation.

When the mother coomes into contact with her infant, whether she is meeting one of his needs, or is simply basking in the feeling of overwhelming tenderness that accompanies her holding or observing him, the feelings of joy and satisfaction are so intense that they could appropriately be called ecstatic. Unless severe pathology in the mother, or in the child interfere, the child himself becomes one of the main sources of revitalization for even the most fatigued of mothers. An oversimplified, graphic representation of this component of the model is reproduced in Figure 8-2.

This aspect of the mother–child interaction requires more description. An ethological model was found to be most useful here in this description.

We can conceive of the child being born with a repertoire of functions and traits that act as signals (and sometimes as symbols and signs) to his environment. His cries, reflexes, movements, expressions, and even his very size and helplessness elicit responses from the people who surround him. In the idealized situation, each signal would fall within the range of his mother's sensitivity and elicit a response from her. These maternal responses may range from the physiological reaction of lactation at the sound of the infant's hungry cry to complex psychological reactions such as tenderness at the touch of his hand. These released responses from the mother soothe and gratify the child, permitting it to return to a state of serene quiescence and gradually allowing mother and child to accumulate memory traces which will permit their next encounter to be more vigorous and secure (Figure 8-3A). The process which Spitz (1957) called "the dialogue" has begun, and its optimal evolution will permit the child to develop what has been called confidence by Benedek (1956a) and optimism by Erickson (1964).

The perfect dialogue exists only in theory, of course. In fact, while most of the signals emitted by the child elicit gratifying responses from the mother, some do not. What father has not arrived home at some time to find mother frazzled and perplexed while Johnny is shattering glasses with his piercing cries. The baby is thrust into father's arms as mother says,

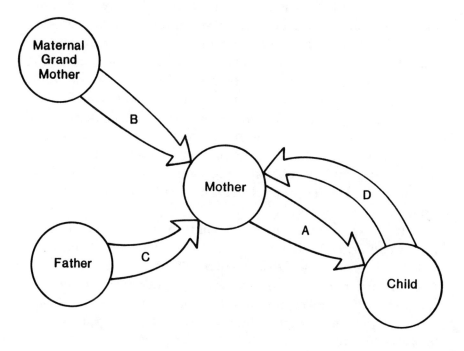

Figure 8-2. Representation of sources of replenishment (B, C, D) for the mother's commitment of energy to her child (A). (Reprinted from H. Coppolillo (1975), Drug impediments to mothering behavior. *Addictive Diseases*, 2:201–208.)

"Thank God you're home. He's been a monster for the past two hours. I simply don't know what he wants. I've tried everything." The mother is reporting that for some reason the child's signals have been unclear or have been undecipherable by her, and she has not been able to institute those actions which would bring them both relief. Mother and child have thus both been left in a state of chronic need tension. If relatively brief and not too frequent, these episodes in communication breakdown are useful because it is in this setting that the child begins to learn to tolerate frustration, and is introduced to that sometimes painful awareness we call reality. Most often after a brief disruption, communication is reestablished and mother and child function as a mutually gratifying unit once more (Figure 8-3B).

What has been described thus far is what is believed to be the optimal development of the mother–child bond leading to a necessary symbiotic relationship. Needless to say, the situation is not always so felicitous. "Derailment of dialogue," to use Spitz's phrase, does occur.

There are instances in which children are born with a valid and broad array of signals or releaser mechanisms. Their signals, however, fail to elicit gratifying responses because the maternal partner's range of sensitivity or repertoire of response mechanisms has been stunted by nondevelopment or constricted by chronic fatigue, illness, depression, drugs, or some catastrophic event (Figure 8-3C). As child psychiatrists, we must at times wonder what problems we may be creating when young mothers are being sedated into semistuperous states of insensitivity to their infants through the abundant use of tranquilization that sometimes protects against or substitutes for human relatedness.

Conversely, we see instances in which a mother's adequate sensitivity and responsivity lay distressingly fallow because the infant is born without the ability to stimulate and elicit mother behavior from its caretaker (Figure 8-3D). This can be a temporary circumstance or more tragically permanent. T. B. Brazelton (1962) gave us an excellent example of the former when he described instances in which mothers attempted to feed ba-

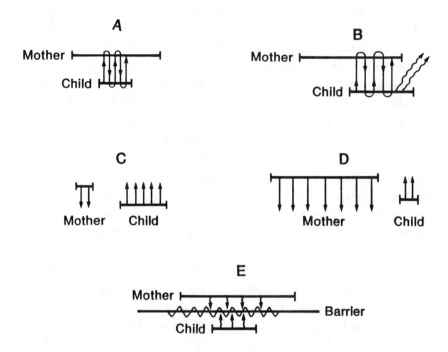

Figure 8-3. Ethological model of mother–child engagement. Idealized and optimal engagement (A, B). Forms of pathological engagement (C, D, E). See further description in text. (Reprinted from H. Coppolillo (1975), Drug impediments to mothering behavior. *Addictive Diseases*, 2:201–208.)

bies who were hypotonic and lethargic due to the anesthesia used in delivery. He noted that even after the first feeding attempt, these women were disheartened, and anticipated the next encounter with their babies with dread.

A more refractory and somber example of the latter situation may be found in cases of early infantile autism or children born with severe central nervous system damage. Not only is it difficult for their biological mothers to respond appropriately to them or to decipher their signals, it is also virtually impossible for any other person to do so.

Finally, we must recall those situations in which the relationship between mother and child was impeded, not by any interpersonal difficulties of their own, but by artificially or accidentally introduced barriers which separate the two. Spitz's (1945) work on hospitalism speaks to this topic. More recently, Klaus and Kennel (1970) followed a group of children who were separated from their mothers during the neonatal and early infancy period because they needed to be kept in a premature or newborn nursery for care. They compared these children to a group of children who also needed to be in the nursery but whose mothers were urged to visit several times a day, to handle and fondle their young. They found on follow-up that there was a higher incidence of child abuse, "failure to thrive," abandonment, and giving up for adoption in the group that did not have early contact with the mother as compared to the group whose mothers were supported and urged to visit the nursery. These studies support the position that mothers and children must be available to each other as soon and as consistently as possible, if a productive symbiosis is to occur. Barriers such as plate glass windows, intrusive grandmothers, obstructionistic medical personnel, poverty, physical distance, and inadequate living conditions can impede the development of dialogue and interfere with a mother's capacity to be stimulated and gratified by her child.

By thinking of the models that have been presented, or others like them, the clinician may be reminded to search his protocols for information that would reveal how the impact of the pregnancy, and the child's infancy affected the various members of the nuclear family. The mother's store of gratifying memories, the father's ability to tolerate maternal impulses, the mother and child's capacity to stimulate and move each other can all be evaluated to estimate if the period during pregnancy and the patient's infancy was a solid base from which future development could proceed, or not. Unresolved problems from this phase can haunt the family for years.

These two models have been described in interpersonal terms. It must be remembered that interpersonal events have intrapsychic consequences. Much of what we call personality structure becomes organized in the context of interpersonal relationships. In the evaluation, the diagnostician should keep his attention on both points of view. This involves how relatedness led to structure, and how structure affected relationships.

THE MODEL OF EGO PSYCHOLOGY

THE AUTONOMOUS FUNCTIONS

Hartmann (1939) and Hartmann, Kris, and Loewenstein (1946) elaborated the concept of the autonomous functions of the ego. These workers had come to the realization that certain basic personality functions developed as a result of the person's biological endowment and its interaction with the external world. In these basic functions they included perception, motor activities, ability to store and retrieve memory traces, and the ability to synthesize and integrate various personality functions. While these operate in conjunction with drives, their development is relatively *autonomous* from the drives. Their development is heavily dependent on stimulation from the external environment and on the nature of this stimulation.

The contribution of these authors is important, if for no other reason than that it allows us to place into one model concepts involving a human being's biology, psychology, and transactions with the world. We can represent the model of the mental apparatus as proposed by Hartmann and integrated with Freud's fundamental structural concepts, in Figure 8-4.

In this diagram the autonomous functions and the id are shown as originating from what Hartmann and his co-workers called an undifferentiated matrix.

The autonomous functions are represented in Figure 8-4A. There is evidence that environmental stimulation is critical to the development of these functions. Stimulation is necessary not only to ensure the development of the anatomical and physiologic substrata of these functions, but also for integrating them with other personality functions at various levels of organizational complexity. For example, research demonstrates that kittens kept in the dark from birth would soon develop optic nerve atrophy. It is evident that inadequate stimulation early in life can cause anatomical impairment of the perceptual apparatus. But this relationship does not stop there! As the kitten continues to develop sight, the nature of the environ-

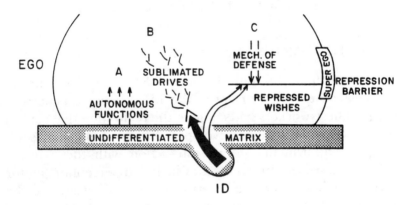

Figure 8-4. Following Hartmann, some aspects of ego development can be represented as:
A. Maturation and development of autonomous functions.
B. Sublimation and neutralization of instinctual drives.
C. Repression of component instinctual drives, defenses against their emergence and subsequent compromise formation.
(From H. Coppolillo (1976), The transitional phenomenon revisited. *J. Amer. Acad. Child Psychiat.*, 15:36–45.)

mental stimuli will determine how it will perceive and react to humans, siblings, its mother, and the inanimate surroundings. In humans it is relatively easy to find clinical data to illustrate the effects of gross distortions of environmental stimulation on the development of autonomous functions. More difficult to document is the way that the environment helps to determine the profile of the autonomous functions to provide individuals with amazing skills in some areas while leaving them less competent in others. That this happens is obvious. How it happens awaits further research.

Let us imagine identical twins that were separated at birth. One is taken to live with a middle-class, healthy family in midtown Manhattan, while the other is raised by a middle-class, healthy family in the Black Hills of South Dakota. Each child is allowed to explore and master his environment in a way that is safe and yet permissive. Then let us imagine that at ten years of age, with preparation, the boy from Manhattan is sent to spend two weeks in the Black Hills, while the boy from the Black Hills is sent to spend two weeks in midtown Manhattan. We can imagine that without help each child would be hardly able to adapt. The boy from South Dakota would suffer massive stimulus overload if he tried to walk two blocks. Conversely, the boy from Manhattan would probably be hopelessly lost if he strayed out of sight of the ranch house. There are many ways that comparisons of the skills provided by the autonomous functions can be made. Common sense supports the notion that people do best in environments to which they are accustomed, but further exploration is needed to determine how the anatomical, physiologic, and functional changes which accompany these differences in upbringing occur.

That different cultures stimulate their children in different ways, and that there are, therefore, consequent differences in the way the autonomous functions develop seems so self-evident that it need not be argued. Yet in the past decade there have been heated and acrimonious debates over the significance of differences in IQ scores from tests administered to various racial and ethnic groups. Seldom in these debates was the concept of the autonomous functions and their development mentioned. The diagnostician must not fall into the same trap. When evaluating those functions in the child that have been grouped and labeled the autonomous functions in this model, the diagnostician must assess them in the context of the environment in which they developed. We would be as much in error calling an Eskimo child, who was raised in a world that was colored mostly white, retarded because he could not distinguish and name pastel shades, as we would be calling a child raised in Florida retarded because he could not distinguish and name the fourteen or fifteen shades of white the Eskimos know.

Within this context then, these autonomous functions can be evaluated to determine their competence. When a deficit is found in one of them the question becomes whether the deficit is due to a defect in the matrix from which the function developed, as in brain damage, or in the way the child was stimulated as he grew, or in the manner in which the function became integrated with other psychological functions of the individual. The hyperalertness and hyperperception of the paranoid patient and hysterical blindness are examples of how the autonomous functions can be distorted in the process or by the failure of integration.

SUBLIMATIONS AND REPRESSIONS

In this model Hartmann's autonomous functions are juxtaposed to the functions that Freud described in his structural point of view. Structural theory states that certain ego functions develop as a result of the child's perception of what happens when he attempts to gratify an instinctual drive. It must be underlined that it is the child's *perception* of what occurred that is the determinant and not the actual occurrence. Let me take an example of a five-year-old child to describe the process.

Johnny has just discovered the charms of what he considers comparative anatomy by catching a glimpse of his mother or sister in the bathtub. Just as he is about to take a second look through the door that was inadvertently left open a crack, he is interrupted by the presence of that intruder into all human affairs who is known around the house as Dad. Now the story can be traced in two ways.

The first of these ways is that John can perceive Dad as being disturbed and angered by his having peeked. The perception may be entirely realistic in that Dad, because of moral or religious convictions, or because of some conflict with sexuality is indeed disturbed and angry. It may also be that the child's guilty conviction that Dad should be angry makes him misperceive Dad's real reaction. Either way the child is convinced that if he were to indulge his impulse, catastrophic consequences would follow.

We must recall that the cognitive competence of a five-year-old boy does not permit him to differentiate between wish and deed. He expects the same response to a wish as to a deed. This can be verified by listening to a five-, six-, or seven-year-old declare with conviction "You better not *wish* that something bad happens to someone, or that bad thing *will happen* to you." This inability to distinguish wish from deed leaves our Johnny vulnerable. The *fear* that he experienced when father witnessed his act of peeking, now becomes *anxiety* even in father's absence. Since anxiety is a corrosive affect, Johnny must now repudiate the wish as well as the act of peeking. The process of repression has begun (Figure 8-4C).

There is a second way that this story can end. If, in fact or in the perception of the child the tone of the father's response is, "Hey there fella! You can't go around looking at your mother or sister when they're nude. We don't do that around here because everyone has a right to their privacy, and we don't go sneaking around. What is it you want to see? You want to see what a nude woman looks like? Okay." At this point, depending on the father's conviction about what is best for his son, he may promise the boy that there will be ample opportunity for these explorations when he gets older, or he may show the child a picture of a nude woman. It may surprise the father to find that the picture of a nude woman is not new to his son. The physician father of a seven-year-old boy was alerted that it was time for a discussion with his son about sexual differences and curiosity. The boy listened patiently and dutifully looked at the anatomy plate of a woman that the father had used to illustrate the lecture. After the father had finished, the boy politely said that he understood what the father had told him, but asked not to be shown the "picture from the doctoring book because it makes me want to vomerate." He then graciously offered to borrow a girlie magazine in his father's name from one of his friends, and they could try the lecture again.

It is not the substantive information which is exchanged that is important. It is the child's perceptions of the attitudes and affects that communicate what is and is not permissible. In the latter, less anxiety-laden example, the father forbade the child to peek through the bathroom door just as the father of the first example did with his son. Yet, in this latter example two important additional messages were perceived by the child. The first message was that, although the impulse could not be gratified in the manner in which the son was attempting to indulge it, the son had a right to be curious and excited by sexual matters. Second, the father indicated that there was a time, a place, and a manner by which these legitimate wishes could be gratified. In this way the child may have to abandon an act, but not the wish, and certainly not disavow or denigrate a part of himself. Curiosity and sexual interest were kept alive, anad utilized for further engagement with the culture at a later time and in a more mature way. Sublimation made repression unnecessary (Figure 8-4B).

Let us assume that the child did accept the sublimatory step offered by the father and for awhile began perusing every magazine with nudes or every anatomy text he could obtain. After awhile, either because the father would growl, "There's other things in that book besides naked women, you know," or more likely because the child's own interest would be captured by a pictorial story of an exotic animal, or the story of intellectual accomplishments of a beautiful woman, his curiosity would once more be stimulated. It would now be rewarded by a bit more subdued but no less useful gratification. In this way sublimations continue and experiences grow. Twenty years later, as we walk through the halls of the microbiology department of a university, we see Johnny, now grown into a young man, peering into an electron microscope, studying the multiplication of viruses. Those who understand psychoanalytic concepts of development poorly, or perhaps not at all, might say, "Oh look there is Johnny looking through a microscope. He is doing that because he really wants to peek at his mother behind the bathroom door." This is popular, misinformed superficiality. Of course a statement like that cannot be made. That statement would assert that because two points are on the same continuum they are identical points. The function of curiosity at five with a nude mother or sister behind a bathroom door was integrated with one set of cognitive acquisitions, memory traces, affective states, and motives. The function of curiosity, while sitting in front of a microscope twenty years later was integrated with a very different set of functions.

Certain statements, based on clinical observations and on direct child observations can be made, however, and attest to the utility of this model in clinical work. Focusing on the component of curiosity from the clinical example, we are authorized to make the following inferences.

1. Curiosity, and the visual functions which were put in the service of gratifying it, remained available in the young man's repertoire, and were used in increasingly more mature and adaptive activities. They were not repressed nor inhibited as they might have been had he been exposed to massive anxiety or fear as in the first example.
2. In remaining available for further use curiosity retained a *plasticity* or *pliability* that permitted it to be integrated with other functions and other activities. This provided our young man with a variety of choices as to how he would gratify curiosity in later life. The opposite would be true if curiosity had been repressed and could only be expressed in a covert manner and accompanied by shame and fear.
3. In the course of development the young person in question

experienced optimism that his curiosity would be rewarded. This allowed him to tolerate frustration and hard work in the pursuit of his goals.

4. Supported by this optimism, curiosity became a catalyst to add power and zest to work as well as continuing to serve pleasurable pursuits.

By scrutinizing functions of the personality in the context of this model of ego psychology, the clinician can trace their longitudinal development over the years as well as determine whether or not they had remained flexible and had retained their ability to be integrated into more mature patterns of behavior. This permits a more thorough assessment of that regulatory portion of the mental apparatus that we call the ego.

THE SECONDARY AUTONOMIES

The final aspect of this structural model that requires description is that section of it that describes the inevitable sacrifices of impulse life that any society requires (Figure 8-4C). As a child grows and matures, inevitably the culture will demand, for example, that aggression be modified so that it harms no other. It will demand a degree of cleanliness that during a child's early years had no meaning for him. It requires that exhibitionism and narcissism be modified to the extent that others can be noticed. These achievements on the part of the growing child almost invariably require some repression and the erection of defenses against expression of the original wishes. These defenses in their turn are so rewarded by the society that they become the reason that a trait or practice is retained as part of the personality's repertoire, even after the original impulse or wish against which they were instituted has disappeared. An example of this is the three-year-old child who has had an unambivalent love affair with dirt and messy play. As he begins to recognize that the adults he is attached to shy away from him after he has spent an hour making mud pies, he begins to imitate their commitment to cleanliness and to repress his love of dirt. That the reaction formation he employs as a defense to bolster his newfound commitment to cleanliness is paper thin at first, is evidenced by his efforts at self-care. When he attempts to clean himself, the bathroom appears as if he had brought the mud-pie making activity there rather than being the place where cleanliness was enshrined. Gradually, however, the pleasure at being bathed by his mother, and the praise for looking and smelling clean begin to make these activities valuable and pleasant in their own right. In this way the wish for cleanliness has become autonomous (not dependent on the impulse or the drive for its existence). By the time the child is in school cleanliness and neatness may well be traits that are kept alive for their own sake rather than a reaction formation against love of dirt. Kind people are more often kind because they cherish the feelings that kindness brings, and not because they are in an incessant struggle against their own sadism.

These secondarily autonomous functions are usually useful, unconflicted, and part of the adaptive strength the patient brings to the therapeutic situation. They become a matter of concern when the child moves from a culture in which they were useful and adaptive to one in which they are seen as alien, strange, or maladaptive. They also require attention when patients regress profoundly, and the old conflicts from which these traits took their origin reappear.

THE TOPOGRAPHIC MODEL

The last model that will be presented in this chapter is a representation of the psychoanalytic topographic model. This is one of the original models of the mental apparatus that Freud (1917) introduced, and although much has been discovered and described since its introduction, the topographic model has remained the most useful way to organize and describe certain fundamental clinical concepts.

In the topographic model consciousness is considered an organ of internal perception and participates, in any given moment, only in a miniscule portion of what is occurring in the mental apparatus. Freud compared consciousness to the lens of a camera which receives stimuli and passes them on to the film. The lens is not altered by the stimuli, but is left free to receive new stimuli and again pass them on. Similarly, consciousness clears itself of the images it held for a moment and goes on to be receptive to new stimuli to which it directs itself (Figure 8-5).

The organ of consciousness can direct itself with relative ease to memory traces, percepts, and activities which are called the preconscious. Freud (1900) did not mean to convey the idea of an anatomical locus for the preconscious, but rather to describe a group of mental images supplied by perceptions which can *readily be brought into conscious awareness.*

The mental images and perceptions that are designated as preconscious do not exist in chaos, but are regulated by rules of logic and are in the service of adapting to and addressing reality. They are governed, as Freud (1900, 1917) said, by the secondary process. An example might be a man who for twenty

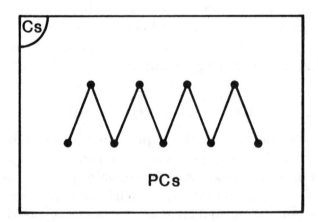

Figure 8-5. The organ of internal perception (Cs) can direct awareness to preconscious memory traces governed by logic and the reality principle.

years awakens every weekday morning at 6:30 A.M. to go to work, walks into the kitchen to turn the gas on to make coffee, and shaves and showers while it is percolating. He then turns off the gas, has his coffee and cereal, puts his cup and bowl in the sink, walks to his car or the bus stop and leaves for work. Each activity is purposive, undisturbed by distraction or conflict, and almost automatic in accomplishing what he had set out to do in order to meet the requisites of the day and his daily wants. Each activity and each wish in the sequence can be brought into awareness at any given moment by directing the organ of consciousness to it.

Let us suppose that on a given morning our working man awakened as usual, undertook all of his usual activities, and left for work. This morning, however, was different from past mornings in that as he reached the bottom step of his front porch, he was bothered by the suspicion that he had not turned the gas off under the coffee. He quickly retraced his steps, and touched the gas jet to make sure that it was turned off. On reaching the bottom step again, he was again suddenly assailed by a doubt. "Wait," he said to himself, "the gas jet was off when I came up. Did I mistakenly turn it on?"

He may have even added that he was acting foolishly. The discomfort he felt, however, was sufficiently troublesome to occasion a patient sigh, and force him back up the stairs to seek reassurance with a ritualistic touch that the gas was indeed off. He even moved the coffee pot to another burner to "leave no room for doubt." Once more he started off to work and to his own amazement was again met at the bottom step by the anxiety-filled doubt that the gas might be on. This time he, like most of us would in a similar situation, decided he had indulged his craziness enough and forced himself to leave for work.

It was in this kind of unexplained, illogical behavior that Freud (1901) found evidence to support his thesis that a part of mental life that was not readily available to conscious scrutiny could effectively disturb adaptive, logical thought and behavior. In three works, *The Interpretation of Dreams*, (1917) *The Psychopathology of Everyday Life* (1901), and *Jokes and Their Relation to*

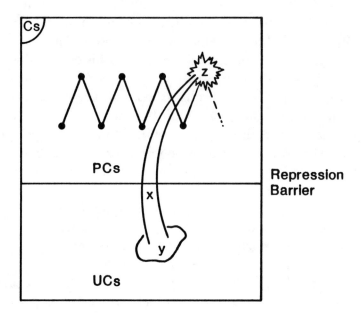

Figure 8-6. Depiction of how preconscious mentation (PCs) can be disrupted (z) by transference (x) from unconscious (UC) impulses, ideas, and affects (y). Further description in text.

the Unconscious (1905), he described the dynamic unconscious, and gave evidence for its universal effectiveness in determining certain behaviors.

   If we were to return to our working man and ask him to cooperate with us in getting at the cause of his irrational thoughts, we might find that a wish or a thought of which he was not aware, or of which *he wished* not to be aware, was the reason for his anxiety and doubt about the gas jet. We could then say that a wish or impulse (Figure 8-6Y) that had been rendered unconscious, exerted its influence, and altered conscious, adaptive behavior in a way that reflected the presence but not the aim or goal of the wish. It transferred its thrust from the unconscious to the preconscious where it could find disguised expression (Figure 8-6Z).

Freud, in the three works mentioned above, described the mental apparatus as consisting of consciousness as the organ of internal perception; those forms of mental activity that were preconscious and readily available to consciousness and which were regulated by the secondary processes; and the unconscious which consisted of those mental activities which were repudiated or unwelcome to the conscious standards of the individual and were barred from direct expression or representation by the censor of mental activity, the repression barrier. He presented further evidence to support his thesis that the forms of mental activity that have been repressed do not simply lie dormant and inert, but exert pressure and seek expression and representation in the life of the individual. In studying the way that they found expression and representation in behavior, Freud discovered and described how unconscious mentation was regulated. Among the regulatory principles of unconscious mentation, which he called the primary processes are:

1. Condensation. Several or even many mental images can be represented by one symbol. A dream in which a top sergeant appears may represent struggles with mother, father, second grade teacher, coach, and other *authority* figures.
2. Displacement. If the target of a wish or impulse is taboo, the wish or impulse may be displaced to another more permissible target. I am angry at my boss, whom I fear, and come home and scold my dog.
3. Symbolization. The symbol of an object or a wish may be treated as if it were that object or wish.
4. Timelessness. There is no concept of time in the unconscious. Prior events may be represented as simultaneous even though they occurred years apart. Events that were rendered unconscious in childhood are experienced as currently relevant.
5. Absence of negation. There is no "no" in the unconscious. One can't unconsciously "*not* like" someone or something. One hates him or it.
6. All or nothing quality of the unconscious. There are no gradations in the unconscious. When a person is hungry, he

is ravenous. When not hungry, he is totally satiated. This may be illustrated by watching a baby eat. Every bite up to the last is avidly fallen upon as if the little one were starving. After the last bite is taken, the baby acts stuffed and any attempt to feed him more is met by tightly clenched lips.

The primary process mode of mental activity thus makes it possible for many objects to become the target of drives and for the protean quality of the expressions.

A part of this model that I have found to be sometimes misunderstood has to do with how that which has been rendered unconscious exerts its effects on the preconscious. Freud (1900) felt that in states of fatigue, during sleep, in those conditions when playful attitudes prevail (1905), or when the unconscious mentation can be sufficiently disguised (1901–1905), the censor relaxes its vigilance and unconscious wishes and attitudes can *transfer* their qualities onto a situation or object in the preconscious. The concept of *transference* was articulated in this way. In later years transference was used largely to describe the wishes and attitudes a patient experienced in relationship to the therapist. While this definition may indeed be accurate when the patient makes the therapist the target of an unconscious wish or attitude, it is not the only circumstance in which it occurs. If the working man, who had the obsessive thought about the gas jet, was found to have harbored unconscious, destructive wishes about his house or the people in it, we could say that these destructive wishes were *transferred* to the act of turning the gas jet on or off.

The organ of consciousness perceives the doubt and anxiety when the activities of the preconscious are disrupted by transferences from destructive or unacceptable wishes. When the situation occurs, the individual finds himself in a state of discomfort that is caused by the intrusion of the unwelcome wish, and not because gas jets are not safe. This is why reassurance about gas jets do little to alleviate the anxiety. Since human beings do not tolerate anxiety well, it is at this point that other mechanisms of defense are automatically and unconsciously brought into play, according to A. Freud (1946a).

Among these we might imagine that our "worried" man might invoke denial that a gas leak could cause an explosion, or projection in feeling that if anything happened it would be the fault of the stove manufacturer, or reaction formation in making a resolution that everything in his beautiful home would always be in perfect working order.

This mental complex of defenses, *erected against anxiety* which is stimulated by an unwelcome or repudiated impulse or wish is called a compromise formation. I will return to elaborate the concept of the compromise formation in the section on treatment, because understanding it is essential to the process of interpretation.

The topographic model gives the diagnostician a frame within which to judge how permeable the child's daily life is to intrusions from the unconscious. Transferences to people and objects can be placed in context, and it is in the understanding of the concepts contained in the topographic model that we can begin to appreciate the capacity of the mind to be self-contradictory, seemingly irrational, bizarre, and uncanny.

CHAPTER 9

Classification, Diagnostic Understanding, and Recommendations

Having collected the data from the diagnostic interviews, the clinician is now ready for the tasks of classifying the psychopathology, making a diagnosis of the child's situation, and coupling that diagnosis with a series of recommendations that can be understood and utilized by the adults responsible for the child and to some extent by the child himself. I qualify the child's understanding of the recommendations with the phrase "to some extent," not so much because the child may not have the cognitive capacity to understand concepts of psychopathology, but rather because the child may be ashamed or angry and therefore resistant to the idea that he has some form of psychopathology. If these resistances and concerns can be overcome during the diagnostic process, so much the better, and the child can then be given a simple, direct description of the therapeutic recommendations that will be made to his parents. If it has been impossible to overcome the child's concerns and reluctance, the clinician must be able to stand by his convictions and announce to the child without deception what he will recommend to the parents. If there is a temptation on the part of the clinician to water down his recommendations or what he

175

tells the child in order to keep his benevolence, this may jeopardize future treatment, or may place the parents in an impossible situation. If the child is very resistant, the first therapeutic alliance may have to be with the parents.

CLASSIFICATION

In distinguishing classification from diagnosis I have followed the useful lead of Ashburner (1968) since I share with him the conviction that the two activities, while related, may serve different purposes. There has been no classificatory model that has satisfied everyone and yet a system of classification is required by the field at large. The practical reason for this is that many insurance companies today require a coded number representing a described pathological entity, be supplied them before they will pay a claim for a mental illness. In addition to this, the field needs a way of classifying psychopathology in order to produce and provide statistical information to epidemiologists, other researchers, and to planners of therapeutic programs. Though classification may be of little aid in the process of describing the psychodynamic forces that have conspired to produce illnesses in the child, we have a responsibility to the current field and to the generations of patients and therapists of the future to attempt to classify pathology as accurately as our skills and classificatory tools permit.

In 1979 the task force of the American Psychiatric Association on Nomenclature chaired by Dr. Robert Switzer, developed *The Diagnostic and Statistical Manual* (DSM-III) (1980). This manual succeeded DSM-II which had been deemed inadequate and even damaging to the cause of understanding pathology and promoting mental health for children. J. G. May (1979) summarizes the most telling arguments which were raised against the DSM-II system of classification in the area of childhood psychopathology. DSM-III is a multiaxial system of classifying mental illness and was designed to be integrated with the International Classification of Diseases (ICD). The multiaxial system follows and extends the work of the World

Health Organization seminarists. They had developed a triaxial system of classification, while DSM-III offers five axes. The first three are designed to serve as the official diagnostic assessment, while the last two are provided for use in special clinical situations and for purposes of research. The five axes are:

1. Clinical Syndromes, Conditions not Attributable to a Mental Disorder that are a Focus of Attention or Treatment, and Additional Codes.
2. Personality Disorders and Specific Developmental Disorders.
3. Physical Disorders and Conditions.
4. Severity of Psychosocial Stressors.
5. Highest Level of Adaptive Functioning in Past Year.

This system provides for listing of multiple psychopathological conditions on axes 1 and 2, and for the inclusion with axis 3 of physical conditions that may have precipitated or exacerbated the condition listed in the first two axes. While DSM-III offers opportunity for a more complete and rigorous description of the individual and his states, it is still not the ideal classification system. Therefore, while we must meet our responsibilities in classifying the conditions we find in the children that we diagnose and treat, we cannot expect DSM-III to serve as the working tool that will guide our therapeutic hand.

Another classification system which has been of undisputed utility was produced by a committee of the Group for the Advancement of Psychiatry, chaired by Dr. Dane Prugh. This group produced their report in 1966. It has been widely used and closely scrutinized since then, and has stimulated progressive and creative integration of concepts regarding health and disease with contributions from a number of disciplines. The GAP classification has a number of features that distinguish it from other systems of classifications. It was developed with the child as the central object of concern. It contemplated both health and disease in the context of development. It conveyed, more than any other, the concept that there is a continuum between healthy responses and maladaptive reactions. It makes it possible for the person using the system to place a symptom in various developmental stages, and thus demonstrate that symptoms cannot be given meaning without considering the physical and social variables that are their concomitants. The GAP classification thus comes closer to conveying a living quality to the categories into which the child's traits, qualities, and problems are placed. Despite these advantages the GAP system remains one designed for classification, and cannot provide the flexibility that would permit us to undertake what we would more properly call diagnosis.

Recognizing some of the limitations of any classificatory system, Prugh (1973) has worked toward bridging the gap between classification and diagnosis by proposing an approach to the psychosocial disorders of children which includes concepts pertaining to function, developmental progression, and regression, and social forces that influence health and disease. The report not only shed light on the process and problems in classification, it also integrated substantive information on physical and psychological development into one work.

DIAGNOSIS

Thus, we pass to the issue of diagnosis, which has as its central aim, not the application of a label to the child or his ailment, but the thorough understanding in living terms of the many facets of the current status of the child. In addition, the aim is to appreciate the forces, events, or experiences woven together in the past to bring the child to his present, and as nearly as possible to predict what psychological competence or vulnerability his future will hold. Certainly, this is no small order, and perhaps the diagnostic part of the relationship between child and therapist may not be concluded until the end of therapy, or perhaps never. But it is to this diagnostic fulfillment that the therapist must aspire, if he is to be sustained through obscure and difficult segments of the therapeutic process by an attitude of inquiry which will insure that knowing and understanding will precede directing and controlling, whenever possible.

If knowing and understanding can occur to both patient and therapist, directing and controlling are rarely necessary for the therapist to undertake because the little patient will, with the environment's help, regulate himself. For this reason then diagnostic understanding becomes a component of regulation in the therapeutic endeavor, which leads to further diagnostic understanding, and the spiral toward health can thus proceed.

Organizing the diagnostic data will at once reaffirm that the child's anatomy and physiology contribute to his psychological state, and that this in turn determines the nature of his role as child in a family, student in a school, and member of a society at large. It is widely acknowledged that lower orders of organization contribute to determining the nature of higher, more complex levels of organization. What has been more easily forgotten is that social roles influence psychology and biology and that psychology can influence social roles and biology. In organizing data, then, we cannot think in terms of an ascending order of organizational complexity with causality starting at the cellular level and proceeding in the direction of the social organism. Rather, we must conceive of constant, multidirectional interactions between the individual, his various subsystems, and his surroundings. Our attempts to look at systems and processes independently may be heuristically necessary but a possible source of distortion.

In beginning to organize the diagnostic information, the first consideration can be the general health of the child, and how this influences the rest of his life. Ill-health leading to psychopathology is only one aspect of this component of the diagnostic formulation. An example of a surprising, but understandable variation of the way health affected a child's psychology can be found in the following vignette.

> As a mother was being interviewed in connection with problems she was having with her nine-year-old daughter, she revealed that she had a twelve-year-old son who had suffered from chronic leukemia for the

past six years. As she spoke of her daughter, she tear-
fully confessed that the girl's excellent health and exuberant spirits were sometimes felt by her to be
constant reminders of the catastrophic unfairness that
her son had suffered. She was fairly certain that she
had not revealed this to her daughter. In her own
interview, the angry and depressed nine-year-old said,
"Sometimes I think Mom wished I was sick instead of
Dick. She acts like it's bad for me to feel good."

The state of poor or good physical health needs to be placed
into the total clinical picture before inferences about its significance can be drawn.

Following the consideration of general health and illness,
we can begin to utilize some of the models described in the last
chapter to help organize the information that is germane to the
psychological state of the child. We can look first to the autonomous functions as they were described in chapter 8.

Information from the developmental history, a description
of the child's current ability to function in various environments, and direct observation of the child, can be integrated
to get a good estimate of the competence of these autonomous
functions. The child's ability to perceive and give meaning to
his perceptions, to move in a manner that permits adaptation
to environmental demands, to have a store of memory traces
that can be retrieved by the child as needed are aspects of the
evaluation that can be assessed relatively easily in most cases.
In addition to the current state of the autonomous functions,
the developmental history will describe the fit between environmental stimulation and the child's readiness to use the stimuli for development. The fit between environment and child
may have been nearly perfect during infancy, only to become
discordant and filled with conflict during the toddler phase,
for example. During each phase of development these autonomous functions achieve new levels of organizational complexity in their refinement and in their integration with other
functions. If there had been a developmental period that was
remarkably troublesome for the child or his environment, par-

ticular attention should be devoted to the evaluation of functions that are expected to develop during that period.

A five-year-old kindergarten student was referred for a possible "learning disability." The diagnostician was surprised that this should be the presenting complaint in one so young. The parents revealed that they had brought the child at the suggestion of the kindergarten teacher because she had noticed that during free play the youngster functioned well, but whenever the teacher attempted to organize an activity in which all the children participated, the child became unable to participate or perform. With the permission of the parents and the child the teacher was interviewed by phone. She described the child as being lively and alert whenever he was playing alone. She noted that he could draw and color well and his movements were free and well-coordinated as long as no demands were placed on him. When she sat the group down in front of her, held up cards with the alphabet on them, and asked the children to reproduce them, he would either remain motionless or when pressed, produce a squiggle that had no resemblance to the figure on the cue card. History revealed that the child was born to professional parents in the thirty-fifth year of their life. They were highly organized people who had both counted heavily on their organizational abilities to achieve success in their professional field. The first two years of the child's life required only some changes in the way they had organized their life to produce satisfactory results in the growth and development of all three members of the family. Beginning with the third year of life, however, the child's demands and activities became much less easily managed. There followed a period in which there was considerable disruption. The mother admitted with a great deal of guilt that she frequently became impatient and perplexed as to how to manage the child's disruption of their routines. She recalled with great regret having lost her temper on numerous occasions and having frightened the child with her shouted admonitions when he touched her papers or scribbled on the walls with crayons. The father was equally saddened by his admission that he had retreated into his work in order to avoid conflict with his wife and child. They both agreed that things had improved after a period of six months. When a detailed description of the "improvement" was obtained, however, it became clear that the child had learned to "freeze" and become virtually without initiative whenever an adult made a demand. The parents in their turn had learned to take over almost entirely and provide all of the initiative in interacting with their son. Competent integration of motor and perceptual functions with initiative and responsiveness became impossible and was replaced by passive resistance or incompetence when adults demanded anything of the child.

The fear of the parents in this situation was that the child suffered from mental retardation. The kindergarten teacher was almost certain that he had a perceptual deficit. In fact, perception and motor functions could be demonstrated to be intact when the child was not being pressed to respond to the demands of an adult. It was his inability to integrate perceptions and motor behavior in order to respond to environmental demands or to initiate activities in an effort to get positive environmental response that was flawed. This flaw was the result of psychological discord in an earlier phase of development, and had been camouflaged by the parents "filling in" for the child when he refused or was unable to respond or act. In a setting where the parents could not "fill in" the pattern of "freezing" was all the child had available.

There are times when subsequent developmental phases will heal the conflicts acquired earlier. At other times the conflicts, inhibitions, or deficits may manifest themselves in ways that are more subtle and difficult to detect than in the case examples just cited. The safest posture that the clinician can assume, however, is that functions that were once troubled are vulnerable under stress.

In organizing the data to assess the competence of the autonomous functions, we must remember that we are in a period when parental guilt, economic considerations, and mal-distribution of competent child therapists have made it very easy to maintain that virtually all the problems in the motor or perceptual sphere are due to a defect in the anatomy or phys-iology of the motor or perceptual apparatus. I can only say that in innumerable cases previously diagnosed as learning disabil-ities or hyperactivity, we have in our clinic found compelling evidence of experiential or environmentally induced malfunc-tion of these systems. Competent psychotherapy then, reduced the symptoms and the vulnerability. Is this problem sufficiently widespread to warrant concern? A school official in a com-munity which did not have one trained child psychiatrist, child psychologist, or clinical social worker in it told B. Miller (per-sonal communication, 1980) that 25 percent of the grade school student population in his school was on Ritalin or ampheta-mines. This kind of information causes concern that organic learning disabilities and the hyperkinetic syndromes are too frequently invoked, often without sufficient diagnostic inves-tigation. Without getting into speculation about the incidence and prevalance of these syndromes, it would be legitimate to say that learning disabilities, retardation, and hyperactivity can be the result of faulty interaction between the developing au-tonomous functions and the environment. Many times these faulty interactions cannot be detected or revealed without a detailed, thorough work-up which includes a psychodynamic evaluation as one of its components.

Pathological conditions which are the results of impairment in the anatomical and physiologic substrate of the autonomous functions do exist, of course. When diagnosed, the clinician must then go on to see if environmental or intrapsychic prob-lems are complicating the clinical picture. Psychotherapy, pharmacotherapy, remedial education, parental psychotherapy, and vocational guidance are but a few of the interventions that may be employed to help a retarded child enjoy as much dignity and satisfaction from his life as is his due. The autonomous functions are the part of the model that require closest scrutiny when working with children that have organic handicaps. In our internal scrutiny we need to recall that our track record for treating organically impaired children with enthusiasm and optimism has not been exemplary.

Moving on in the assessment of the child's state, we can address that portion of the personality's traits and functions that has developed through the process of sublimation. This is represented in the model in chapter 8, Figure 8-4B. Here we can begin by appreciating the breadth and variety of ways the child has available to him to express wishes and impulses in modes that are acceptable to himself, and his environment. Some children, for example, can express competitive or exhibitionistic strivings excellently well on the playground or athletic field, but have developed no skills for standing out in the classroom or in verbal exchanges. A child with few modes available to express himself, or to seek satisfaction runs the risk of investing in these few modes in a single-minded manner, and is vulnerable to depression or regression if one modality becomes unavailable to him, through injury for example. One can see instances of this in cases of the child who has put all of his hopes for gratification in athletic or motoric endeavors, only to find in adolescence that athletics has become a nonproductive pursuit.

We would want to know also from our assessment of this personality component, if the aspirations of the child for future gratifying pursuits are consistent with his physical and psychological equipment. We have all seen the pain and sadness that ensues when a youngster with an IQ of 90 is driven and badgered by his own wish or a parent's dream that he become a theoretical physicist; or the many physical and psychological bruises that a sixteen-year-old adolescent suffers when he aspires to a brilliant football career with his 5 feet 5 inch, 126-pound frame.

As psychiatric treatment for children becomes available to more people from various cultures and socioeconomic groups, the evaluation demands an assessment of whether or not there was congruence between the culture at large and the family's mode of sublimating. Anyone who has ever had to straddle two cultures knows that the pain can be exquisite when adoption of one cultural mode produces isolation or shame when he is living in the other culture. While we can acknowledge that our own culture can be enormously insensitive in ignoring or denigrating other cultures, it is the child's internalized, self-depreciation and anger at that which makes him different from his school or playmates that may be most destructive to his self-esteem.

> A fifty-year-old man recalled vividly how out of step and "typically low class, foreign," he felt that he and his family were when, as a school-aged child, they insisted that on Saturday afternoons he accompany them to operas or concerts rather than go to the movies with "American kids."

In many activities, the impetus and zest that characterized early forms of expressing wishes or seeking gratifications are necessary. In play, or when expressing passionately felt convictions, for example, an individual must be able to tolerate some regression if the expression or activity is to bring satisfaction. The diagnostician must evaluate if this flexibility is available to the child and if he can utilize these temporary forms of regression to reduce tension and to express exuberance. Many children who have matured from fear, frustration and despair rather than from pleasure in mastery and competence, cannot permit themselves any pleasurable regression.

Evidence for sublimations and change in functions is sometimes not readily elicited through the history or by tapping the child's memory. It must be inferred from what can be observed. If, for example, the youngster exhibits the capacity to be tender and loving to a parent, sibling, or companion, we can safely assume that possessive or sensual love was not repressed, but modulated and groomed. If he enjoys being admired, we can surmise that the wish to be seen and noticed became a motive for achievement and productivity. Competitiveness may well have come from mastering destructive impulses, and brought with it the desire to be the best as well as the conviction that destructiveness is unnecessary. Thus, we look for derivatives of original impulses and look further to see if these derivatives need to be further refined and differentiated, or if they have reached their age-appropriate potential. It is this area of personality function, in concert with competent autonomous functions that supplies the plasticity that ensures growth throughout life, healing after hurt, and optimism that serenity and gratification are enduring and predictable.

The diagnostician can now begin a survey of the data that has been collected to seek evidence for impulses, wishes, or developmental thrusts that have been repressed. This could be graphically conceived as scrutinizing section C of Figure 8-4 or Figure 8-6 in chapter 8, remembering always that these models portray the living situation about as well as a road map of Arizona portrays the beauty of the Grand Canyon.

It is useful when assessing the state of the child to look for evidence of repression in two ways. The first is to be alert for the *absence* of a function or trait that a child of his age should have available. The second way is to look for the persistence of immature (for his age), primitive behavior which should have been integrated into more complex, adaptive organizational patterns earlier in life. This double scrutiny is much like the way a neurologist evaluates the lesions of an upper motor neuron. The paralysis is noted by the *absence* of a motor function that should be there. The presence of the Babinski reflex represents the persistence of a behavior that should have been integrated into more complex, adaptive, and controllable patterns of behavior.

Examples of absent functions are: an inability to feel or demonstrate tenderness or nonsexualized affection in a post-oedipal age child; the inability to behave in a way that indicates awareness of triadic relationships in a school-age child; the apparent unwillingness or inability to find pride or satisfaction in some degree of self-regulation in a child beyond the toilet-training years. A clinician must, of course, have an image of the traits and competencies typical of a child of his patient's age in order to make these observations.

Examples of the persistence of early, immature patterns might include intense sexual or aggressive components to interactions that should be free of them, experiencing unfounded concrete fears of people, and expectations of treatment from people that would be appropriate for a much younger child. These persisting, immature tendencies are often expressed in inappropriate settings and to inappropriate people, and can be thought of as transferences as described in chapter 8, or as character traits if no part of them is repressed.

In an unconscious effort to justify these disguised wishes, impulses, or attitudes, and to avoid anxiety or shame, defenses are called into play to aid repression. The mechanisms of defense can be many and varied (A. Freud, 1946a), and the child will often seek the aid of adults in the environment by enlisting them to take complementarity to the defenses. The clinician will note that defenses, anxiety, and the transferred wish or attitude have a particular quality which reveals them to be different from a realistic adaptation, a legitimate fear, or an age appropriate wish. They are rigid, monotonously repetitive, even in widely different situations, and unaltered by new experiences. Reasonable persuasion falls on deaf ears when the child's environment attempts to "persuade" a transference away. A convincing illustration of the absence of expected functions and the appearance of the archaic wish from which these should have grown, occurred in the analysis of a young adult. This case was reported more fully in an earlier report by Coppolillo (1967), and more details are available there.

> Mr. T., a 26-year-old man, came to analysis because of anxiety and depression. Although his education had earned him a master's degree, he was virtually incapable of communicating feelings verbally, and was seldom gratified by the verbal expression of

care or concern from others. For him to feel any sense of gratification physical contact was necessary, and this led him to a series of homosexual contacts, which he deplored. In the course of his analysis he revealed not only a lack of development in his ability to communicate verbally, but also a staggering absence of cultural erudition of any kind. He had never heard of Tom Sawyer or Huckleberry Finn. Gulliver and Pinocchio were unfamiliar to him, and only those current events that had a direct impact on his life and work evoked interest. In the course of the analysis he could reveal that verbal or conceptual interchange had had little meaning for him throughout his life. He recaptured memories of his childhood during which a deeply depressed mother held him for hours, making her own existence endurable. Whenever he attempted to become interested in a picture book or magazine, she would intrude, take it from his hands, and read it to him while holding him on her lap with his head pressed to her breasts. The holding and fondling were so stimulating that he ignored her words. Verbal communication and interest in images of human beings, as might be found in literature remained poorly developed. Physical contact more appropriate for a child of three or four was his preferred mode for human contact.

The question of whether the absence of a mode or function is due to repression born of conflict or the result of the individual having reached the limits of his competence needs to be asked. While at times the problem may be sufficiently obscure to warrant formal psychological or neuropsychological consultation, at other times the history and the direct examination of the child may suffice to distinguish one state from the other.

First of all, evidence from the developmental history will reveal if the child had reached a higher level of function and then regressed. Also, the regression is seldom total, and vestiges of the achieved developmental level remain. The overall picture in a regressed child is one of unevenness, while in a child who has been arrested in his development, it is one of uniform incapacity. A child who has regressed from a resolution of oedipal conflicts, for example, may be able to demonstrate excellent ability to be tender and loving with peers or with pets and show awareness of triadic modes of relating even as he shows immaturity in being seductive, exploitative, manipulative, and fearful with adults. If the extent of the regression is difficult to determine, observations made in direct contacts with the patient may resolve the issue. Of course, children with retarded or arrested functions can also be disturbed psychologically, and until these latter problems are alleviated, it is almost impossible to ascertain the extent of the handicap without formal testing. Here the comparison is made between a psychologically impaired child without organic dysfunction and a child with organic retardation without psychological damage.

In attempting to teach a new skill or a new task to the retarded child, it becomes apparent that the child calls up all his resources to comply with the instructions. He attempts the task, watches the examiner's reactions, attempts to please, seeks hints and help, and generally reaches out for an alliance and affective contact. In fact, the joy of human contact and the appreciation for attention and care that some of these children display is profoundly moving. If these children show frustration or irritation, it will come only after many futile attempts to comply. If they succeed, their happiness is ecstatic.

In asking the same thing of a child who is negativistic or a nonperformer due to conflict, a very difficult clinical picture results. The child will "freeze" and stop trying even before the examiner has finished describing the task. One defensive reason after another is given to avoid expending effort. Sometimes the reasons given for noncompliance are contradictory to each other. He can't do it because he has not understood what the examiner wants him to do. When it is explained again, his attention wanders to noises outside or cracks in the wall. He protests that he has *never* been able to do what the examiner asks, and in the next breath asserts that the last time he accomplished what the examiner asked him to do he was tired and grouchy all day. If the examiner insists or cajoles, each attempt brings further isolation or alienation rather than a bid for help. If the child fails the task or fails to even try and the examiner abandons the effort, there are signs of relief. If the child is pushed and succeeds, there is little joy or satisfaction. Rather the child acts as if he had been coerced and exploited. Psychological conflict condemns the bearer to joylessness and dissatisfaction far more than a handicap.

The clinician thus searches for evidence of forces that cause the child's affects or behavior to be rigidly repetitive, nonadaptive, refractory to change through experience, and accompanied by dysphoria and lack of satisfaction. Perplexing as it may seem, these behaviors are defended by the child as if they were cherished possessions and not encumbrances of which he would be well rid.

Next the data needs to be reviewed to determine the stability of those functions that were called secondarily autonomous (Figure 8-4). In the child these functions require special scrutiny because some are in the process of having recently become autonomous from the drives from which they took their origin. It is not unusual, for example, to see a three- or four-year-old, who had had excellent bladder control for one or two years, begin to express distress or chagrin in the form of enuresis after the birth of a sibling. At times the reinstinctalization is disguised. For example, a child may have mastered aggression and sadism through reaction formation, and converted it into kindness and concern. In a regressed state, due to the birth of a younger brother, he may become so "kind" to his younger sibling that he gives him no rest. If left to his own devices, he would approach that well-known condition of killing with kindness. When disguised, the original impulse is expressed symbolically or in its effects.

What needs to be scrutinized about the secondarily autonomous functions is not how they *originated* but their current efficacy. If they have remained stable and efficient, they achieve their aim without conflict, difficulty, or even notice. If they

have once more become the vehicle for the expression of unacceptable impulses, these will be reflected in their effects. A
person struggling with their sadism tyrannizes those around
him with goodness. The expression of goodness becomes the
vehicle for irritating the other person and ineffective as a function to promote relatedness. It is the ineffectiveness or ambi-
valency of a function that we must address, since in diagnostic
and therapeutic efforts we are not authorized to assume that
a trait is the result of concealing an unwelcome impulse unless
we have evidence for the persistence of that impulse.

A seven-year-old girl brought a flower to her therapist after he had had to cancel a session due to illness.
She had learned of his illness from one of the clinic
secretaries, and said that the flower was to make him
feel better. After accepting it and thanking her, the
therapist asked about her reasons for making people
feel better and the ways she accomplished this. The
child's association to the flower clearly indicated that
this kindness was based on positive identifications with
her caring, nurturant mother. The therapist remarked
that she had a lovely way of making people feel good.

In contrast a nine-year-old boy, who also had had
to miss a session due to this illness, called at 10:30 P.M.
to say that he was so worried that the therapist would
die that he couldn't sleep. In the next session the therapist, after learning more about the boy's worries, was
able to show him how these "worries" had played a
trick on the boy's mind, and spoiled his wish to express
concern to his therapist.

The therapist felt authorized to assume that the nine-year-
old boy's concern for him was being contaminated by anger as
the call became a disturbing one, and the script which the boy
had written in his own mind had the therapist dying.

FAMILY DIAGNOSIS

Using models, like those described in chapter 8 as a guide,
the clinician will have organized the information from the his-

tory and diagnostic interviews into a comprehensive picture of the child's current psychological state. The next task is to achieve an understanding of the psychological environment that surrounds the child. Although this ambience is most frequently supplied by the family, it is not invariably so. When children are living in foster homes, boarding schools, or other institutions, attempts must be made to assess the psychological climate that predominates in their life space, since it can influence what is seen in the child.

When the child is living in the family, it must be repeated that the strengths and stability of the family should be noted with as much diligence as it liabilities. Pathology is so seductive and fascinating that we sometimes fail to note that the very act of coming to our consulting rooms can be a demonstration of a family's strength. Stability, role definition, aspirations, commitment as a unit to protect the individual member, are examples of the assets that families bring with them. Not only is it imperative that the clinician be aware of these assets, it is also imperative that the *family knows* that these are recognized.

In considering the child in the context of the family, the clinician may find it useful to turn back to Figure 8-1 to look for sources of identifications that the child has made. Mentioned earlier were a number of possible identification sources based on the model. They were briefly:

1. An identification with a trait or traits of one parent as perceived by the child;
2. An identification with traits of one parent as those traits are perceived by the other parent;
3. An identification with the idealization of a parent;
4. An identification with the oneness that parents can achieve.

The clinician must suspend judgment on the utility or value of the child's identifications until they can be evaluated in the context of the child's own sense of self and self-worth.

The depressed adolescent son of a widely admired and much loved public figure acknowledged that he was like his father in many ways. He said, "Yeah! Wherever I go people like me, just like him. I can talk to anyone just like he can. I'm kind to everyone just like he is, and I'm as big a phony as he is. It's more important to him that everybody thinks he's great than it is for him to give anything to me and Mom."

An identification that could have easily been thought of as a source of strength, was to this boy a source of pain.

In addition to evaluating the family as a source of identifications, the clinician must have a picture of their composition, internal alliances, the overt and covert roles each member plays in the family, the family's development as a system, and the family dynamics. The information gathered in the evaluation either supplies this information or points to areas that need more scrutiny. The great variability of family pathology places its description beyond the scope of this work, and I would refer the reader to one of the excellent texts on this subject. Here, however, I will mention several conditions as illustrative of forms of family pathology that are particularly germane to the child therapist.

As mentioned in chapter 7, Berman (1973) in his book *Scapegoat* describes a form of family pathology in which a child member is unconsciously designated as the one to express his family's fear and anguish. As long as the child was troubled, they could avoid the dreadful pain of impending death that hovered over the family.

A variation on this theme can be found in the family that designates the child as the one who is to be evaluated, but is unconsciously using the evaluation to direct diagnostic attention to another (usually adult) member of the group. These conditions must be detected and managed because unless the family's fear or pain can be alleviated, the child cannot be adequately evaluated, and the family may not be able to let treatment be effective.

Another form of family pain that deserves mention is a condition that, I feel, has been encountered more frequently in the past twenty years than before. These are families, who in the diagnostic sessions, appear communicative and con-

cerned about each other. When this concerned role is examined
minutely, however, each member is found to lead a lonely existence in which closeness and intimacy is longed for but can
neither be achieved nor tolerated. The children they present
to us for treatment are depressed and isolated due to intrapsychic factors to be sure. But as the child's conflicts and isolation begin to be resolved by interpretive and remedial
measures, the more basic therapeutic task begins to loom. The
therapist is challenged to find ways to make the family tolerant
and responsive to the healing child's pleas for closeness. If the
therapist can be alerted to this eventuality, he may be able to
plan the therapy differently, perhaps to include other members
of the family, and thus save himself and the child disheartening
surprises later.

Finally, a family trait that must be reckoned with, if the
child's therapy is to succeed, is that of family passivity or indifference. These families seem to say from the first, "Here is
my child. Make him be less bothersome, but expect no help
from us, because we cannot or will not change." Usually the
problem the child is referred for is misbehavior, because in
these families the child's failures or quiet suffering is not perceived as troublesome. This situation must be distinguished
from those families mentioned earlier in which fear or conflict
designates the child as the patient. This latent fear or hidden
conflict can be used to motivate families to change their views
or to undertake therapy. Passivity or indifference is much more
difficult to engage.

A child in a family with passive or indifferent parents is
often very difficult to treat because the symptomatology evokes
no negative reaction or distress in his environment, and is therefore perceived by him as unremarkable or even expectable.
Little anxiety or fear of negative reaction is attached to his
misbehavior. The therapist then must be ready to take a somewhat hardhearted but realistic position. He must first acknowledge that people have the right to be as they wish to be. They
then have the responsibility to reap the reward or pay the pen-
alties that accrue from their behaviors and attitudes. Our task

can only be to make our patients aware of the connection between their discomfort and the hidden motives and convictions that give rise to that discomfort. We must then make them aware of the options they have available to reduce the pain or discomfort. In the last analysis, the choice must be theirs.

When the child patient begins to develop a character structure that causes others to suffer while he himself is not suffering, it is his *environment* that must render the undesirable traits, a "foreign body" in his personality makeup; otherwise, there is little reason for the child to change. The therapist cannot successfully treat a patient for behaviors that the environment rewards, or to which it takes complementarity or remains indifferent. These considerations prompt me to recommend that when this condition is detected in a family, the therapist should inform the family of these principles and provide them with the opportunity to discuss them as thoroughly as they wish, as well as the opportunity to review their choices as to how *they* *want* to help *their* child to heal. If they decide to proceed, therapy has begun. If they demure, the therapist should advise them of the difficulties that will probably be encountered.

PATTERNS IN PATHOLOGY

Neurotic patterns of adjustment tend to recur. The setting may be different, the characters involved may have changed, but the script remains the same. This occurs because the neurotic can perceive his interactions, and even the unhappiness involved in them, but the motivation for behaving as he does remains unconscious, and therefore unchanged by experience. For this reason, it was suggested earlier that with diagnostic data in hand, the clinician should start looking for patterns of interaction that occur either in the child's life or in the lives of the parents. While some of these patterns can be subtle and be detected, at first, only as hunches awaiting confirmation, some others are blatant, leaving the therapist to marvel at his patient's inability to perceive them.

An eleven-year-old boy was referred by the school

authorities with only passive compliance on the mother's part. He was referred because of poor schoolwork despite his excellent intellectual potential. Three older siblings had made better than adequate grades and good personal adjustments. The mother had been recently divorced from a man who had had an industrial accident before the marriage, and had been incapacitated during much of his married life. As the history unfolded, it became evident to the therapist that this mother, devoted though she was to her son, frequently sabotaged his efforts to be competent in school. The therapist first assumed that the undermining was due to unconscious hostility toward the boy, but this assumption was not supported by evidence and was challenged by her genuine concern and unambivalent love for the youngster. Understanding began when the therapist was able to discover that the mother had, as a schoolchild, inherited the care of an ailing father after her own mother died. Her sense of worth and self-esteem were heavily predicated on her service to persons near her. Her husband, whom she had slavishly taken care of, was gone, and her other children were grown. Her eleven-year-old son was now her last hope to maintain this sense of worth. As long as he failed in school, she needed to keep helping him. It was when the *pattern* of "self-esteem only through service" became apparent to the therapist that the aspect of the relationship that was hurting both mother and child could be addressed.

PSYCHODYNAMIC FORMULATION

After establishing the current psychological state of the child and the family, the diagnostician can turn to the development of a psychodynamic formulation. This task attempts to conceptualize the psychological forces that acted on the individual's development to produce the patterns of intrapsychic and interpersonal adaptations he currently employs. Although formulating how these dynamic forces affected the individual in the past and influence him in the present, begins during the diagnostic phase of the clinical encounter, it should continue throughout the therapeutic process. The formulation should constantly be revised, questioned, and amended until both patient and therapist find it a stable and convincing account of the patient's inner life.

The reasons for formulating the psychodynamics of a child are several. When an affect or an attitude is recognized as a transference, knowing the forces that have acted on the child may help place the source of the transference. Some behaviors or attitudes cannot be undone by learning a new pattern of acting or a new attitude. The conditions that produced the behavior or attitude must be relived, understood, and discarded as irrelevant before new views can be espoused. The dynamic formulation alerts the therapist to the situations that may have to be relived and worked through rather than repeated (Freud, 1914). In the course of therapy, prediction is helpful to avoid the pitfalls of repeating a traumatic experience with the patient. The dynamic formulation describes some of these traumatic situations, and signals potential pitfalls.

The raw data for the diagnostic formulation comes from the developmental history, the behavior of the patient during diagnostic and therapeutic interviews, and the patient's reports of transferences that they experience toward the therapist or others. How these are put together to produce a dynamic formulation varies with each diagnostician. Here I can only share the visual imagery that would describe how I formulate psychodynamics. Others may well experience and describe it differently.

From the material that describes the current state and the living conditions of the patient, I imagine a two-dimensional picture emerging as if on a television screen. From the back of this viewing screen extends a receptacle much like a photographic slide box with a light in the end farthest away from the screen. This represents the patient's developmental history

(Figure 9-1). As each new bit of information emerges, I treat it in one of two ways. It may be seen as a jigsaw piece to be fit on the front of the viewing screen to help complete the picture of the child's current life, or it may be thought of as a photographic transparency. It would then be placed somewhere along the long axis of the box to participate in modifying the light as it is cast on the screen. Like a transparency, it is modified by the slides between it and the light, and in its turn modifies those between it and the screen. These transparencies are the dynamic forces that influence development. A bit of information that I cannot fit anywhere remains at the periphery of awareness, nudging me constantly to find it a place somewhere on the screen or in the slide box. When I see a recognizable picture on the screen, and can see a degree of continuity between the slides in the box, I feel I can formulate how the child came to his current state. This is the imagery and feeling tone that accompanies my attempts to formulate the dynamic psychological forces that have acted on the patient. Each therapist will have his own image of the process.

RECOMMENDATIONS

When the diagnostician is ready to describe his findings and make recommendations to the family, time should be set aside for a formal interview. Recommendations should not be made by telephone or during some time tacked on the end of one of the diagnostic sessions. It is a time when great tact is required of the clinician, and we should not underestimate the courage required of the parents. This completion interview demands a time of its own.

If therapy is to be prescribed, the therapist must be prepared to assess the response of the parents to his prescription and to discuss the form of treatment he will recommend.

It can be expected that the child and the family may be fearful and ambivalent or question their commitment to the therapeutic process. This may even be acknowledged by the diagnostician who recommends therapy. Questions that the

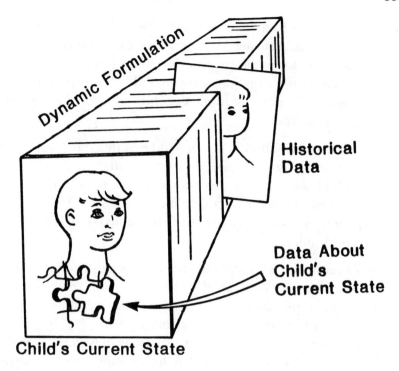

Figure 9-1. Representation of the process of formulating psychody-namically. See text.

family may have about the significance of therapy, the time it will take, or how it will be conducted will be invited. Until the family can make a reasonable well-informed commitment to the form of therapy that has been suggested, interviews with the family in which their doubts and fears are expressed, and their questions are answered should be continued. E. J. Anthony (personal communication, 1964) maintains that in the psycho-analysis of children this is sufficiently important to warrant seeing parents for as long as six months before beginning the child's treatment.

As to the form of treatment, here we can consider four of the possible choices. The four are: hospitalization, day treat-ment, individual psychotherapy, and family therapy.

1. Although inpatient treatment of a child is costly in time

and money and often frightening to the child and family, a hospitalization may ensure the successful outcome of a therapeutic endeavor, as well as protect the child's health or even his life. Indications for inpatient care include those instances in which a psychosis may endanger the child's life or the welfare of those around him.

> An autistic child of seven had been in a day treatment setting since the age of four. Although improvement had occurred, he was still vulnerable to outbursts of rage and virtually uncontrollable behavior. He had to be moved to an inpatient unit after injuring his two-year-old sibling.

In other instances, inpatient care may be required for dangers that emanate, not from the child but from the environment. For example, danger of physical or sexual abuse to the child may be an indication for hospitalization.

There are also less dangerous situations in which, possibly brief periods of hospitalization may in the long run be useful for progress in therapy. The interference with destructive family patterns is an example.

2. The day treatment of children in a setting in which milieu therapy and remedial education are combined is a valuable addition to the therapeutic repertoire. Day treatment is particularly useful when academic problems and emotional problems coexist. In addition to seeking remediation to these problems, a day treatment center also protects a child's reputation. Unfortunately, the reputation that a child may acquire as a poor student or troublemaker may precede him in a school system, and become a self-fulfilling prophecy. A day treatment center in which the staff of educators and therapists are sophisticated in understanding transferences and countertransferences may avoid or interrupt these spirals of pathology.

Day treatment may be of immense help to the therapeutic process when the child's capacity for self-observation is limited or nonexistent, and pathology can only be revealed as it is being manifested in behavior. Here the milieu in concert with the therapist can address pathology as it emerges, and therapeutic or remedial action can be taken on the spot. Day treatment, of course, has the added advantage of maintaining the child for at least part of the time in the home and neighborhood environment. This permits the process of working through his problems to occur more naturally and with less distortion than occurs in an inpatient setting. The availability of the family as participants in the working through process is also enhanced.

I have avoided consideration of "the least restrictive" environment in considering day treatment and an inpatient setting because this has become a catch phrase that really does not do justice to the complexity of issues in the clinical setting. Of course there have been children whose liberties have been curtailed by an inpatient and day treatment placement. At the same time, any inpatient or day treatment worker can point to numbers of children who have never been more free than when they were placed on an inpatient ward or a day treatment unit, and removed from an environment that could not tolerate their growth, development, or even their expression of individuality without reacting with coercive measures. The ultimate decision of the setting in which a child is to be treated needs to be made in a clinical frame of reference with legal safeguards and not in a legal frame of reference with clinical consultation.

3. Individual psychotherapy of children in an ambulatory setting is the most frequently used form of psychotherapy today. When conditions of the child and his environment permit it to be used, this treatment is the least artificial of all forms of therapy and provides the child with the best opportunity to do his healing where it needs to be done; in his daily world and not just in the office of his therapist.

Decisions must be made in outpatient therapy as to the frequency of visits, and when they will occur. With this consideration comes that of deciding whether psychoanalysis or psychotherapy is more indicated. In the next chapter, I will compare these two forms of treatment and supportive psychotherapy. A discussion of the indications for each more logically follows their descriptions.

Once it is decided that the child will be involved in outpatient therapy the therapist must also decide whether the parents will be seen *as parents* in separate sessions, or as *patients* themselves. By and large I have found that if parents are identified as patients, a separate therapist for them is indicated. To treat both parents and child has always felt like a contamination of both therapies to me, and the question of whose agent the therapist is becomes complicated. At times, however, the therapist may have little choice in the matter. If parents and child are treated by separate therapists, an active decision should be made regarding the extent of the collaboration between the therapists, and child and family should be informed of this decision.

4. Family therapy has become a more frequently utilized treatment modality in the past two decades. The techniques and indications vary with the different schools of thought. Here I will say only that family therapy has appeared to be most useful in instances in which the interdigitating pathology between family members was the *principal* pathology, and the intrapsychic difficulties of the individual were kept alive by it. The family was powerless to interrupt the destructive transactions as a group or as individuals. In seeing these patterns of interaction unfold before the therapist, his interpretations of them can be liberating for the family.

On a number of occasions I have felt that a family therapy approach had been selected because the therapist had neither the understanding nor the necessary technical competence to treat the individual child. It was then asserted that child psychotherapy was neither necessary nor preferable. This is not an indication for family therapy. This is simply another example of children's needs being rationalized out of existence because we do not have the tools, or will not take the trouble, to meet those needs. When the diagnostician decides that there are positive and legitimate indications for family therapy, either as the sole treatment of choice or in connection with an individual's psychotherapy, it becomes a productive tool.

It is by now evident that successful diagnosis and treatment of the psychological illnesses of children rests on a tripod of knowledge. The first leg of the tripod is thorough, dynamic understanding of psychological growth and development. Fraiberg's (1959) *The Magic Years* and Lidz's (1976) *The Person* are excellent guides in this area.

Recognition and understanding of psychopathology is the second support of the tripod. Clinical experience, guided by a seasoned clinician is indispensable for this phase of training. Good preparation for this is available by a study of Achenbach's (1974) book *Developmental Psychopathology* and volume II of Noshpitz's (1979) *The Basic Handbook of Child Psychiatry*.

The third area to be mastered is the clinical art of diagnosis and treatment. As said before, actual treatment with an experienced supervisor is the basis for development of this art. A book such as this can only prepare the student to learn.

CHAPTER 10

Psychotherapeutic Choices and Some Essential Tools

Unexamined, unconscious mentation may coerce behavior more unremittingly than a tyrant's threat. The therapist's task is to free the patient from this internal tyranny so that he may *choose* how he will behave and think. I find the word *shrink* offensive when used to describe a dynamically oriented therapist. This is not because I resent any disrespect that may be implied, but because it misrepresents the aim of psychotherapy. In addition to other implications, like comparing a therapist to a head-shrinking sorcerer, *shrink* implies that a person's opinions are reduced through treatment. It is this misrepresentation that I find misleading and objectionable, whether or not the word is used. The aim of therapy is not to replace the internal coercion of the unconscious with an external coercion of rules and directives. Its aim is to free the person to use self-knowledge and self-awareness so that he may achieve *self-regulation*. Only through self-regulation can the individual hope to optimize his ability to put together components of his resources to meet the new and changing demands of the environment and new requisites of his own development. When it is determined that self-regulation is impossible for the individual to achieve, psychotherapy alone is not the treatment of choice.

In the previous chapter four settings in which psycho-therapy could take place were examined. These were an in-patient therapeutic milieu, a day treatment unit, the outpatient individual mode, and ambulatory family treatment. Here, the therapeutic strategies of psychoanalysis, uncovering or conflict reducing psychotherapy, and supportive psychotherapy will be described. Any of these can be used in an inpatient, day care, or ambulatory setting. Family treatment requires its own ex-position, and I would refer the reader to texts on its techniques.

PSYCHOANALYSIS

Two major schools of thought that have predominated in child psychoanalysis are the Kleinian and the Freudian schools. Each has made valuable contributions from different points of view as expressed in the writings of Melanie Klein (1932) and Anna Freud (1946b). Both schools depend on the child's ability to recapture and examine unconscious wishes and thoughts for their therapeutic efficacy.

Psychoanalysis is particularly indicated in psychoneurotic conditions afflicting children with relatively intact egos who are living in an environment that is sufficiently stable to permit frequent therapy sessions, and which will not expose the child to major changes in their living conditions during the course of their analysis. These conditions are most often met by chil-dren living in intact families, and who are not suffering massive environmental trauma like abuse, life-threatening illnesses or abandonment. They should have developed a capacity for re-latedness to other human beings, some ability to observe and report their feelings and wishes, and be able to tolerate enough frustration to permit them to discuss an impulse before in-dulging it.

The pathology that responds to psychoanalysis best is the one which is the result of having regressed from a develop-mental phase, with repression of wishes and distortion of de-velopmental acquisitions typical of that phase. Developmental arrests due to psychological trauma frequently require teaching in addition to analysis.

The strategy in psychoanalysis is to provide enough contact with the analyst to permit the child to live out his problems in the relationship with him. This usually requires four to five sessions per week. There are those who maintain that this "transference neurosis" cannot occur in children. I am with those who are convinced that children can and do develop transference neuroses in analysis. When this develops, the analyst and child then work in the context of the transference neurosis to define how the child defended himself against the fear, wish, or conviction that caused the child's problem. Once the defenses against the anxiety and its repressed cause are defined, the child–analyst team seeks to recall or reconstruct the situation that occasioned the repression of the conflict.

I believe that further comparative study is required to delineate clearly which children must have a psychoanalysis to reach their maximum potential, and which can be adequately treated with competent, conflict reducing psychotherapy. In the remainder of this work we will focus on the techniques of psychotherapy and add only that when the diagnostician is convinced that psychoanalysis is the treatment of choice, the child be referred to a certified child analyst directly or through an institute for psychoanalysis that has a child analytic program.

CONFLICT REDUCING PSYCHOTHERAPY

Conflict reducing psychotherapy or insight psychotherapy borrows widely from psychoanalytic technique, psychoanalytic concepts of development, and dynamically oriented theories of personality functions. Sessions are usually one to three per week, rarely more. The strategy is to use accounts of the child's daily life as well as his interactions with the therapist to inquire into the reasons for repetitive, stereotyped behaviors that are troublesome or maladaptive. While transferences are utilized as objects of this inquiry, the therapist does not encourage a transference neurosis, nor interpret predominately within its context as in a psychoanalysis. In psychotherapy the therapist must be ready to intervene in more realistic ways in the child's life with school consultations or suggestions to the family, while in psychoanalysis this is less frequently done. Supportive measures (which will be described in the section on supportive psychotherapy) are more frequently used than in psychoanalysis, and what Eissler (1953) called parameters are more widely employed.

Even as child psychotherapy has profited from its psychoanalytic borrowings, in some settings it has suffered from its proximity to psychoanalysis. In these instances the attitude that has insinuated itself into the teaching and practice of psychotherapy is that great attention to technique is required to conduct an analysis, but psychotherapy permits the therapist such great latitude that discipline virtually disappears. If this attitude is present and persistent, it can destroy the efficacy of psychotherapy. While support, realistic interventions, and parameters may be more widely employed in psychotherapy, the therapist must scrutinize their introduction and effects as closely as he scrutinizes the productions of the child. They are used only when necessary, and dispensed with when no longer necessary.

Psychotherapy is indicated in children who fall on both sides of the children who would be referred for an analysis. On the one hand, there are children whose pathology is sufficiently severe, or involves so much environmental management that an analysis would be impossible. On the other hand, there are children whose pathology is so circumscribed or limited that an analysis would be too much treatment. These children can be managed and successfully treated in dynamically oriented, individual psychotherapy. In a word, psychotherapy provides flexibility in making care available to a broader segment of the child population than could be served by psychoanalysis. Also, a number of children for whom psychoanalysis is not possible because of cost or unavailability of an analyst, can be adequately treated by psychotherapy.

SUPPORTIVE PSYCHOTHERAPY

If unwarranted and regrettable attitudes have crept into the field of child psychotherapy, they have thundered into the area of supportive psychotherapy. This area has received probably less attention than any other available treatment approach. And yet, on reflection it is impossible to imagine that treatment could be conducted without supportive measures. The regularity and predictability of the therapy hours, the privacy of the sessions, the nonjudgmental attitude of the therapist are all basic principles of any psychotherapy, even as they also serve as support to the patient. It would appear that supportive psychotherapy has come to be considered the antithesis of uncovering psychotherapy and associated with severely disturbed patients for whom there can be no cures, only props. As such, supportive psychotherapy was seen as something less effective, that could be left to persons with less skill and training. These are misconceptions that have interfered with recognizing the importance and ubiquity of human support in the process of psychotherapy or psychoanalysis.

The adolescent boy, referred to in chapter 9, had in an earlier phase of treatment encountered resistances, which were both stubborn and vigorous. As the reader will recall, his father had done so many good works that he was considered saintly by his admirers. His mother was a kind, reliable person who in comparison to her husband was considered somewhat colorless. The patient felt that many of the mother's fine qualities had not been recognized because they were overshadowed by the father's energy, idealism, and social attractiveness. During his childhood and early adolescence, the patient had despaired of ever being able to emulate his father, and had unconsciously identified with many solid, productive qualities of his mother. He was in conflict over these identifications, however, since he considered them effeminate, and they did not live up to his father's expectations. Whenever recognition of the sources of these identifications threatened him, he would begin to act like a bigger than life replica of his father with a constantly hovering conviction that he would not be able to carry it off. In one of the sessions, he announced with a belligerance that revealed his defensiveness that he would miss his next appointment because he was going to join a group of welfare mothers marching to protest what they felt was mistreatment by the department of social services. Attempts to elicit associations to his plan to miss his session were met with increased belligerence and accusations that psychiatrists were selfish, uncaring, and did not live in the real world. The therapist was told that rather than chiding him for missing an appointment he should be out marching with the mothers too. All attempts to help the patient look at his affects, or the possibility of latent motives failed until the therapist said, "I know that you sincerely care about these mothers and children who are not being treated fairly, and this does you credit. I know also that you have many good reasons for being in that protest march. But, among these many logical reasons of which you are aware, there may be one reason for going that you know nothing about. Wouldn't it be helpful to you to know all the reasons for feeling and doing things?" With this the patient calmed and began to be more self-observant. He asked for and was given a different appointment time that permitted him to explore the ambivalence in his identifications with his mother, and the anger he felt toward his father's competence.

In acknowledging his "many good reasons" for wanting to join the protest march, the therapist was doing supportive psychotherapy. He was supporting the patient's awareness that he was not only an anxious, conflicted person, he was also a person with ideals and competencies, even when these were derived from ambivalent identifications with both his mother and his father. Without this support the patient would not, at that time, have been able to look at his own conflict. Supportive psychotherapy thus accompanies conflict reducing psychotherapy as it addresses difficult or painful segments of the work. It is not only for the patient who constantly needs props to survive.

There are few efforts made to conceptualize a model that will address principles of supportive psychotherapy. I think it possible to conceive one, and it seems worth doing in view of the frequency that psychological support is needed and used in patient care. Here, I will offer a brief description of a model that has helped me visualize supportive interventions, and that will, I hope, be helpful to the reader.

To begin with, the support that is offered a patient is directed to a function. Functions process stimuli that originate either in the external world or from within the organism. These latter are not only drives and their derivatives, but also thoughts, affects, and images of the self. Rapaport in 1951 and 1958 formulated some elegant ideas on the freedom of the ego to function efficiently in this task of processing stimuli. He begins by underlining the fact that though human behavior is determined by instinctual drives, it is not simply a passive expression of drive activity. Man can respond to the external environment, and his behavior can adapt to its requisites or appeals. He achieves this freedom from instinctual drives through the primary and secondary autonomies of the ego. Rapaport (1951) called this freedom the "autonomy of the ego from the id." Today we would be authorized to say that man achieves autonomy not only from drives. He can also become relatively autonomous from idiosyncratic thought, inappropriate affects, and distorted self-images through the autonomies of the ego.

Conversely, man's behavior is not entirely dependent on the external world. Social and psychological observations clearly describe the persistence of both pathological and normal behavior forms in adverse environmental conditions. Rapaport (1958) says, "To the medical man, it is a commonplace that nonliving matter cannot escape the impact of . . . [the] environment and its reactions are strictly (or statistically) predictable, but that organisms can escape such impacts, can avoid responding to them, and when they respond, they can do so in a variety of alternative [vicarious] ways" (p. 16). Later in the same article, he writes, "Man's constitutionally given drive equipment appears to be the ultimate (primary) guarantee of the ego's autonomy from the environment, that is, its safeguard against stimulus response slavery" (p. 18). Again, I feel that today we are authorized to say that in addition to man's "constitutionally given drive equipment" his internalized values, commitments, and sense of self can free him from slavery to the stimuli from the external world.

Finally, Rapaport (1958) asserted that the ego's two autonomies (from the internal and external world) exist in inverse relationship to each other (p. 23–24). Any alteration in the state of one autonomy is inevitably accompanied by a change in the other. If the ego is forced to be autonomous from the environment through sensory deprivation, for example, it soon becomes inordinately permeable to internal stimulation. The person can even hallucinate and become delusional. A more commonplace example is the mild ache that becomes a pain difficult to tolerate when the lights are turned off in preparation for sleep (Figure 10-1A). Should the environment become incessantly intrusive on the other hand, as in brainwashing, the ego can become so autonomous from a person's inner world that he can abandon all of his own desires, strivings, values, and commitments (Figure 10-1B). The converse of these two states can be seen clinically. Increased drive tensions, or fanatical conviction can render reality oriented perception and behavior difficult (Figure 10-1C). A child having a temper tantrum does not observe the niceties of etiquette. In those conditions in which there is blocking of drive tension or insensitivity to internal stimuli as in obsessional neurosis or in schizophrenic waxy flexibility, the individual may become a slave to external stimuli (Figure 10-1D).

It is obvious that when the ego is in any of these extreme states it has suffered a breakdown in a number of the functions that it deploys to cope with internal or external reality. Most of the situations in which the ego requires support can be conceptualized in this manner, and these ideas of Rapaport are offered as the basic ingredients for a model of supportive psychotherapy. When the patient's ego is being overwhelmed by impulses, affects, or internally generated convictions, the ther-

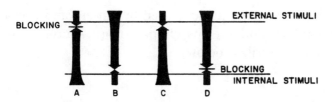

Figure 10-1. Representation of Rapaport's concepts of the relative autonomies of the ego. See text. (From H. Coppolillo (1976), The transitional phenomenon revisited. *J. Amer. Acad. Child Psychiat.*, 15:36–45.)

apist offers himself as a support for those ego functions that perceive external reality. For example, a comment to a child who was overwhelmed by anger, or is actually experiencing intense anger in the sesson could be, "Yes, I know how angry you are, but can you imagine how people feel when you scream at them?" Conversely, to a child whose ego is being oppressed by events in the external world the therapist could say . . . "You've told me what happened when Mom and Dad were fighting, but you haven't said what was going through your mind."

This then, is a model for supportive psychotherapy. It does not cover all of the possible ways that support might be needed, but I think the principles involved are sufficiently generalizable to be able to say that when support is needed it can be viewed in the context of this model. If the patient is responding largely to his inner world, the therapist supports the functions that perceive the external environment; if conversely, the patient seems to react mostly to the external world, the therapist addresses the necessity to take internal states into account.

TOOLS OF PSYCHOTHERAPY

The tools of dynamic psychotherapy are mental operations. Some of these are the development of attitudes, while others involve verbal techniques. Still others are ways of listening and assigning significance to what is heard. Of these tools, some are used predominately by the therapist, some used mainly by the patient, and some are shared. The therapeutic alliance collects them into an armanentarium used by patient and therapist to detect, explore, and alter psychopathology. A number of these tools will be described below.

INQUIRY

An attitude of inquiry is a potent way of assaulting the barrier that keeps mental phenomena unconscious. While this attitude is usually the therapist's at the beginning of the treatment process, a major therapeutic achievement is marked when the patient begins to question his own motives or behaviors. The patient's inquiry indicates that wishes, attitudes, or actions that were automatic and givens in his mental life are now foreign bodies, and the patient has taken the responsibility for scrutinizing them.

The idea of maintaining an attitude of inquiry is deceptively simple, and more difficult to put into practice than would appear. There are a number of reasons for this difficulty. One reason is that many of us were trained to *do* rather than inquire. The patient's pleas and our own anxiety sometimes combine to force inquiry aside in favor of action. As we inquire, we must live with uncertainty. This is no easy matter and most of us are relieved by early solutions, and then action comes to the fore. Inquiry also demands that appropriate questions be asked. As we know, the appropriate question is often more difficult to find than the answers that ensue.

Finally, when inquiry threatens to reveal a painful insight, the patient or his family may precipitate some crisis to force the therapist into action and away from questioning. If this defensive maneuver succeeds, the therapist will find that soon the treatment consists of ricocheting from one crisis to another without the time to ask how each crisis occurred. Crises demand action, and thus inquiry disappears.

The therapist then, must make an adjustment as treatment begins if he is to institute and maintain an attitude of inquiry. He must learn to live with periods of uncertainty. He must be ready to resist the temptation to spring into action, and if forced to do so by a crisis, follow the crisis intervention with curiosity about why the crisis occurred at the time that it did, and how it was precipitated. The therapist must put aside the satisfactions to be found in being an expert and telling his patients about themselves in favor of being curious about what the patients think about themselves.

If the therapist has been the diagnostician, there is a particularly important shift to be made when therapy begins. In the course of the diagnostic evaluation he, as diagnostician, was in a posture of continually extending himself mentally with inferences and formulations to achieve understanding, and create a mental image of the patient's development. Now he must sit back and change the pace. The therapist, if he is to be effective, cannot cram the patient into a preconceived mold of development, or make him fit the known dynamics of a pathological entity. He must allow the patient to rediscover anew the forces that go into healthy and pathological development. If, for example, the patient is kind and considerate, he should wonder about these traits, but should not assume that the kindness is only reaction formation against sadistic impulses. If there are sadistic impulses against which the patient struggles, these will be revealed by symbols or actions. Only then is the therapist authorized to conclude rather than wonder.

In addition to challenging repression, the attitude of inquiry is useful for other reasons. It guarantees that the therapist will respect the individuality of the patient. Each person came to be the way he is through personal experiences. It is the personal experiences that must be understood in therapy and not the textbook's articulated principles of development. Inquiry probably comes closer than any other tool to ensuring that misconceptions of the past will not be revisited on the patient in the present. If the patient supplies the data for fresh conclusions, as these are recognized, therapeutic endeavors will stay current with social changes as they are reflected in the patient. The therapist will consider and treat the ills of today and not what was discovered thirty, forty, or seventy years ago.

Probably the most important reason for an attitude of inquiry from the point of view of its therapeutic implications is that the *process* of discovery is as useful to the patient in restoring health as that which is discovered. In the process the patient actively renders rigidly entrenched defenses useless, masters anxieties, and becomes aware of the many options he has available to attain satisfaction. In so doing, the patient learns the processes of self-observation and regulation, and makes them his own, eventually dispensing with the need of a therapist to regulate his life or his behavior.

EMPATHY

In being empathic the therapist evokes in himself *memories* of experiences that he believes the patient is living through or has experienced. I avoid saying that the therapist feels what the patient feels, because often our little patients feel, or describe having felt, terror, impotence, rage, or despair. While it is necessary for the therapist to know the experience of being in one of these states, it would be counterproductive if he were to actually experience them during the therapeutic hour.

Steinberg and Simons (1981) have suggested that empathy requires an identification with the patient, while others propose a partial identification. I think it worthwhile to split some hairs here and propose that there are mechanisms at work other than identification that make productive empathy possible. Kohut (1966) provides a valuable insight when he lists empathy as one of the outcomes of the healthy, developmental transformations of narcissism. In so doing, he underlines that we look inwardly, to our own experiences in development, to find the resonance that characterizes empathy. To achieve this in working with child patients, an exquisitely dosed amount of regression is required. The therapist cannot on the one hand dismiss a child's night terror, for example, as being foolish because he cannot permit himself enough regression to recall the pain associated with terror. On the other hand, he also cannot become so identified with the paralysis that is associated with terror in the child that he, when confronted by a child's nightmares, for example, insists that the parents allow the child into their bed. By dipping into his own developmental experiences, the therapist can recall terror rather than experience it. At the same time he can re-evoke the optimism and confidence that came from mastering terror. If he identifies with the child, he may become too immersed in the helplessness that accompanies the terror to be optimally helpful.

Empathy is a powerful tool for appreciating how another person's shoes feel. It is also a tool that is vulnerable to blunting. Unrecognized countertransferences may so distance the therapist from the child that empathy is impossible, or they may mire him so deeply in an identification with the patient that he loses the ability to distinguish his own reactions from those of the child. Fatigue or a persistent worry may erode empathy by putting the therapist in the position of feeling, "I can't worry about your troubles, kid, I've got some real ones of my own." A particular pitfall for some child therapists is what occurs when his own children may be doing, saying, or experiencing the same thing as his child patient. Empathy again can turn into an identification or be rejected entirely. The ability to empathize can be seriously compromised when the child expresses a trait or quality that the therapist has repudiated in himself. A young, black therapist, for example, was unaware that he treated his black patient's poor school performance and misbehavior coldly, even as he was ready to understand a white boy's bad grades and anger as a product of his depression. When, in supervision, this discrepancy was challenged, the therapist could recall how often he had felt that he had had to defend his race (himself) against the accusations of laziness and lack of restraint, and how he felt his black patient threatened his defense.

Empathy, therefore, can be undermined, and sometimes so subtly that we are unaware of it. Some signs of this erosion are boredom or irritability on the part of the therapist during the hour. Another indication that I have learned to detect in myself is perplexity or pessimism about a therapeutic intervention. When I feel that anything I try is not going to work, I am fairly certain that something that is burdening the child is being missed by me. The therapist should also be alert to a possible breakdown in empathy in those instances when sessions degenerate into arguments. Finally, the therapist can note if he thinks about his patient as "a case" or a pathological entity or as his "three o'clock appointment." If this happens repeatedly, a review of the relationship is called for.

In treating children I have noticed that when my own empathy for the child's plight was unencumbered, the child who was previously self-preoccupied, would begin showing empathic responses of his own. While this may be imitation at first, in the course of treatment it becomes identification, and an excellent indicator that the therapist's empathy has been appreciated.

Empathy's value does not only lie in making understanding more complete for the therapist. Perceiving empathy in the therapist permits the child to feel understood. For this reason empathic understanding needs to be reflected back to the patient. Long discourses or contrived expression of the therapist's feelings are not the way to achieve this. A nod or a brief rephrasing of the child's description of one of his states, or a phrase like, "That must have been sad," gets the job of communicating empathy done without interfering with the child's activity and individuality. That is what I believe the essence of empathy to be, the ability to show the child that he, as a separate, autonomous human being, can be understood and elicit concern and care from another human being who is separate but not distant.

INTROSPECTION

The process of introspection is not frequently associated with children for a number of reasons. It is somewhat difficult for children to split a mental operation into a component that experiences or recalls an experience, and a component that can observe this experience or the memory of it, and then report the observation. It is also difficult for children to articulate a cognitive construct or affective experience that has not been validated for them by others. Since the convictions, wishes, or affects that may be troublesome to them also cause them shame or pain, they are often unexpressed, and so remain unvalidated and obscure or ill-defined. Reporting them, therefore, is difficult. Children are accustomed to having adults tell them what their values, reactions, and feelings are, or should be, and are therefore perplexed when an adult inquires rather than asserts something about them. Conversely, we as adults are ready to assume that a child cannot or will not introspect, and we convey little interest to the child about his self-awareness. Despite these impediments, the utility of this tool should not be summarily dismissed even when doing therapy with preschool children. Although they may not have formally conceived of it, children introspect frequently. As understanding between child and therapist grows in the process of treatment, the child can be taught to introspect and report what he discovers. At times the therapist can teach this by example. He can, when appropriate, say something like, "When you told me about that, a picture of another boy I knew came into my head. It made me wonder if you sometimes felt like he did when such and such happened." Conveying the importance of introspection in the therapist can make it an important activity for the child to emulate. At other times the therapist can do some fundamental, step-by-step teaching that will formalize the process for the child, and make it available for his use when it is needed. He can do this by putting words to experiences that the child has already had, but may not be able to describe. "Have you noticed that when you think of your little sister, you get a picture in your head? And that picture is not just of your sister. It has other parts to it: where she is, what she's doing, who is with her. Look at that picture inside of your head, and tell me about it, since you are the only one who can see it." In so doing, the therapist and child find another source of data from which insights are gleaned. In addition, the child will acquire another tool for self-awareness and self-regulation, and also have demonstrated to him that his subjective states are a valid part of his condition as an individual.

ASSOCIATIONS

The value of the child's associations as a tool to reveal unconscious or suppressed mentation seems to have diminished as we invested more in play techniques. Although children have a more difficult time understanding and complying with the principle of free associations than adults do, it would be a mistake to ignore the process completely. Children, of course, make associations and connections constantly in their thinking. It is in the articulation and reporting of these associations that the difficulty arises. Yet any child I have treated for any length of time indicated that they could appreciate the significance of an associative connection when it was pointed out to them.

In some instances the connection between the associations is clear and unmistakable, even if the youngster remains unaware of it. The therapist can then make a simple declarative statement about the connection for the patient's scrutiny. In other situations the help of the patient must be enlisted if any sense is to be made of the perceived association.

An example of the first situation is to be found in an interchange with Don, an eleven-year-old boy who had come to treatment to alleviate chronic anxiety, poor school performance, and truancy. On several occasions when he had suddenly fallen silent in earlier sessions, he was able to say that some things that happened in his family were "so fierce" that he couldn't talk about them. In the session being described, Don had just acknowledged with some embarrassment that on one occasion when he skipped school, he and his friends went to his house to look at pornographic pictures. He then added hurriedly, and with some anxiety, that his older sister was not at home that day, since she was attending her high school class. The therapist recalled that this was the third time that Don followed a memory of some kind of sexually exciting situation with an association to his sister. He said to Don, "I think that what's so hard to talk about because you feel it's so 'fierce' has something to do with sexy feelings and your sister." He nodded sadly, and over the next several sessions told of open sexual activities between him and his older sister.

An incident that illustrates how the patient can help in understanding an association happened in an hour with an eight-year-old boy named Teddy. He was being treated for aggressive and unruly behavior, which had started after the sudden death of his father. Despite the hard work and long hours that the father spent at his butcher shop, he had always managed to find time to spend with Ted, and a relationship of mutual adoration existed at the time of the father's sudden death. Because of his own character style and for other reasons that involved the mother, Teddy was not able to express healing grief, and adequately mourn his father. The rage and misbehavior were a manifestation of his unexpressed pain. In a session when he was describing a teacher's mediocrity, he said, "Well, he ain't no Harmon Killebrew, or anything like that." Teddy and his father had been great baseball fans and Killebrew was one of their heroes. The therapist said he wasn't sure that he knew what Teddy meant. "Ya know," he answered, "Not the greatest, like Harmon Killebrew. He just ain't no Oscar Mayer, or anything like that."

"Oscar Mayer?"

"Yeah. The greatest. My father used to tell me that Oscar Mayer was the greatest. Best hot dogs and everything. Well, he ain't that good. He ain't no Harmon Caballero or anything. (For the younger reader, Carmen Cavallero was a pianist of great popularity when this session took place.)

"Teddy, is that the way that these three people are alike? They're the greatest."

"Yeah! They're the best. My father used to say that. He liked Harmon Caballero the best, too."

"Ted, I think you're also saying that your father was the greatest, and since he died, you just don't see how anyone can be as great as he was for you."

At this Teddy lowered his head, and began to cry softly. Only in later sessions did further associations reveal that as mourning progressed, his therapist's name sounded more and more like "Harmon Caballero's" to him, and that his major conflicts were around longing for and feeling guilty about wanting to love and be loved by someone like his father.

As these vignettes demonstrate, associations can be used to detect and demonstrate conflicts and other forms of mentation to our young patients. In addition, when the therapist can review his own associations to the patient's productions, he will find that they will lead him to a hypothesis that can easily be verified or rejected by asking the appropriate questions of the youngster.

COUNTERTRANSFERENCE

It may appear strange to the reader that countertransference is included in a section on the tools of psychotherapy. The reason for including it here is that in recalling my own training and in supervising residents and fellows, I see how often countertransference is listed as a clinical sin rather than a clinical tool. I list it here to underline my conviction that it is a universal phenomenon, and rather than judge, deny, or repudiate countertransferences, the therapist would do well to utilize them as a source of information. This is not to say the countertransference manifestations should be indulged or expressed to the patient. It *is* to say that when these manifestations are perceived and understood, they can supply important information about the state of the therapist's empathy and sensitivity, reveal blind spots that may be hindering therapeutic efficacy, and reveal subtle ways that the patient may be affecting the therapist.

The term *countertransference* is not a precise one, and has been used by various authors and at various times to describe different psychological events that influence the attitude of the therapist toward his patient. In some cases authors have called any reaction of the therapist toward his patient a countertransference, arguing that any current feeling that a therapist may harbor toward a patient has had antecedents which are usually unconscious. Other authors have used the term to describe any transference, whose origins are unconscious, that the therapist may develop toward his patient. Still others have reserved the concept for the reactions that the therapist has to the infantile wishes of the patient. However the therapist chooses to define the word in theory, in practice, the important issue is to detect and understand the significance and origins of the feelings he has for his patients. The significance of the term must not be allowed to obfuscate the significance of the process.

In working with children, I have found that positive, affectionate countertransferences are more insidious than hostile, angry ones. These latter are more often dystonic and cause discomfort in the therapist, and therefore more readily become a cause for concern. Tender, loving feelings are sanctioned by our upbringing and culture. This sometimes keeps us from seeing that when they are not understood they can create mischief.

The therapist must also be aware that countertransference can be directed toward family members. Although this can happen in adult therapy too, it is more frequent in child work.

The four-year-old named Tommy, described in chapter 3, was the recipient of a countertransference attitude that brought his treatment to a standstill until it was discovered and diluted. Tommy had always been charming and appealing in his interactions with adults. When we began to work on some of the feelings that made him anxious, he found it difficult to stay in the office during his sessions, and would often bolt through the door, and run around the clinic seeking refuge behind secretaries or running into other offices. As mentioned before, Tommy's therapist experienced some pressure from colleagues to contain his little patient. In addition to Tommy's anxiety and hyperactivity, there was a period of a month when the weather in the area had become quite severe and he missed a number of sessions. The therapist on a number of occasions found himself irritated that Tommy's mother was not being as cooperative as she needed to be if the treatment were to succeed, and found himself ready to blame her for the missed sessions as well as Tommy's flights. One day Tommy's father brought him to his hour instead of his mother. Tommy began showing signs of his usual reluctance to come into the office and fearfulness about staying. Quite spontaneously, the therapist said that Tommy's father could accompany him to the office and stay a minute or two if Tommy wished. Then when he was comfortable, Dad could leave.

After the hour the therapist had to confront himself with the awareness that he could be flexible and understanding with Tommy in the presence of his father, but became involved in a power struggle when his mother brought him. Following the self-confrontation, the therapist could see that he had been unrealistically protective of Tommy in looking to assign responsibility for the therapeutic stalemate because he was so fond of the little charmer. His fondness inadvertently fostered in the therapist attitudes that were more parental than therapeutic, and these, in turn, created a posture of competition with the mother. Once this was detected and defused the treatment returned to a productive course (Coppolillo, 1969).

As many of us know, psychiatrists are not the only healers beset by countertransferences. There are instances in which medical treatment is dictated more powerfully by unconscious forces than the requisites of the patient. Henry Bellamann's book *King's Row* movingly describes how Doctor Gordon catastrophically indulges his countertransference when he treats Drake McHugh.

PLAY AS A THERAPEUTIC TOOL

The activities that we have come to know as play have, from all available evidence been a boon to human development and to the restoration of psychological serenity in daily life. In psychotherapeutic endeavors play has become a mixed blessing. While it has on the one hand permitted treatment of younger children by providing a vehicle for expression and reduction of anxiety, it has on the other hand often been misused. Some have invested so heavily in the *process* of play that the significance or reason for it has been lost. In numerous instances play became such a deeply entrenched expression of resistance to understanding that the child refused to do anything but play. Some therapists have acted as if play in and of itself had therapeutic efficacy, and while so doing, they failed to ask why the child had not cured himself with the countless opportunities that the environment offered him to play. Selma Fraiberg (1965) presented a useful observation she made after a follow-up visit by an eighteen-year-old, who had been in analysis with her as a child. The young woman acknowledged that she had often regretted not having found the courage to speak to her about her masturbatory preoccupations during the analysis. Fraiberg was surprised since they had played out these preoccupations repeatedly with dolls during the session. Obviously, however, the child had been able to compartmentalize the play, and had not translated it into principles and ideas that related to her real life.

Of course play has a place in the psychotherapy of children. For it to be useful, however, play must be put in the service of the therapeutic effort, and not be used as a substitute for it or as a resistance to it.

The literature on play activities has encompassed:

1. Biological concepts of play as proposed by Spencer, Hall, Colozza, and Groos;
2. Interpersonal aspects of play exemplified by the writing of Sigmund Freud, Piaget, and Erickson;
3. Intrapsychic phenomena involved in play as documented by S. Freud, Piaget, Solnit, and others;

4. Sociocultural theories of play that can be found in the writings of Roberts, Kendon, and Sutton-Smith.

The literature reflects a variety of ways that play can be seen to be significant to human beings. In this section a narrow segment of the activity will be explored in addressing only those aspects of play which can be related to the psychotherapy of children.

In observing school-age children in play, it becomes evident that there are at least two forms of the activity, and each of these reflects different ground rules. The first group consists of those games that seem to be bound by a rigid set of rules and regulations such as table games and sports. In the second group of games the play seems to have no rules other than the ones the children create in an *ad hoc* way to make the play more enjoyable, more exciting, or to prolong the game. Playing cops and robbers or war or pretending to be an astronaut, with a packing crate to represent Apollo I or Soyuz II may take this form.

Each of these forms of play offers material for useful hypotheses. In the first instance we can imagine a group of eight school-age children who have met in a park or an empty lot with a baseball bat and a softball. A game is proposed, and when the sides are chosen there are four players on each team. Although there is no hope that all the positions can be covered, our big league aspirants cannot suspend or alter the rules. One player positions himself between left and centerfield while another takes his place between center and rightfield. Another player tries to be creative in his assignment to cover the whole infield, and the pitcher prays for a strike even as he dashes to cover first base with every pitch. It is only when utter exhaustion or a score of 32-0 recurs, and with the passage of time, that the youngsters will begin to modify the rules. They will institute provisions like any ball hit to the rightfield side of second base is an out, or a putout can be made by throwing to the pitcher. These rules in their turn will require adherence that is more important than the game itself or the skills involved.

How can this be explained? One plausible explanation is

that the rigid rules provide a safeguard against regression. This safeguard against regression promotes progression in the child and permits him to mold aggression into competitive competence, and self-preoccupation or narcissism into pride in creative accomplishment. Adhering to the rules also preserves interpersonal order and avoids chaos.

An additional, and to me profoundly human explanation is offered by Peter Berger (1969) in his book *A Rumor of Angels*. In one passage Berger speaks of transcendence (pp. 65–66). He means by this "phenomena that are to be found within the domain of our 'natural' reality but that appear to point beyond that reality." Berger then discusses the human propensity to organize or to order his reality and an "intrinsic impulse to give cosmic scope to this order" (p. 70). In discussing ways that human beings achieve this ordering of their reality, Berger cites the transcendence in religion and in the utilization of play. He reviews the ludic, or joyous, exuberant component of play and follows the historian Huizinga, and C. S. Lewis in considering man a joyful, playful, pleasure-seeking being in his very nature. He then argues that in play this joy and exuberance can emerge because the players can suspend a portion of reality. He states that the portion they suspend is pain and death. In *A Rumor of Angels* (p. 74) he described a scene that expressed his views on play beautifully.

> Some little girls are playing hopscotch in the park. They are completely intent on their game, closed to the world outside it, happy in the concentration. Time has stood still for them or more accurately, has been collapsed into the movements of the game. The outside world has, for the duration of the game, ceased to exist. And, by implication (since the little girls may not be very conscious of this), pain and death, which are the law of the world, have also ceased to exist. Even the adult observer of this scene, who is perhaps all too conscious of pain and death, is momentarily drawn into beatific immunity.

Although I will argue a bit later in this section that Berger has been too specific in stating that it is pain and death that are suspended in play, I find his concept of transcendence a useful one that stands up well under clinical scrutiny.

In summary then, one explanation for play that is bound by rules is that children, *by their own initiative*, can bring order to their immediate surroundings. This order then transcends the baseball diamond, the hopscotch markings, or the table game board to become the promise of an orderly, safe world in which understandable rules insure the individual as well as the group a safe place in an orderly universe. In this way the child avoids that terror of chaos that Emile Durkheim called anomie.

Do I believe that children consciously think of an orderly universe? No, I do not. But clinical evidence convinces me that they are terrified by an absence of order or structure. Also, while they welcome the order provided them from the outside world, they aspire to create their own order from within, and play is one of the important activities that contributes to the erection of their own citadel of order.

Let us turn now to the less structured and more creative play, characterized by rules that children make up as they go along. This play, often so revealing of the child's otherwise hidden wishes and percepts can open the inner world of the child to the therapist. In this activity too, the child can become "lost in play." Whether he is in the above mentioned packing crate or in his backyard adorned with a superman cloak, the child can swoop from galaxy to galaxy and from fantasy to fantasy creating new worlds to explore and enemies to conquer. How do we understand the utility of this play and its place in psychotherapy?

It was primarily this kind of play that I sought to understand and describe in a paper on transitional relatedness (1976). In 1953, Winnicott published his classical paper "Transitional Objects and Transitional Phenomena." He wrote that besides the human capacity to perceive external as well as internal reality, the individual can experience in a third mode. He said, "The third part of the life of a human being, a part that we cannot ignore, is an intermediate area of experiencing to which inner reality and external life both contribute" (p. 90). For example, a teddy bear can be appreciated for its size, its expression, the softness of its fur, and its durability. As it is brought into the intermediate area of experience, it becomes much more. It is now a transitional object and as such becomes a *loyal* companion, or an *appreciative* recipient of loving hugs. It can be the *repenting* miscreant tolerating a scolding or the *triumphant* victor of a duel with Darth Vader. To the inanimate physical reality of the teddy bear, the child has added the vitality of his inner world endowing him with lifelike qualities like loyalty, appreciation, repentance, or joy in triumph. Winnicott clearly indicates that any object, thought, or concept can become a transitional object. It need only be experienced in the "intermediate area of experience" (p. 89). He goes on to say that, "By this definition an infant's babbling or the way an older child goes over a repertory of songs and tunes while preparing for sleep comes within the intermediate area as transitional phenomena" (p. 89). Winnicott further defined this phenomenon as continuing throughout life. "It is assumed here that the task of reality-acceptance is never completed, that no human being is free from the strain of relating inner and outer reality, and that relief from this strain is provided by an intermediate area of experience which is not challenged (arts, religion, etc.). This intermediate area is in direct continuity with the play area of the small child who is 'lost in play' " (p. 96).

If we now integrate the concept of the transitional phenomenon with the concepts of Rapaport reviewed in the section on supportive psychotherapy in this chapter, we can see that play as a transitional phenomenon offers the child an optimal regulatory system even as it soothes him and permits joy and exuberance to be expressed.

When a child takes a toy with him into the intermediate area (whether it is a packing crate or a teddy bear), he takes a manageable bit of reality with him to do with as he wishes. Any aspect of that reality can be suspended or ignored. The fact that the teddy bear is inanimate is of little or no importance to

the child who is having a conversation with it. The suspension
or reintroduction of segments of reality is entirely up to the
child. No one can demand an accounting. To repeat the words
of Winnicott, this area is "not challenged" (p. 96). In control,
as he is, over the introduction of external reality into his play,
the child, based on the principles described by Rapaport can
modulate the amount of his inner world that he permits to
emerge, or come into awareness. If a trait, affect, or wish that
is unwelcome, frightening, or repugnant to the child, begins to
emerge in the course of play, he can invest in more of the reality
of the object, and thus reduce the thrust of the internal stimulus.
If the reality of the object becomes too restrictive to the play
and its use too boring, more of its reality can be suspended and
its interest and utility reexpanded. As this occurs, the child
comes to be familiar with those internally generated wishes,
drives, values, and other traits which coalesce to form images
of the self. The child can thus function in an optimal zone
without being overwhelmed by internal or external forces (Figures 10-2).

To return now to the concepts of Peter Berger, we must
wonder if clinical evidence does not suggest that virtually any
aspect of reality can be suspended, and not just pain and death,
when the child is living in the intermediate area of experience.
It may be that the soothing aspects of transitional objects and
the ludic, joyful quality of play is to be found largely in the
ability to construct a reality that is appealing, interesting, non-
coercive, and useful to the child at the time that he creates it.

For therapeutic purposes then, either type of play can be
useful when through its regulatory functions it permits the
child's perceptions of his inner and outer world to be viewed
by the child and the therapist without undue threat or disruption. Thus, play can be likened to a supportive system that
permits evolving revelations of the patient's inner world and
his views of his outer reality.

Of course play has other functions in treatment that the
therapist may exploit. At times play may be used to permit the
child to rest after a painful revelation or an arduous period. If

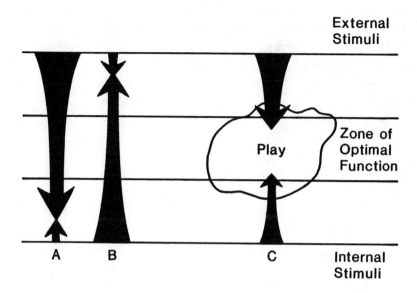

Figure 10-2. Play provides an arena in which tides of stimuli from the outside world and from the inner world may be blended and used to protect the child from being overwhelmed from either source. Further description in text.

we are to be honest we must acknowledge that sometimes it may be used to allow the therapist to catch his breath, or to protect himself from the onslaughts of the child. At other times play permits mastery and working through a hard won, labile insight. Play may sometimes shore up a therapeutic alliance or reveal an impediment to it. All of these are legitimate uses of play as a transaction. What must not happen is that play is undertaken routinely and without purpose. Play should not be the indulgence of an *unexplored* countertransference of the therapist or the resistance of the patient. Above all, it should not be used to comfort the threatened therapist when he feels that unless he amuses the child he will not return. There are not many places in the world where the child can receive forty-five or fifty minutes of undivided attention from a helpful adult. Seduction by play should not be necessary. If the therapist feels that the child cannot appreciate this, a review of the importance of the relationship to both the therapist and the child is in order. Or perhaps the therapist needs to review his own convictions about the worth of his attention and therapy.

Part IV

Therapy Proper

CHAPTER 11

Beginning the Therapy

The terms *management* and *treatment* are used interchangeably in the description of virtually every therapeutic endeavor. In speaking of the psychoanalytic psychotherapy of children, a distinction should be made between therapy and management. I would propose that the term *treatment* be reserved for those interchanges between child and therapist that offer the child the opportunity to alter his personality structure or responsivity through insights and learning. *Management* should be reserved for those activities that the therapist must undertake to make treatment possible. The reasons for this distinction will become clear in the following paragraphs. Some management activities are easily distinguished from the treatment process as, for example, when a therapist arranges transportation to the sessions for the child with a social welfare agency. Other activities can be almost indistinguishable from treatment proper, and almost all management will have repercussions on the treatment process.

MANAGEMENT ISSUES INVOLVING THE FAMILY

One of the first issues to be settled before treatment begins is the way the child will get to the sessions, and the times that he can be brought. When both parents must work this can become an arduous problem. Even if the therapist is able to work late into the evening, those hours will quickly fill with appointments and there will surely be another instance in which still another child will need a "special" time when he can be brought. Some child therapists will work late into the evening one day per week in addition to Saturdays in order to see children at a time when parents can bring them. A certain amount of this is expectable in our field, but beyond a certain point the therapist's own fatigue or desire to be with his own family may encroach on the sensitivity and equanimity that he would wish to carry with him into the hour.

An idealistic child advocate once suggested that our clinic begin its workday at noon and remain open until 8:00 P.M. There were several reasons why the plan was impractical. Among the clinic staff there were a number of parents of young children who wanted to be with their own children during the evening hours. In many cases it was not clear that it was truly impossible for the parents to bring their children to their sessions. For some parents it was simply inconvenient for them to interrupt their daily routine, and it was much easier to ask the therapist to inconvenience himself. In other instances the employer was unduly insensitive to the importance of the treatment and preferred to shift the burden of responsibility to the clinic staff rather than explore the possibility of an adjustment of the parent's work hours. In still other instances, we found that even when some after-work hours could be provided, the parents had another reason why they could not bring the child. This is not to say, of course, that there are not times when it is indeed impossible for some parents to bring children to their sessions repeatedly during working hours. But the therapist must be sure that in providing a special hour, they are not burying in management an issue that would more properly be dealt with in treatment or in scrutinizing social policy. Parental resistance to children's treatment, or unwillingness of a parent to be inconvenienced by a child's needs is a treatment issue, not one of management.

In those cases when there is a well-documented and realistic inability of the parents to transport the child to his sessions, and the therapist cannot adjust his schedule to the family's timetable without discomfort or hidden resentment, I would recommend that community agencies be contacted to see if they can be of assistance. If this fails, extended family members can often help.

A related issue is establishing the hours of sessions when children need to be seen several times a week. Both normal and emotionally troubled children need time to play, to be alone, and to be with their peers. A child who spends three or four hours a week in therapy in addition to music lessons and practice, religious school and homework, may be so locked into prescribed activities that there is little unstructured time available to work through conflicts and institute new and creative strategies of behavior after old neurotic patterns are abandoned. Therapeutic flexibility will be important in establishing the hours of therapy in a way that will permit rest and recreation to be available to the child. Sometimes it may be necessary to recommend that an activity like music lessons be suspended until the child terminates his treatment. Simply writing off an overburdened child's fatigue or reluctance to attend his sessions as "resistance" is too glib and does not address the true issue.

In adult work, establishing a fee is part of the therapeutic process. When treating children, fees, more often than not, fall into the category of management. A realistic appraisal of what the parents could afford should have been part of the diagnostic evaluation and helped to determine where the child would be treated. Often the fee is set without difficulty and this part of the management becomes automatic. It can, however, constitute a hidden hazard.

At times, after an evaluation the therapist discovers that the family cannot realistically afford a full fee. In recommending a clinic or agency where the child can be treated at a reduced rate, the therapist may find reluctance on the part of the child or family. He may then decide to treat the child at a reduced rate. Care must be exercised that this does not return to haunt the treatment. After the enthusiasm of the new encounter is blunted by hard work and transferences, the therapist may inadvertently begin to resent the financial sacrifices he is making in fee reduction. Resentment may also occur because the issue of the affordability of treatment is a perennial problem, and the number of cases that one carries on a partial fee basis may become a burden that had not been anticipated. If a therapist manages a fee problem by reducing his fee, his scrutiny cannot end in the management. He needs to scrutinize the treatment process to make sure the fee reduction did not produce countertransference.

The fee setting aspect of management may also acquire significance in therapy in another way. The parents may subtly punish the child for having to spend their money, or the child may enjoy forcing his parents to make special expenditures for him.

> A nine-year-old boy expressed reluctance to be treated and protested the recommendation despite his awareness that he was unhappy and despite the parents' avowed commitment to his psychotherapy. After a painful month of protest, he shouted angrily that his parents could not afford his treatment. On inquiry, he revealed the number of times his mother had, with regret, told one or another member of the family that some activity could not be enjoyed now that the family had the added expenses of his treatment. He, himself had had to forego some of his recreation because "it was too costly." Exploration of this issue with the family revealed that the cost of the treatment was not too burdensome, and that the mother's complaints were for other reasons. The fees which had seemingly been a simple matter of management were used as a vehicle to express psychological problems that belonged in the treatment.

In another case it was the patient and not the parents who converted the management issue into a therapeutic one.

> A fifteen-year-old seemed quite happy to come to

her appointments, but also missed appointments without regret, or sat for the entire hour silently or addressing trivial issues. In a conference with the therapist, her mother said that the daughter had openly acknowledged to her that she wanted to stay in treatment so that her father would have to "pay through the nose" for having left the family two years earlier. Not only was the symbolic significance of her statement noted, to be addressed later, but the situation regarding the fees had to be managed. The adolescent was asked to contribute by paying an appropriate portion of the fee, in an effort to bring the issue into the treatment realm.

Management includes aspects of setting some ground rules with the parents. A policy regarding vacations and trips that the child may take should be discussed. I do not have a fixed policy on this. I indicate to the parents that there are advantages for both me and the child if we can coordinate vacations. When this is realistically impossible for the family, I do not charge for the missed sessions. Missed single sessions are also scrutinized individually. If missing is inevitable, or there is a sound reason for the child to be elsewhere, I expect to be notified as early as possible and to have an opportunity to discuss the absence with the child. If there is a *bona fide* emergency and notification is impossible, I do not charge for the hour. I do charge for the hour if a session is forgotten or there is evidence that negligence or lack of respect for the time occurred. Management of responsibility for therapy hours is a personal matter, and the therapist should develop a sound philosophy of his own about it that is resonant with the standards of the community in which he works. My own preferences were offered only as examples.

Assurances should be sought that once treatment is started, the family will not terminate the contacts without discussion. While there is no way to ensure that they will not do so anyway, a discussion of how this could be potentially painful or even damaging to the child, reduces the possibility of a precipitous termination by them.

Major changes in the family's life-style or living arrangements can profoundly affect a child's treatment. If these are necessary, they should be discussed with the therapist in advance. The therapist is not demanding that his permission be asked before the change is made, but only that he be kept informed. If a major change is being planned for shortly after the beginning of treatment, the therapist should consider the possibility of delaying the start of therapy until after the change has occurred and the child and family have had a chance to adjust to it.

An agreement with the child's pediatrician to keep each other informed about the child's physical and mental health may be contemplated. Both parents and child should know that these communications will not compromise confidentiality, and the family's wishes about this will be taken into account. The child should be told what information will be shared with the pediatrician before it is communicated. When information must be sought or exchanged with a school, welfare department, insurance company, or other agency, the family should be alerted and invited to discuss the question if they have any reservations.

The question must be addressed as to whether the parents need therapy for themselves or will require parental counseling, or should simply be kept informed about the child's therapy. Sperling (1979) has written a helpful chapter on this issue.

Finally, if his age permits, the child should be given the opportunity to participate in solving any management problems that exist. Optimally, he should also know of any agreements made with anyone that involve his treatment.

MANAGEMENT ISSUES INVOLVING THE CHILD

A number of management issues may need to be raised with the child before therapy starts.

The extent and limits of confidentiality should once more be reviewed. The therapist should make no promises that he might be unable to keep. Imagine the dilemma of a therapist who has promised absolute confidentiality and then discovers that the child is involved in some activity that endangers his life or health, or is contemplating suicide. The therapist can only assure the child that confidentiality will be maintained unless it would compromise the child's welfare to do so. If there are agencies with which the therapist must communicate, the child should be aware of what will be said to whom.

Management should include a reiteration of the purpose of therapy in general terms with only sparse references to the child's specific conflicts. Something like this may suffice.

> "You've already told me, Betty, that you some-times have sad thoughts and scary feelings. During our meetings we'll try to find out the reasons why these thoughts and feelings keep coming back. Sometimes the person who worries doesn't even know the reasons for the worries. That's what you and I will work on together. If we can find out the cause for the worries, we can then see how we can make them go away."

The therapist may once more wish to describe the methods that will be used to conduct the treatment. The idea that the child can feel free to discuss anything he wishes, and that the job will be to understand, and not to react to the communications should be presented. The therapist may also wish to reiterate here the principle that play will be for the purpose of detecting and understanding conflicts and hidden thoughts.

I have found it useful to ask children to call me if they need to change an appointment time or to cancel an hour. Allowing him some say in canceling or rescheduling an appointment fosters a sense of respect, responsibility, and mastery in the process. Also, there are times when, as therapy progresses, activities that may have been impossible for the youngster to perform before treatment can resume or begin. For example, a camping trip with a school group for a child who came to treatment because he could not separate from his mother should be a welcome interruption for child and therapist.

PERILS OF MANAGEMENT

Although management is necessary to permit psychotherapy, pitfalls need to be avoided, as these can trip both the
therapist and the patient. The therapist must be alert to the
possibility that he may turn toward management as a relief from
the tedium or anxiety of psychotherapy. At other times, covert
reservations about the efficacy of psychotherapy in general, or
in a specific case, may push him toward managing a situation,
issuing a directive, or providing something for the child or
family that they could have provided for themselves. The desire
to be responsible for effecting a change can sometimes be so
pressing that the therapist initiates a process that should have
been left to the patient or addressed therapeutically.

A young therapist requested supervision for her
treatment of a child who had been deprived and
abused. The child had reached a stage in the treatment
in which she both expressed and disguised the anger
and sadism she felt by being silent and withholding.
The therapist had tried valiantly for a number of hours
to reestablish communication by various appropriate
measures, and some which were not so appropriate.
When these failed, she began to buy new dolls and toys
for her office even though she already had more
equipment than most children could use. When this
also failed, she "lent" the child her tape recorder in
the hope that the child could "talk" to her when not
in the treatment situation. The child promptly broke
the tape recorder, and it was then that she requested
help. It became clear to the therapist, as she presented
some of her feelings and thoughts about the treatment
that she had failed to appreciate the defensive component of the child's silence. She had seen only the
child's anger and had become ashamed, frustrated,
and guilty at her counteranger. In an effort to undo
this, she began to provide for the child, and to "manage" the situation by refurbishing her office. Once she

saw this she could readdress the defenses, and give the child the responsibility of overcoming the silence.

Some families can be so burdened with realistic problems that they need to be counseled and guided as the problems are managed. When this occurs, the therapist must first ask if he is the one best equipped to counsel, guide, and manage this family, or if they should be referred. If he does the family management, he will have to determine if after the management efforts are no longer necessary, psychotherapy is still indicated for one or more members of the family. If it is indicated, he must decide if he, as the former case manager, can now shift gears and become a therapist, or if the management had rendered him a "real" person to the extent that transferences necessary for therapy, would be inhibited. Management must not insinuate itself into the relationship in an unplanned manner as a refuge from the discipline or difficulty of psychotherapy.

Management can become quite appealing to patient and family too. It can be gratifying to have a therapist show concern and solve problems for you. In addition, the child and the family can, without conscious awareness, use the therapist's management activities as a resistance against having to explore their own longings, fears, or feelings of inadequacy. This can become a chronic tendency, and whenever treatment comes close to revealing an unwelcome insight to child or family, a crisis is created that requires the therapist to leave off treating and begin to manage. Family and therapist can thus careen from crisis to crisis without the time or serenity to contemplate or inquire how the calamities occur.

TREATMENT PROPER

Five important achievements that are optimally attained in the first phase of psychotherapy are these:

1. The child attains a degree of comfort that permits him to be productive in the sessions.
2. The child communicates as a matter of course.

3. Child and therapist achieve a working alliance or therapeutic alliance.
4. The child becomes aware that some of his mental activities are internally generated rather than elicited by external circumstances.
5. Child and therapist begin to share modes of representing his internal states with words, images, and symbols.

This phase may vary greatly in duration. In some cases, these five goals will be reached in a matter of weeks. In other instances, it will take longer. There have been cases in which the attainment of a therapeutic alliance occurred virtually at the end of therapy. Once the child overcame his isolation and suspiciousness sufficiently to feel allied to his therapist, he had accomplished his therapeutic task, and his symptoms dissolved in short order. Achievement of the five goals does not guarantee that they will be continuous tHroughout the treatment. For example, addressing a new problem that emerges in the course of therapy may render the former Modes of communication obsolete and require the development of a new and expanded mode of representation. Below, these five areas will be explored briefly

COMFORT OF THE CHILD

The extent to which the child reveals himself depends, of course, on the range of comfort in which he operates. He cannot be so anxious or feel such threat that he becomes immobilized. Even though the therapist poses no realistic threat, the child may bring his own convictions of threat with him, and immediately transfer them onto the therapist. The therapist must find ways to convince the child that what he communicates will not result in punitive social consequences. He will not be reprimanded, punished, failed, or ostracized. His revelations will occasion scrutiny and not reactions.

On the other hand, the child cannot become so complacent about what he communicates that it becomes meaningless. There are times when youngsters make the therapy a "pretend game" to the extent that they simply spew forth words that they feel have no significance or convey no message. While abstaining from being judgmental, punitive, or demanding, the therapist must interfere with this degree of nonchalance.

Jeff was a twelve-year-old latchkey child for whom therapy hours were a welcome relief from the tedium of waiting at home after school for his parents to arrive from work. He thought of his treatment as entertainment, and was not willing to tolerate much discomfort during the hours. The therapist urged him to be less guarded about what he revealed. In a way that was almost mocking, Jeff began to utter anything that came into his mind without bothering to see if it made sense. He showed little inclination to explore the significance of anything he said. In one session his therapist had interrupted a game of solitaire that Jeff began to play with a deck of cards that he himself had brought to the hour.

Therapist: "Do you suppose that by playing solitaire you're showing me how it feels to be ignored?"
Jeff: (Picking up cards) "No solitaire, no solitaire. (With no affect) Just sit here and talk with this old shithead son-of-a-bitch." With this he walked off to pick up some items from the bookshelf and handle them in a disinterested way. After several minutes he turned and said jokingly, "Hey, you old son-of-a-bitch, you want to talk?"
Therapist((Not smiling) "O.K."
Jeff: "Hey, are you mad at me?"
Therapist: "No."
Jeff: "Well, you look worried, like, maybe mad."
Therapist: "No, I'm not mad. But I don't like to be called a son-of-a-bitch, and I guess that's why I looked serious. Especially since I don't know why."
Jeff: (Anxiously) "Are you going to see me next week?"
Therapist: "Of course! But I'll still be wondering what made you call me a son-of-a-bitch."

During the session the following week, Jeff first tried to avoid the subject, then said it was a joke. Finally, he looked crestfallen and said that he didn't know why he had called the therapist names, but acknowledged that sometimes he did have angry, mischievous feelings. The therapist had successfully interfered with the defense of "too much comfort."

The attention, respect, empathy, and serious consideration of the therapist do much to keep the child in a range of comfort from which he can operate effectively.

THE TWO-WAY COMMUNICATION SYSTEM

Most children will, after a few moments of shyness, share enjoyable conversation with an adult. They find it fun, exciting, and have few qualms about revealing themselves and, as embarrassed parents sometimes discover, when their five-year-old becomes engrossed in conversation with a stranger, reveal intimate family secrets. Despite this, some therapists think it characteristic of children to be silent when they come for an appointment. Often a therapist does not wait long enough for the shyness to thaw, and begins to shove crayons, paper, games, or toys under the child's nose and hope that they will be vehicles for communication. This is unwarranted: If the child has been prepared and knows that his verbal communications are expected and respected, the therapist can assume he will begin talking. If he does not, his silence should be found remarkable and a cause for it should be sought in the child, his home, or in the therapeutic environment.

Silence may be but one component of the behavior of a passive child. Any therapist knows how frustrating and defeating a truly committed posture of passivity can be. There are situations such as these when, for a time, all we have to offer our patients is patience. It would be a mistake for the therapist to equate his patience with counterpassivity, however. Active observation of the patient coupled with inquiries about the silence, and what might be done to dispel it, may break the ice jam.

Understanding silences in specific clinical situations is, of course, what is needed, but a general premise may also be helpful. Passivity must not be thought of as the opposite of activity. Passivity is a specific form of activity. This can be confirmed by noting the creativity and effort that some patients put into the work of maintaining a passive posture. This authorizes the therapist to assume that the silence component of a passive posture is meant to convey an attitude or maintain a state. Questions, then, about what the silence conveys or what is being maintained by the child, let him know that discovering reasons for the silence and passivity is also his responsibility, and that the therapist must make inferences about it, without blaming or scolding.

Except for rare instances, the child who has been adequately prepared for his meetings with a therapist, will not be silent from the start. Usually a child falls silent in reaction to something that has happened, or he imagines has happened in the relationship with the therapist. A careful scrutiny of the session or the segment of a session that preceded the silence may reveal its cause.

The preschool or early school-age child may use play to break a silence, or to dilute the impact of revealing something unpleasant. The therapist can continue his posture of inquiry even as he participates in play.

Brett, a five-year-old enuretic boy had been silent and listless for the past two sessions. With mild discomfort, he began playing with dolls. The therapist asked what was happening in the play.

Brett: "Here, you be the Dad. I'll be the Mom." (This identification is scrutinized later.)
Therapist: (Taking the father doll) "O.K., what are we going to do, Mom?"
Brett: "We got to take the baby to the doctor."
Therapist: "O.K., Mom, let's go. You show me where the doctor's office is."
Brett walks to the desk, carrying the mother and baby doll.

Brett: "What's wrong with my baby?" (Looks at the therapist for an answer, obviously assigning him to the role of the doctor.)
Therapist: (In a conspiratorial, off-stage whisper) "What does the doctor say?"
Brett: (Whispering back) "He's sad."
Therapist: (Pontificating) "He's sad." (Then, going back to the whisper, asks) "Why is he sad?"
Brett: (Whispering) "Because they whip him when he wets the bed."

After Brett took the family back home to the doll-house, the therapist said to him that he thought that Brett was afraid or embarrassed to tell about his bed-wetting and spankings, but that he was worried about both. Brett nodded sadly, and told about trying so hard not to wet at night that he sometimes stayed awake as long as he could. When the therapist expressed empathy for Brett's helplessness, the dialogue resumed and therapy progressed.

Relating the play to the child's life and problems may not always be immediately possible when the therapist is attempting to break the ice jam of silence. The significance of the play and what it reveals about the child's perception and conflict should then be addressed later when the child can bear it.

DEVELOPMENT OF A THERAPEUTIC ALLIANCE

Building on the work of Freud (1912), Richard Sterba (1934) described "a split in the ego" of the patient undergoing psychoanalysis. He maintained that the patient divided his ego functions into a group that experienced and one that observed these experiences, and reported them to the analyst. Bibring (1937) later associated the observing portion of the ego with that part of the patient's personality that developed a therapeutic alliance with the analyst. Since then, there have been a number of authors, such as Zetzel (1956) and Greenson (1956) who have summarized and added to this concept.

The concept currently defined is that there is a segment of the patient's personality that can ally itself with the therapist in the task of observing and evaluating his own affects, ideas, wishes, values, and convictions as they emerge or are exposed during therapy. This alliance has been thought to be the counterbalance to neurotic conflicts and their transferences, allowing the patient, with the aid of the therapist–ally, to examine them. Though most of the descriptions of this alliance come from the analysis of adults, psychotherapy with children requires achievement of an alliance with the child and an understanding of its development in childhood terms. Alliance with a child may require special efforts, depending on the developmental level and experiences of the child, and once achieved may have characteristics different from those that are entered into by adults.

A working alliance with a child requires that the child be aware that some aspect of his life is not going well, that it would be to his advantage to have control over the causes of his troubles, and that he and the therapist *together* have the wisdom, strength, and will to gain this necessary control. The child must also know that an alliance with the therapist will not constitute disloyalty to others to whom he may be attached or that he loves.

To ensure that the child is aware that there are areas of his life in difficulty, specific questions need to be asked about how he views the difficulties that his parents or teachers report. If the environment has been too lax, anxious, or uninvolved to reflect the child's behavior or attitudes back to him as problems, the child may be feeling no discomfort and therefore not feel in need of an ally. The alliance, thus, has no reason to exist. If the child's environment conveys to him by word or deed that something about his behavior or state is not as it should be, the therapist has a reason to invite an alliance.

It is more difficult to convey the notion of unconscious wishes or strivings causing conflict to a child when this is the issue the alliance must address. Knowing the child's capacity for imagery and the experiences that are evocative to him helps the therapist to choose a way to describe unconscious mentation in those instances when it is necessary to do so. I have found something like the following helpful. "You know, sometimes people's minds play tricks on them. A thought or a feeling way at the back of your mind, that you hardly know is there, can cause you to be afraid or to act in a certain way. When you find out what that thought or feeling is, it's not scary or bossy anymore. It's like when you woke up at night and saw a scary shape near your bed. When you turned on the light and looked at it, you saw it was just the way you piled your clothes on the chair. Once you saw it clearly, it couldn't scare you anymore. I'll bet that together we can figure out what that thought is." By using a shared experience as an image and the words *we* and *together*, the therapist invites an alliance.

The therapeutic alliance that some children develop is not as stable and persistent as that of adults. Each new problem that is addressed may require some degree of bolstering or even a reestablishment of the alliance. At other times, changes in the family or school situation, or even a developmental step taken by the child may require that the alliance be revitalized.

RECOGNITION OF AN INTERNAL WORLD

Children come into the world exquisitely sensitive to stimuli. It appears, however, that it is difficult for them to determine whether a stimulus reaches them from the external environment or is generated in their inner world. Even after they have achieved the ability to distinguish a headache from a bump on the head, they still find it difficult to acknowledge that impulses, wishes, and convictions originate from within. "Why did you eat all those cookies?" a mother may ask a six-year-old. His reply will likely be "Because they are good." The taste of the cookies is more readily and honestly available as an explanation than a perception of his own appetite. A parent or therapist asks a child why he mistreated a younger sibling, and receives an answer like " 'Cause he's a dope," or "He bugs me," or "Because he was looking into my eyes." The awareness that an internally generated motive can occasion overt behavior or conscious feeling is usually not prevalent until the age of nine, ten, or eleven. Before then, most children feel that affects or behaviors were evoked or seduced by external events or people.

Often, children come to a diagnostic or therapeutic meeting with a conviction that there are problems in their lives, but these will be solved if the therapist changes the environment. Sometimes this is true, but more often it is the child who must make the change. In order to keep the youngster engaged, the therapist cannot reject his ideas out of hand. They must be heard, and then, whenever possible, the child must be helped to come to an awareness, through his own observations, of the need for an internal change.

> Thirteen-year-old Sam had been doing failing work in school for several years, in part due to abysmally low self-esteem and, in part due to rage at demanding parents. He was adamant in insisting that his therapist get the school and his parents "off his back." "If they stop bugging, I'll be O.K." he protested.
>
> Therapist: "If they did stop pressuring you, do you think you would do the work?"
> Sam: "No! I just don't wanna do schoolwork."
> Therapist: "How will you know if you can do it then?"
> Sam: "I can do it."
> Therapist: "But Sam, do you remember when you told me that sometimes when you tried to do your homework you felt like a feeb?"
> Sam: "Yah, a retard, but I can do it."
> Therapist: "Knowing that for sure would really be good. Otherwise, *you* would always wonder whether you *couldn't* do your work or you *didn't want to* do your work. Why don't we put our heads together, and find out for sure?"
>
> Despite some bluster and protest, Sam eventually began to address his own concerns and to improve.

Paradoxically, the child's need to recognize internal states may be greatest when there is, indeed, something wrong in the environment. In the following situation, frustration prompted me to use a technique that I would not usually recommend, since it is gimmicky and tricky. I hope the reader will understand it is used here to illustrate a point rather than to suggest a technique.

Terry came into treatment because he had uncontrollable outbursts of temper in school. He was nine when he started treatment, but the problem had existed since he began school. The evaluation revealed that the temper outbursts were displaced expressions of intense anger at his mother who saw nothing good about Terry and criticized everything he did. When Terry brought home four As and one B, his reward was to be told that had he not been so lazy, that B would have been an A. Winning a part in the school play elicited a comment from his mother that this would be but one more distraction for him and things would really deteriorate. This constant barrage of criticism was real and not imagined by Terry. The therapist had been present when the mother had indulged the wish to criticize Terry to the extent that the therapist had had to inhibit an angry retort to her. In addition to the direct destructiveness of these comments, further damage was occurring because Terry had begun to use his mother's anger at him as a defense against recognizing any responsibility for his behavior. If he misbehaved in school, it was because of his mother's criticism. If he failed to do his homework and was penalized by a teacher, it was because he was depressed by his mother's comments. Every session during the initial six months of treatment was filled with complaints and recriminations about his mother. Although the temper outbursts in school had disappeared, Terry's rage and passivity had not been touched. In the session in which this exchange took place, Terry had once more begun to describe a maternal atrocity that he felt was responsible for a failure of his. After he wound down his impassioned indictment, the therapist said: "Though you say your mother is the cause of your problems, I really think you have trouble because you're a bank robber."

Terry: (Laughing) "Yeah, sure. Stick 'em up."
Therapist: "No, I'm not kidding. Stop stealing and you'll get better."
Terry: "Come on, what are you trying to pull?"
Therapist: "No, I'm serious."

After several attempts to joke about this, Terry became angry and said: "You're crazy. I don't rob no banks. I don't steal anything."

Therapist: "Terry, how is it that you can tell me I'm crazy when I tell you you're a bank robber, and you can't tell your mother she's wrong when she says you're a schnook?"
Terry: "Well, I know I don't rob no banks . . . and . . . and . . ."
Therapist: "And you're not as sure you're not a schnook (one of his mother's favorite words of denigration for him).
Terry: (Tears) "I hate her. I hate her."

Despite Terry's fury, we could eventually see that if we lessened his vulnerability to his mother's depreciations, he would be hurt less. Although reality can be used as a formidable defense, it can be demonstrated even to a child that how a person reacts to reality is an intrapsychic matter, and even when reality cannot be changed, one's reactions to it can be.

ACHIEVEMENT OF A DIALOGUE

As successfully conducted therapy progresses, increasingly more subtle and abstract concepts may need to be explored. Since abstractions are not easily made by children, the child therapist may find that he needs to rely on his creativity to coin a phrase or a symbol that the child can understand and use to signal or label psychological states and processes. At other times, therapists must be ready to understand and describe a process that the child may have labeled with an idiosyncratic word. Child and therapist, thus, develop a *dialogue* that serves not only as a vehicle for communication, but also to make the therapy a unique relationship for both. The special nature of this dialogue grows throughout the treatment process, and by the time treatment ends, child and therapist have developed a system of symbols, signs, and signals that amount to a private language. Two clinical vignettes represent the development of this dialogue.

Randy was seven when his parents brought him to treatment at the suggestion of his teacher. She had noticed that whenever another child was the focus of attention, Randy became petulant and disruptive. Diagnostic evaluation revealed that the child had suffered narcissistic injury due to his misunderstanding of a complex series of events that occurred in his family during his preschool years, and that had included the birth of a younger sister. By the tenth session, he was able to describe his anger and sadness when he was not at the center of attention, and how he felt unimportant during those times. When he did not express these feelings openly by becoming disruptive, he would withdraw into fantasies of greatness in which he was always publicly acclaimed. The therapist who had been seeking a way to convey the idea of narcissistic injury and attempts at replenishment to the child, found an opportunity in this exchange.

Therapist: "Let me see if I catch on, Randy. When you feel your teacher pays too much attention to someone else, you feel like you're nobody and this feels bad."
Randy: "Yeah, and she always says 'wait your turn, Randy,' and my turn never comes."

(The teacher actually felt that Randy received the lion's share of attention in the class.)

Therapist: "And that's when you either get mad or make up stories in your head where you're the hero."

Randy: "Yeah . . . woosh! (Making a superman flying gesture, followed by a curtain-call bow.)

Therapist: "Tell me a couple more of those stories you made up in your head (his term for daydreaming).

Randy told a few more daydreams which reflected the common themes of greatness and recognition.

Therapist: "Oh! I think I catch on now. Even though all the stories are different, they all have the same feeling. It's like Randy was sitting on a high throne, and everybody in the world was passing before him, and saying, 'Oh, great Randy! You do great things, Randy!' Does that sound right?"

Even before Randy said "Yeah," the therapist could tell that Randy felt the image was accurate by the intensity of his attention and the broad grin on his face. From then on, Randy referred to his "world, come before me" feelings whenever he wished to describe his attempts to heal his narcissistic wounds.

The therapist, in this example, created an image in his own mind, like an artist creates images with words, paint, or stone, and showed it to the child to see if it corresponded to what the child felt but could not say. In the second vignette, we see that the child can present the picture to the therapist, so that he may describe the feeling it represents.

Tami was three-and-a-half-years old when her mother was shot and killed in her home while the child was taking a nap. A month after the mother's death, her father requested an evaluation, since she was continuing to show psychological symptoms. In one of the early evaluation sessions, Tami interrupted the description of interchanges with her mother and began to stomp around the room with her arms outstretched, a ferocious scowl on her face, and to say repeatedly, "Fee Fie Fo Fum." When the interviewer asked what that meant, Tami pretended to scare him. Over the next several weeks, Tami repeated this "monster game." When the therapist noticed that each time she initiated the game, it was to interrupt a description of interactions that had occurred with her dead mother, he provided the concept that the game depicted:

Therapist: (Pretending to be frightened) "Oh, my! Here's that giant again. (Regaining composure) "Say, giant, I know where you come from."
Tami: (In a deep gruff voice) "Where?"
Therapist: "I've noticed that you come out every time Tami and I talk about her mama, and . . ."
Tami: (Interrupting in her own voice) ". . . about when my mama is dead."
Therapist: "Oh yeah! Talking about your mama reminds you that she's dead and that makes you have monster feelings inside of you and . . ."
Tami: (Twisting her little fists in front of her and making an angry face) ". . . and grind his bones to make him dead." (sic)

The rage, regret, and despair the child felt had found a symbol in the stalking giant that growled his threat. In supplying the concept, the therapist expanded the dialogue to include affects that were necessary for Tami to express and have understood if she was to heal. Although the dialogue will continue to become increasingly more expressive throughout the treatment, its growth must start with the initial phases of treatment if therapist and child are to achieve the intimacy and the specificity that will permit treatment to progress.

THE FLOW OF THERAPY

With the desired objectives for the first phase of therapy in mind, the therapist finds himself with the child in the waiting room for the first therapeutic hour. Several therapists have commented that when they first began their careers, this was the moment when they said to themselves, "Now, what do I do?" The answer to this is, do as little as possible, and still keep the child engaged. The less the therapist does, the more of the child is revealed. Also, recall that clinician's anxiety fosters action rather than scrutiny. These rules of thumb must be applied with good clinical sense, however, and if the clinical or social conditions *demand* an action on the part of the therapist, he would be well advised, in this phase of treatment, to act, and scrutinize the transactions later.

There are times during the diagnostic evaluation, when it is determined that a specific goal has been set for the therapy and to achieve this goal, an action or intervention may be necessary from the outset.

> Michael, aged six, was brought to treatment because he became so fearful of leaving his mother after the death of his father, that he refused to go to school. In the diagnostic evaluation it was determined that treatment would be started with the goal of making it possible for him to tolerate separations from his mother. She would then move to another city where her own family lived, an excellent job awaited her, and where the child would get more treatment. In the first session, the child hung back and began to whimper at the approach of the therapist. The therapist unhesitatingly suggested that both the boy and his mother come into his office. Once there, he told Michael that he knew he was frightened to be away from his mother, and that was the problem that they would work on together. He and the boy agreed that the mother would accompany them to his office if He were scared when they came to see him. Each time she would remain with them for a shorter period until Michael felt that he no longer needed to be accompanied. Then they could have their own private time together alone. Repeated reminders by the therapist that they were

striving to reach the goal of allowing the boy to separate from his mother helped them to have solo sessions in the space of two months.

When no specific action is indicated, a simple invitation
like "Please come in," rather than a tentative "Will you come
to my office, Johnny?" will likely get the therapy started.

Once in the office, every therapist should remind himself
that this initial phase, above all others, is a period of inquiry.
The pace of questioning and the number and levels of inferences that characterized the diagnostic sessions should be reduced. The child must now set the pace and the therapist rides
the flow, noting and looking for significance in every verbal
message and nonverbal cue. Communication at this point needs
to be flexible and broadly inclusive rather than precise and
specific.

> Therapist to adolescent patient: "Hi, Joe. How are
> things?"
> Joe: "Bad day. Bad day. It started from this morning.
> Mom yelling and moaning."
> Therapist: "Lots of tension at home, huh?" (This state-
> ment with its lack of specificity is preferable to the
> following):
> Therapist: "Mom was angry with you again?" Or, "Did
> you quarrel with your Mom?"

Although specificity is desirable in treatment, it
should be the child who supplies or describes the specific situation and child and therapist together who
find the signals, signs, or symbols to describe it.

When more clarification is needed on a subject, broad,
open-ended questions are preferable to specific ones.

> Child: (Limping into the office) "I scraped my knee
> at school today."
> Therapist: "What happened?"

This is preferable to asking something specific that
could be answered with a "yes" or:

> Child: "I scraped my knee at school today."
> Therapist: "Did you fall? Or, "Were you playing football?"

Carek (1979) describes how by relating as naturally as possible and being wary of gimmicks or ploys, the therapist can settle back to let his curiosity guide him in elucidating how health and pathology emerge and unfold in the relationship. The therapist can at this stage of the treatment emulate the fine cabinetmaker who is examining a piece of wood that he has just finished sanding. He lightly runs his fingertips over the surface, ready to feel any irregularity. At the slightest suggestion of roughness, he examines the spot more carefully with both touch and sight to see if more work is needed. So, the therapist lets his attention spread over the child, his associations, his actions, movements, sounds, and affects. He becomes sensitized to anything that may attract or jar awareness. When any action or state creates a blip of relative hyperalertness in him, the therapist focuses on the perception to see if it fits into the dynamic formulation as a recurring pattern, or inquires further about it if its significance is not clear.

Authors have labeled some of those interventions that translate the therapist's perceptions and curiosity into words, *confrontations*. I join those therapists who are uneasy with this word. It has an aggressive, adversary connotation that does not do justice to the need for an alliance with the patient. Even if an unpleasant revelation or request must be made, it can be done in a way that will be less likely to alienate or hurt the patient, and still keep the focus on process of inquiry.

> A nine-year-old boy who had already acknowledged that he sometimes wished to be small again, came to his fifth session with shoes covered with wet mud. He was met in the waiting area by his therapist, who walked down the hall with him until they were out of hearing range of the waiting room and then said, "Ron, I've just noticed something that's important for us to understand. Do you think that your muddy

shoes are telling us that you feel like little Ronnie today,
or might it have some other meaning?" The boy
quickly ran back to the waiting area, removed his shoes
and ran back to the therapist's office.

Ron: "I'm sorry. I forgot my shoes were dirty. I was
playing outside."
Therapist: "Yes, I thought you might be embarrassed,
but I think it might help us to understand some of the
worries you told me about, if we could find out how
your mind played a trick on you and made you forget."

Another example of a clarifying intervention may be one
that links or integrates one mental act with another, an emotional state with a behavior, or a motive with a past experience.

In her first therapy hour, Tami, the three-and-a-
half-year-old described earlier who had lost her mother,
denied the loss to her therapist. She continued to press
the denial as she told of being taught to write by her
"mom and dad."

Therapist: "Your Dad teaches you lots of things."
Tami: "And my Mommy does, too."
Therapist: (Surprised) "Your Mommy does, too?"
Tami: (Nods).
Therapist: (Voice inflection between a statement and
a question) "But you looked sad when you said that.
How come?"

Tami gave a brief nod, made a rude sound and
skipped off to do something else. Her contribution to
clarifying the issue would have to await another time,
but the therapist issued an invitation.

As the child's conflicts and pathology begin to be delineated
by the therapist's inquiry and interest, defenses against components of the pathology begin to appear in the form of resistances. These may take the form of any of the mechanisms
of defense or manifest themselves in prolonged silence, re-

luctance to come to therapy sessions, complaints about the hour of the sessions, or any of an endless number of maneuvers the child may employ. While the process of interpretation will be examined in the next chapter, the process actually begins with the appearance of these defenses. It begins with the therapist's interference or refusal to take complimentarity to the defenses.

> Eleven-year-old Mary was becoming aware that her poor school performance and refusal to care for herself or her belongings at home were connected to a sullen, smoldering resentment she nurtured toward her parents. She defended herself against this awareness by assuming a pseudostupid posture, which made her constantly misunderstand what was expected of her. This was in marked contrast to her natural intelligence as revealed by her stories, drawings, and perceptiveness when she was not defending herself. In the third month of treatment, she was telling the therapist about having gotten into trouble because she had not turned in her schoolwork. As she pleaded her innocence because of her inability to understand the work and the assignment, the therapist expressed surprise that anyone who could be as intelligent as she was in so many different circumstances, could convince herself that she was dull in situations that required work.

This was an *active* attempt to interfere with a defense. An example of the therapist interfering with a defense by *passively* refusing to take complimentarity follows:

> A fourteen-year-old boy had defended himself for years against taking responsibility for his diffuse anger and hostility by having become the class clown and joking almost incessantly. For the first few sessions he had amused the therapist with an endless repertoire of jokes, quips, and hostile but witty descriptions of his interactions. After his therapist perceived the controlling quality and hostility behind his humor, he

stopped laughing. It was not long before the youngster began to experience anxiety and then anger at the impassivity of his audience.

As the first phase of the treatment process progresses, a particular defense needs to be mentioned because of its subtlety. As some children become aware that their thinking, behavior, or affects are a problem for them and others, they begin to show evidence of changes to their therapists. They begin to control impulses, disavow unpleasant affects or convictions, and may even achieve valid insights. The trouble is they remain unchanged in their daily lives. This is just the opposite from the course that successful therapy follows as a rule. Improvement is often detected at home or in school before the therapist sees it. When the therapist notes that the reverse is happening, he should be alert to the possibility that the youngster is isolating the treatment from the rest of his life and exerting efforts to control rather than explore in the consulting room to avoid the pain of recognizing unwelcome feelings and wishes. This encapsulation of the therapeutic process is sometimes revealed by a practice the child will initiate that "brackets" the interviews with a ritual at the beginning and at the end. One youngster would come to his hour early and do his homework before the session, and return to the waiting room to finish it after his hour. Another child insisted that his mother buy him a hot dog before each session and a soft drink after it. Bathroom and water fountain rituals are not uncommon signals of this defense. When the therapist detects these patterns, it is not difficult to use them to point out how the child encloses the interviews in a time period that is kept separate from the rest of his life.

A process that may confound the therapist's efforts to interfere with the child's defenses can occur between parent and child. There are instances when parents unconsciously help the child deny the significance of a neurotic symptom by rationalization. Often this is done in a manner that conveys reasonable and realistic concern, and the neurotic components of the conflict are accepted by the child and parent as a given rather than seen as a foreign body in his personality.

What was to become a full-blown school phobia in a six-year-old boy began with his fear of a neighbor's dog. He began to refuse to go into his yard to play and fearfully expressed his conviction that the dog would get into his house and bite him. The dog, an eleven-year-old retriever, had been a citizen of the neighborhood from his puppyhood and was cherished by the children for his friendly, docile, temperament. The extent of his intrusiveness was that he was allowed to sit on his front porch where he would be occasionally petted by children on their way to and from school. Despite this, and despite the child's repeated awakening in the middle of the night, crying with the fear that he might be bitten, the parents began an active campaign to force the dog's owners to keep him confined to the house. Their argument was that as dogs become older they can become vicious. They tried to use logic to avoid seeing that the child was phobic rather than cautious.

This parental reification of a neurotic fear or conviction can make the therapist's efforts to interfere with a child's defensive maneuvers an arduous task. If the *defense sharing* was not detected during the diagnostic evaluation, or begins in the first phase of treatment, the therapist must decide if he will spend more time with the child's defenses, more time with the parents, or refer the parents to a colleague who will collaborate in treating the family situation. In some cases, if the pathology is found to be firmly rooted in the family system, the treatment of choice may be to begin with family therapy, leaving the decision for individual treatment for later.

Thus, in the opening phase of treatment, the therapist perceives the child's communication and is brought by them to a point where he can feel the ambience, the rhythms, and the texture of the child's life. As he experiences this life with his senses, his empathy, and his knowledge of development, he finds irregularities in the texture that signal psychopathology and, in concert with the child, elucidates and delineates the nature of the problem. Using this process as a vehicle he deepens the therapeutic alliance with the child, develops with him a rich, flexible, and personal dialogue and introduces him to the subtlety and complexity of an inner, psychological life. As these milestones are reached, the therapist will find that he has become a part of the child's family system and his inclusion will stimulate more intrapsychic material from the child and interpersonal data from the family. By the end of the first phase of this development, the child will have learned "to be in therapy." The child will not have achieved this through a sterile, rote memorization, but by a living experience with the expanded awareness of self-scrutiny.

CHAPTER 12

The Middle Phase of the Therapeutic Process

Imperceptibly, the relationship between child and therapist changes as the treatment glides or grinds into the middle phase. Essentially the middle phase of therapy has many of the characteristics of any relationship in which two people have come to know each other. The child has come to think of the therapist as a person of his daily life, and the therapist experiences a feeling of familiarity when he thinks of the child. The history and the psychodynamic formulation become less important as orienting devices in the course of an hour or when the therapist recalls an event of the hour, and the child, as the therapist knows him, becomes the familiar image around which the significance of events are organized.

Behaviorally, the therapist finds himself greeting the child in a comfortable, familiar manner, and walking to the office easily and unencumbered by the feeling that he must put the child at ease. Also, he finds that the start of the hour has become more predictable. For the child's part his behavior indicates that the waiting room and the therapist's office have become as familiar as his classroom and his home.

Another indication that the therapy has evolved to a middle phase is that there begin to be bridges of unfinished business

from one session to the next. The child may say, "Like, I told
you last time," for example, or he may return to a project that
he had started in the previous session. The therapist will notice
thematic continuity from session to session more frequently
than before, and the "red thread" of significant psychological
material is recognizable during the hours.

There is an apparent paradox that occurs in the middle
phase of the psychotherapy of children. The child and therapist
who have worked so hard together to make each other comfortable in earlier parts of the therapy, now seem ready to make
each other uncomfortable. The child does so by voicing dis-
pleasure, anger, or dislike at the therapist, or by indulging
impulses during the sessions. The therapist may do so by reflecting back to the child his alienating behaviors or attitudes,
or by asking the child to address painful issues. This apparent
paradox can be explained by recalling that by this time the child
has achieved more confidence in the therapist's benevolence,
and the therapist has developed confidence in the child's
strengths and the therapeutic alliance. It is mentioned here
because on a number of occasions therapists in supervision have
expressed concern that their more confrontative tendencies
during this phase could be in response to the child's more readily expressed anger and aggression.

OBJECTIVES OF THE MIDDLE PHASE OF
TREATMENT

Four main undertakings are central in this phase of treatment. These are the isolation or definition of the child's conflicts
or deficits, articulating these problems in the context of the
child's life, understanding and applying the principle of abstinence, and culmination of the process of interpretation. The
overall goal that these objectives serve is to bring the child's
behavior and mentation under the child's conscious control.
The route to this goal is through the determination of how
conflicts or deficits fit into cycles of pathology, prevent the
indulgence of this pathological behavior, and arrive at con-

sciously articulated choices of how desires can be fulfilled and adaptation achieved. It must be quickly added that this approach to a description of therapy, in which aims and objectives are described for the various phases of treatment tends to depict it as having almost mechanical progression. This is, of course, a gross distortion. Psychotherapy is a fluid process with each therapeutic endeavor evolving with its own characteristics and it is as unique as the people who participate in it.

ISOLATION AND DEFINITION OF PROBLEMS

In undertaking this objective the therapeutic task is to elaborate the true nature of the symptoms and an understanding of *how the child experiences* his problems. This must be done in terms that refer to the child's daily life. Technical jargon is of little help here. The terms that are needed are terms that conjure up in the child's mind images of the time and place that the problems occur and bring with them the concomitant affects. The child may supply the words to describe the symptoms or problem, or he may borrow words and terms from meaningful people in his environment. At other times, the therapist may tap his own creativity to offer a term for use.

> Sammy was seven when his father left the family. Although Sammy was deeply pained and angered by the abandonment, his own character style in collusion with his environment permitted him no way to express his grief and rage. Shortly after his father left, he had developed a number of compulsive rituals, and was frequently plagued by obsessional thoughts. His ability to reveal his obsessions to the therapist was hampered not only by resistances, but also by his difficulty in finding descriptive terms. In one session, when he was deploring the fact that his teacher had accused him of daydreaming in class when in reality he was being beseiged by obsessional thoughts, he burst out with "She doesn't care if the thoughts go through my head like machine-gun bullets." With inquiry Sammy revealed

that the thoughts were incessant and uncontrollable. Later the hostile, destructive components of the thoughts could be explored, but at the time that Sammy described them the quality of the thoughts being a foreign body, and Sammy's helplessness to stop them was the central issue. The machine-gun bullet image that he created gave us not only a label but an emotionaily rich description of a symptom.

Thomas, a fifteen-year-old boy, whose parents were immigrants from Mexico, was being treated for depression. In the course of his treatment he revealed that he was troubled and ashamed at the way he had treated his first girl friend. With great regret he said that he had accused her of being unfaithful to him, and had called her a "whore." His thoughts returned to this incident repeatedly without being able to further explore the significance of it until the therapist, recalling that the family spoke Spanish in the home, and suspecting that his pain had something to do with comparing himself to his verbally abusive father, asked, "What did you feel when you called Julie a 'puta'?" Tommy flushed and began to make connections with the sadness and shame that he felt when his father used terms like *puta* in the home, sometimes referring to Tom's mother or sisters. Using the Spanish word helped Tom place the problem where it belonged, in the identification with a hated trait of his father.

A twelve-year-old boy with an abysmal self-concept had in earlier sessions told his therapist about his miserable career as a soccer player, and described himself as a perennial "benchwarmer." He was also a devoted defender of schoolmates that he considered "underdogs," but who were almost always labeled troublemakers by teachers. As a result he was often in trouble with teachers and school authorities himself.

In a session in which he was complaining about feeling "like a loser" his therapist attempted to get him to see that he took on impossible causes when he identified with depreciated people. This interpretation was not convincing to the patient until the therapist found a phrase that carried with it the feeling tone with which the young patient could resonate. He said, "When you take on these causes that are impossible, you must feel not like the *champion*, but like the *benchwarmer* of lost causes." To this the patient first laughed, and then regretfully said, "Yeah."

The description of the problems the patient experiences, whether they are perceptions of his own deficits, interpersonal difficulties, or intrapsychic conflicts must be articulated in terms that are familiar and evocative to him. The examples cited above attempted to show that the descriptive terms for the problems may be coined by the patient, be borrowed from the patient's experience of what people in his environment would say, or be coined by the therapist. The important issue is that the terms be affectively significant and *specific* for and to the child in question.

Especially in the middle phase of therapy, the therapist needs to be sensitive to both the *content* of the child's communication and the *process* of communications in order to help the child isolate and describe his problem. It is usually easier to give significance to the content of the child's communication than it is to detect the significance of the process of communication. A potential stumbling block for the therapist is that the content becomes so fascinating that the significance of the process can be neglected. To keep the process in mind, it may be helpful for the therapist to note and be curious about these factors:

1. When does a communication or an act occur in the course of any hour? In placing it the therapist may consider the time during the hour in which it occurs, or may consider when in relationship to other issues the act or association emerges.

2. The therapist can scrutinize if, in previous hours, other similar communications also occurred at the beginning, middle,
or end of the hour or bracketed by similar subjects.
3. The significance of the act or communication may be questioned, not only as to its content, but in terms of its relationship to the communication which preceded or followed
it.
4. The act of communication may be viewed in terms of the
effect that it may be designed to have on the therapist.

A seven-year-old boy, George, had been busily
engaged for several sessions in keeping his therapist
at arm's length. Every effort to engage him with questions or comments was met with inattention or superficial responses. If the boy was drawing and the
therapist asked him what he was depicting, the answer
would be "nothing." If the therapist recognized what
was being drawn and commented on it, the boy would
act as if he had not heard. Finally, the therapist addressed the process and said, "I think I finally understand what you're afraid to tell me in words. You want
me to know how it feels to be ignored like you feel
your mother and father ignore you."

George: (With genuine curiosity, not defiance) "How
does it feel?"
Therapist: "Rotten."
George: "You bet."

In this instance the therapist could sense that it had become
impossible to relate the detachment to the content of the hour,
and could feel the frustration and lack of relatedness that
George felt. If he had persisted in attempting to discuss the
content of a drawing or of a verbal response that George gave,
he would have only continued to be ignored.

Sometimes content and process need to be addressed si-
multaneously.

Bruce came to treatment when he was five, for

night fears, insomnia, and outbursts of anger. His parents had been divorced about six months earlier because of his father's drinking. The mother accused the father of being rowdy and unpredictable when he was drunk, and the father accused the mother of being domineering and shrewish all the time. In the two months before the start of psychotherapy, the father's visits with Bruce had been erratic. Many visits were missed, and Bruce was left feeling disappointed and sad. After several months of therapy Bruce began to do something that was perplexing to the therapist. In the midst of a transaction he would begin to whirl around until he made himself dizzy. Then he would begin to stumble around the office, falling down or bumping into furniture. When the therapist remembered his father's drunken "rowdiness," he could look a bit further, and see that the spinning invariably began when Bruce was talking about activities with his mother. The therapist was thus able to address both the symbolic content of the wild gyrations as well as the process by pointing out that they occurred whenever Bruce was wondering if he should be like (identify with) his mother or his father.

Another instance in which the communicative process revealed as much as the content of the communication was in the case of Dwain. He was an articulate, dramatic thirteen-year-old who presented the therapist with pseudomature, "profound" and elaborate insights regarding his problems. He was a whiz at "insights," but was failing in school. His very busy parents were a contrast in styles. The mother from whom Dwain had gotten much of his flair was an emotional, attractive, free spirit deeply involved in her career as a model and actress. The father, a hard-driving professional man, was quiet and self-contained to the point of being dour. The mother was often away from home on trips that her profession required.

Mother revealed that she was involved in an affair that she was sure neither Dwain nor her husband knew anything about. After about a year of treatment, Dwain was able to say that he resented his mother's absences from home. He was able to add that his resentment was often accompanied by a fear that she would not return. In a session shortly after he had made this revelation, he spoke briefly about his mother making another trip and his resentment at her taking her profession so seriously that she would never stay home. He seemed only to want to register his complaint and explore it no further. When queried, he answered that he was getting used to it anyway so there was "no sweat."

Therapist: "But you also said that you were afraid she might not come back. What's that about?"
Dwain: "Oh, I don't know. (glibly) Maybe, I'm just insecure.—Oh, say! Did I see a neat musical. It was great! There was this woman, Evita, and she was Peron's wife. She had some great songs. There was this one song about her suitcase that I really liked.

Following this, he quickly went on to plays that were going to be done in his junior high school, and the roles he would play in them. In several sessions that followed, thoughts of his mother were followed by associations with Evita. When the therapist could finally hold him still for a moment, he asked him to notice the connection between thoughts of his mother and Evita. Following this, he was able to both perceive and acknowledge that he worried that his mother would be "unfaithful" like Evita was and leave him. Keeping an eye on the process made the content meaningful.

Content and process are inextricably interwoven. They can contradict or synergize each other's significance or one may serve as the real vehicle of meaning while the other disguises the communication. Only by letting attention hover over them both can the therapist hope to detect that which the patient conveys, but is not yet able to tell.

Child psychiatrists, especially, become aware that using words as symbols is only a small part of the communicative process. Victor Rosen (1969) summarized a good deal of work in this area, asserting that in addition to verbal symbols, important vehicles of communication are signals and signs. A brief summary of these three processes and their qualities, as Rosen presents them, are as follows:

1. A signal is an event, whatever its form, that gives rise to the expectation of the occurrence of another event. The amber traffic light (Event A) alerts the viewer that a red light will soon appear (Event B). The lightning flash gives rise to the expectation of a thunder clap. Signals may be simple or complex events that may reach any part of the sensory apparatus. They may have a natural relationship to the subsequent event, as in the case of the lightning and the thunder clap, or the relationship may be assigned by convention as in the case of a flashing red light and appearance of a dangerous situation. The common quality of most signals is that there is temporal or spatial contiguity, with that which is signaled.

2. A sign is an object or an event "A" that indicates the existence of an event or state "B." The sign, unlike the signal, does not imply the materialization or actualization of event or state "B," but only that it exists or has existed. Finding cigarette ash in an ashtray is not a signal that someone will start to smoke, but rather a sign that someone is smoking or has smoked. One other quality of signs is that there are often similarities between them and what they signify. These similarities, called iconic or pictographic similarities may have become obscure because of changes in a culture, or in the way things are represented, but often the similarities can be rediscovered if the origins of the signs are traced.

3. Symbols differ from signals and signs in one important respect. The relationship between a symbol and what it represents is an arbitrary one, and has been assigned by convention

or common experience. Symbols may have had temporal or spatial contiguity or similarity to that which is indicated, but these aspects of the relationship are rarely reconstructable. Due to the fact that symbols that are regularly used for communication, such as words or sounds, have lost their temporal or spatial contiguity as well as their iconic similarity to what is signified, they must, if they are to communicate thought successfully, possess a common characteristic. They must follow rules which govern their permissible combinations. These rules are codified in the concept of "syntax." The syntactic rules ensure that there will be congruence in the encoding and decoding processes so that what the sender transmits will be understood by the recipient.

When symbols are explicit and enough exist to provide an infinite number of combinations, symbols can offer great economy in coding and decoding. An example of this is the relatively few symbols needed in a phonetic alphabet as compared to a pictographic one.

Thus, symbols are explicit, economical, and flexible vehicles for communication which afford virtually inexhaustible raw material for the process of communicating thoughts and concepts. This is in contrast to the rather limited possibilities of signs and signals. The disadvantages of symbols, as I understand it, are that persons using them must have had a common experience in order for the symbol to mean the same thing to all, and that more maturation is necessary to utilize symbols effectively for communication than for signs and signals.

Expectably, the psychotherapy of a child will usually involve more exchanges of signals and signs than that of an adult. Clinical experience has convinced me that not only does the younger child rely more on signals and signs to convey and perceive messages between himself and the environment, these signals and signs often have more specific meanings than those of an adult, both as he perceives them and as he transmits them.

Specificity of terms, actively considering process and content, and being ready to perceive signals and signs as well as symbols are some of the ways that make it possible to define the problems or deficits in the child, and place them in relief in the child's personality so that they may be addressed.

PROBLEMS AND CONFLICTS IN TERMS OF THE CHILD'S LIFE COURSE

"I interpreted his hostility to him, but he resisted." This statement standing by itself is lifeless as well as meaningless. For it to even begin to convey significance it would have to be placed into a context that defined it, delineated it, described how the hostility manifested itself, and how it altered other manifest traits of the child. The statement would have to take place in a description of a whole person in order to mean anything to others. Clinically, it can only have meaning when it is sufficiently specific to pertain to one human being among the multitude that brush by our daily awareness. If a description pertaining to him is to have any meaning to our child patient, the dignity of individuality must be afforded him even as we offer the comfort of recognizing his mental state.

The middle phase of psychotherapy is an optimal time to place these problems, which have been identified and isolated through the efforts described in the prior section, into the context of the child's life.

As this phase proceeds, the therapist can find many instances in which he can refine the description of problems that have become so prominent that they dominate rather than become integrated with the child's life. Further observations will reveal that there are other problems which do not dominate endlessly, but have an ebb and flow. Sometimes the child compensates for them. At other times he changes one problem into another by virtue of the defenses he erected against the original discomfort. Often if the therapist will review the events of a therapy in the temporal frame of weeks or months rather than hours, he can see that there are recognizable cycles in the way the child, interacting with his environment, will seek new adaptations and compensatory balance in an effort to alleviate his discomfort. The reasons these cycles are recognizable is because, as discussed earlier, there are components to them that are rigid, repetitive, refractory to change in the face of new experiences, and reflect the child's past rather than his ability to adapt creatively to the present or prepare for the future. A case history may help to clarify this construct.

Timmy was referred for an evaluation when he was about seven years old, after his parents and teacher had met and decided to seek help. The parents said that Timmy had started each preschool and school semester with eagerness and enthusiasm. After a month or two, his performance and behavior would deteriorate. He then became irritable both at home and at school. He would frequently fight with peers, become disrespectful to the teacher, be hyperactive, daydream excessively, and refuse to do classwork. His relationships at home suffered too when he became troublesome at school, and the parents were unclear as to whether they had fallen into the pattern of nagging him, or he had become irritable in both settings on his own.

Timmy's gestation, birth, and developmental history were unremarkable, as presented by his parents. On inquiry, they did recall that his mother had two or three weeks of postpartum blues after his birth, and even a bit longer period of depression after his younger brother was born, when Timmy was three. Timmy had started nursery school shortly after his brother's birth, and was said to have enjoyed it for a couple of months when the pattern of irritability and aggression that his parent described started.

Timmy was an enthusiastic patient as therapy started, and the therapist had little difficulty establishing a pleasant, warm relationship. There were times when the therapist was tempted to consider the complaints about Timmy exaggerated until he recalled their universality, and the fact that he was seeing Timmy alone in his office while teachers and parents interacted with him in situations in which he scrambled and vied for attention. In fact, the therapist's problems in the early part of treatment were not Timmy's behavior or attitudes in the office, but rather how to manage the school and the parent's demands that the therapist make Timmy "good" before he could find out what was making Timmy appear "bad" (see chapter 6). Also, the implicit assumption that the therapist was going to be the disciplinarian or enforcer of rules required some exploration and clarification with both parents and teachers. After having worked through these early environmental management problems, the therapist could focus his attention on therapy, and after a year shared enough insights with Timmy to achieve two important goals. The first was to redefine the symptoms in terms that specifically made sense to Timmy. The second was that he could visualize the cycles of the child's states, as he struggled to reconcile his wishes and longings with environmental conditions and reactions. What had appeared as meaningless at the beginning of therapy began to demonstrate the logic of emotions and desires in the context of Timmy's life.

From Tim's communications about his interactions at school and home, and from things that he revealed in transferences, the therapist could detect that Tim's shaky self-esteem was dependent on the constant reassurance of adults who were important to him. As experiences with Tim accumulated and he became freer to express his internal states, the therapist was allowed to see that no amount of reassurances and expressions of affection or respect were enough to soothe Tim's pain. He was trying to heal an internal wound with external balm that never seemed to penetrate deeply enough. Incessant demands on teachers, parents, and therapist inevitably brought Tim to the limits of what was realistically possible, and he experienced these limits as rejections and depreciations. He then felt ashamed and belittled and tried to compensate for his disconsolate state by making himself tough and important through fighting and leading insurrections in class. The expectable environmental response to his misbehavior and aggression produced guilt and more fear in him that he would be ignored and ostracized, with concomitant dysphoria. It was this depression and sadness and his self-soothing fantasies that made him daydream and unable, rather than unwilling, to do his schoolwork. The feelings of worthlessness and depression that went with feeling he was the "class dummy" made Tim even more dependent on approbation from the world of adults, and around went the rigid, repetitive cycle.

This is the kind of understanding of the forces acting on the child that allows the therapist to understand the symptoms, not as a static checklist of complaints, but as components of a living, vital system that is in constant flux. In the ebb and flow of its component parts the child is constantly agitated and disturbed. The pathogenic elements in Tim's problems could be graphically represented as the cycle in Figure 12-1.

As we will see later, when the therapist is fortunate enough to be able to perceive a discrete cycle like this in working with a child, changes in it can provide him with an excellent indicator of the efficacy of his therapeutic interventions and of changes in the child's repertoire of feelings and behaviors.

THE PRINCIPLE OF ABSTINENCE REVISITED

It is surprising to see how infrequently the "Rule of Abstinence" is addressed in the literature in child psychotherapy. And yet it is a problem that arises in almost every treatment. I cannot help but wonder if sometimes it doesn't make its appearance in disguise in the form of therapists wondering whether or not candy should be kept in the treatment room, or if gifts should be given on birthdays and holidays. Exploring

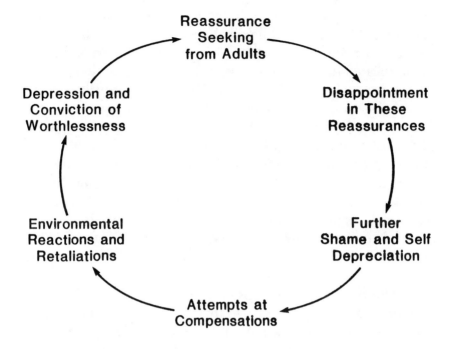

Figure 12-1. Repetitive cycles of a child's reactions to his own pathology. See description in text.

this concept may help provide not only the idea of another principle applicable in this phase of therapy, but also help answer some of these questions about technique on the basis of principles rather than *ad hoc* decisions.

While it is beyond the scope of this work to trace the philosophic and theoretical basis of the principle of abstinence, a word or two about its evolution may help in understanding its utility. Early in the history of psychoanalysis Freud became convinced that a number of psychological ills came from the prohibition of activities that would discharge libido. This "dammed up" libido was then thought to be responsible for certain forms of psychopathology. Later, in proposing techniques for psychoanalytic treatment, it was first thought that

not permitting libidinal discharge during the course of treatment would ensure that libidinal energy would be directed to
verbal expression of conflicts. Clinical observations and more
sophisticated theoretical constructs led to the abandonment of
these general prohibitions and the more specific concept
emerged that the erotic wishes of the patient toward the analyst
were to be frustrated if the analysis was to progress (Freud
1915, 1919). Freud clearly predicated his conclusions on technical rather than ethical or moral tenets, arguing that to gratify
the patient's wish for the therapist's erotic love would simply
indulge archaic wishes and leave the patient's capacity to understand, regulate, and develop them into mature desires, unaltered and incompetent. Sandler, Kennedy, and Tyson (1980)
have addressed this concept in the psychoanalytic treatment of
children.

The rule of abstinence is based on the principle that frustration of a wish is necessary so that the wish may be perceived
and articulated; then the reasons for its compelling impetus can
be explored. Although Freud originally postulated that these
wishes would be of a sexual nature, I think it safe to say that
most therapists would consider it necessary to frustrate any wish
of an immature or inappropriate nature that needed to be
understood rather than indulged. In the psychotherapy of
adults an important diagnostic tasks is to determine if the patient can tolerate frustration sufficiently to undertake a form
of psychotherapy whose therapeutic effects depend on uncovering and revealing unconscious motives. The therapeutic alliance and the nonjudgmental atmosphere of the therapeutic
relationship ease the frustration of abstinence, and render the
revelation of the true origin of the unacceptable wish or impulse
tolerable. Maugham's insightful story, "Rain," offers a picture
of what can happen when these supports are not available to
the self-scrutinizer.

With children, some special problems present themselves
with the rule of abstinence. The child's capacity to tolerate frustration cannot always be predicted accurately. Some children
are well equipped to inhibit aggressive impulses, but are enor-

mously vulnerable if pleas for affection are not indulged. Others may show just the opposite array of strengths and vulnerabilities. At other times children, who are models of temperance when they are healthy, well rested and well fed, become intolerant of any frustration if they are hungry, tired, or becoming ill. The therapist may not always be aware of the diminution of their frustration tolerances. Also, children generally find it more difficult to understand and remember the reason for abstaining from indulging their curiosity, affection, anger, desire for fun, and other impulses that play across their awareness in a labile and even wanton way in the course of each of their days. The therapist's reasons for imposing abstinence may be misinterpreted by the child and perceived as rejection or a reprimand. For example, the therapist's unwillingness to reveal some aspect of his personal life may be interpreted by the child as a cold and hostile rejection of his wish to be intimate. Yet, which therapist who is a parent, has not detected in the child patient's insistent questions about our own offspring and our relationship to them, the obvious expression of their jealousy and competition with their own siblings? This concept of abstinence, therefore, requires some special considerations when the patient is a child. Let it be said from the outset, however, that many of the principles that are pertinent in considering an adult's tendency to indulge a wish through action also hold for the child.

Freud (1915) called attention to the element of resistance in the adult's demands that a wish or tendency be indulged. Where can one see this more clearly than in the child's demand that he be amused and indulged in play during the whole therapy hour? In feeling that he *must* accede to this demand, the therapist neglects to recall the number of situations in which the child must forego fun and amusement in order to tackle the task at hand. The task in treatment is for the child to utilize the benign and unflagging attention of the therapist to alleviate his own anxiety and the interpersonal disharmony with those that surround him. To indulge the wish to play may well mean that the child is rendering the therapy or the aims of therapy meaningless or impotent. This is the aim of most resistances.

Another similarity between child and adult as they press their demands in the therapeutic relationship is that indulgence brings only short-term relief. The cookies or chocolate that the child demanded during the treatment hour soon become tasteless when the demand is nothing but the expression of another unrecognized longing. Soon the demand is back anew, and this time with heightened expectations of success based on past experience.

In those instances when frustration tolerance is not adequate, the therapist finds that he must provide some special supports for his child patient. One of the first considerations, of course, is to make sure that the child's demand is not based on a realistic current need. A child who comes to a therapy hour immediately after school and who clamors for candy or cookies may be reflecting lowered blood sugar rather than past deprivations. Only after investigating what the child has for lunch or if a midafternoon snack alleviates the compelling qualities of his demands, can the therapist begin to explore with the child the way he made (or *did not* make) his demands. In some institutions this problem has been addressed by providing snacks in the waiting room for children. While this may prove a suitable solution for some children, the therapist must remain alert to the possibility that the "realistic hunger" was hiding one that came from earlier privation. The point that needs to be made here is that abstinence cannot be imposed when the child's need is realistic, but realistic needs sometimes cover neurotic wishes.

When the therapist detects, or suspects that the child's demands are the vehicles for bringing unconscious wishes from earlier conflicts into the therapy, he is faced with the problem of judging whether the child can understand and tolerate frustration of the wish *at that time* in the therapy, without shattering the alliance and the child's commitment to therapeutic work. If the therapist is convinced from past experiences, or based on the strength of the tie to him that the child can tolerate imposed abstinences, the task is relatively easy.

Charlie, age seven, had expressed intense curiosity

about other patients. He had discovered some of the reasons for this, and his curiosity had become manageable. After a week's illness during which he had missed a session, the curiosity came back with full vigor.

Charlie: "Did someone come to see you when I was sick?"
Therapist: "Do you wonder if I continued to work?"
Charlie: "No! Did you see someone during my time? Was it a little boy? Did he take my drawing paper?"
Therapist: "Charlie, those old feelings have come back. You remember when we talked before about your privacy and other people's privacy, and the important things we found out when you told me what and why you wanted to know about other kids."
Charlie: "Yeah! But once when I was sick my mother . . ."

Off Charlie went into a series of associations that were important and revealing enough to him that the "real" issue about whether or not the therapist had filled his missed hour become uninteresting.

Many other times the child is much more insistent and the therapist senses, but cannot fathom the cause of the urgency. A technique that has frequently solved the problem is a compromise.

An eight-year-old boy named Brett became adamant about discovering whether his therapist had a cabin in the mountains, and if he took his children there. The therapist wondered aloud why he wanted to know, thinking that such a specific curiosity was probably predicated on a more important concern. He was surprised to find that Brett's curiosity was both intense and compelling. The boy simply could not or would not leave the subject. The therapist then told the child that this seemed so important to him that they really needed to put their heads together to find

out what the question meant to him. If, after they
discovered what the question meant Brett still wanted
to know, the therapist would tell him. Brett first pro-
tested that he did not know why he asked, and when
he was persuaded to associate to the question (a technique that he had successfully used before), he revealed the significance of the issue. Brett had heard
a story about the Arapaho nation in school. In it the
author or narrator had used the term *happy hunting
ground*. Brett, knowing that the Arapaho were buffalo
hunters associated to a place in the mountains where
the highway passes a pasture where buffalo are often
brought to feed. The image in his mind was that, if
someone went up to the *happy hunting ground* in the
mountains, they would never return. As this fear (later
to be understood as a wish) about the therapist and his
children going to the mountains (*happy hunting ground*)
never to return, began to be recognized, the question
became irrelevant and needed no answer.

In this example the therapist, sensing the anxiety involved
in the wish, felt that he had to offer additional support in order
to maintain a posture of inquiry with the child. The support
was in the promise to relieve the child's anxiety if the inquiry
did not relieve it, and in the therapist's very recognition of the
discomfort the child was feeling.

There are times when the original intent of the principle
of abstinence and the origin of the child's wish to be indulged
are swept into the background by child and therapist becoming
involved in a power struggle that is the by-product of the therapist's attempts to apply the rule. In the ensuing fray the child
forgets that the aim of treatment is self-awareness, and the
therapist forgets that abstinence is in the service of discovery.
The power struggle acquires a self-perpetuating life of its own.
This is an excellent place for the therapist to shift from content
to process. If he has been able to detect that he has been lured
by the child or driven by his own countertransference into an
oppositional position, he can begin to explore with the child

how the content of a problem becomes less important than the power struggle that was born with it.

In this issue, as with virtually every other technical consideration in treatment, no regulation or rule can be a substitute for the therapist's clinical judgment. There are times when the few suggestions listed above must be put aside. There are times when it is not only technically indicated, it is humane and decent to indulge the child. The disconsolate child may need to be held. The bereft child may need to be comforted, the hungry fed, and the cold child warmed.

> Tessie was four when her mother died. In the course of her treatment, previously suppressed grief began to be mobilized and expressed. With it came fears that the people she loved would become lost to her forever, as she had begun to feel her mother was. In one session in which she expressed grief and rage at her loss, she suddenly asked the therapist if he had a phone at home and if his children used the phone a lot like her older brothers did at her home. She was told that the therapist did have a phone and, although there were young people who used it often, it was free often enough that a young girl could reach the therapist if she needed to do so. Tessie was supplied with a piece of paper with the therapist's number, which she solemnly put into her jumper pocket. Although she never called, she showed it to the therapist when treatment was terminated, and told him that she was going to keep it in case she needed to call in the future. Rather sadly she added that she knew she could never call her mother.

Children, of course, have more difficulty than adults in self-imposed abstinence outside the treatment hours. Yet, the tendency cannot be ignored. The case of Billy (chapter 3), who managed to get a secretary to give him a ride home, demonstrates how the therapist must be sensitive to these issues not only in the office, but also when children, much like adults, begin to carry frustrated demands into their environment in their plea for a reduction of tensions. Whenever indicated and without violating confidentiality, the therapist would be well advised to alert the child's parents and teachers to the possibility of increased demands during a segment of the treatment when abstinence may be difficult for the child and to suggest that their readiness to indulge be predicated on their assessment of the appropriateness of the wish rather than the persistence of the demand.

By keeping the principle of abstinence in mind the therapist is more able to answer for himself that recurring question of whether or not to give the child a gift on birthdays, promotions, graduation, Christmas, or Hanukkah. By and large the privilege of giving a gift to the child is reserved for family members and close friends. The therapist need not intrude on their territory and do things that they often do admirably well. But the therapist can best decide what is kind, humane, and appropriate by placing the question in the context of the treatment goals.

Abstinence, like all other principles that we consider in this chapter, is placed here because we hope to have instituted it by the time that we reach the middle phase of therapy. This is not to suggest, however, that the process of applying these principles has not or should not have begun earlier in the treatment.

THE PROCESS OF INTERPRETATION

Interpretation, which in the minds of many, is practically synonymous with psychoanalytically oriented psychotherapy, may be one of the most frequently misunderstood and casually applied processes in the psychiatric repertoire. On reflection, this is not surprising since the interpretive process is fairly easy to understand when reading about it, and this ease of understanding lulls us into complacency about its use. The analogy to chess is again applicable here. The moves of chess pieces are learned relatively quickly, and one is charmed by the fluidity and mobility of the game. Then, one begins to play, and is surprised to see how much time and thought are required to achieve excellence and elegance. We are awed when we begin to understand the parsimony, harmony, and effectiveness that is reflected in each move an expert makes. So it is with the principles of interpretation. They are easy to read, but the clinical situation demands that they be applied elegantly and with parsimony. The process of interpretation is well described by Wallace (1983) in his book on adult psychotherapy. Many of the principles he describes will be repeated with an eye to their application to children. First, however, I would like to address a few concepts that I have found elusive and from what I can tell from the supervision of young therapists, are frequently not easily integrated into the practice of psychotherapy.

Interpretation is a process. It is not an act or an event. The process of interpretation begins with preparatory acts which must precede it, such as clarifications, elucidations, isolating and describing traits or acts of the patient, and involving the patient in determining the significance of his traits or acts which reappear in his relationships to the therapist or others. It is important that this be recognized because when the unprepared, single-shot interpretation is tried and fails, as frequently it must, the reaction of the therapist is to try harder and more convincingly, and in the process he risks becoming a nag. Conversely, some therapists lose confidence in the process and give it up. We will attempt to describe the process in a way that will help avoid either extreme.

There has been a growing tendency to call most things that the therapist says to the young patient an interpretation. This is erroneous. Most communications are directives, admonitions, invitations, elucidations, explanations, or trial balloons. The term *interpretation* should be reserved for the verbal summary of a process that has allowed the patient to experience and understand the defenses (or resistances) that were erected against the anxiety engendered by an impulse, wish, conviction, desire, or fantasy. Because of the length of the process and the time it takes for the patient to perceive and understand the relationships between components of a conflict, interpretations

are few in treatment. If the therapist finds himself firing off
several interpretations each session, something is wrong.

In order to develop a mental image of the interpretive
process, a microscopic look at the "anatomy" of an internal
conflict is helpful. A number of internal conflicts will emerge
in the course of therapy. Loving or protective feelings toward
a younger sibling will vie with angry, destructive tendencies in
a young patient's mind. The desire to eat a piece of candy may
conflict with the wish to hoard it. The wish to win the parent's
love and approbation is challenged by the pressure to indulge
an impulse. Among these, the kind of conflict that needs to be
best understood in order to develop a basic technique of interpretation is the neurotic conflict. We can define this simply as
the defenses erected by the ego against the *anxiety* which would
ensue if an unconscious wish, plan, or conviction were carried
into action or *recognized* consciously. Classically, the wish, plan,
conviction or fantasy is thought to be the derivative of one or
another instinctual drive, or a fusion of both (Freud, 1924).
Graphically, this can be represented by Figure 12-2.

In this figure we can see a defense or series of defenses
(A) deployed as a bulwark against the anxiety (B) that would
be generated if the impulse were to become conscious through
thought or behavior. Behaviorally, these defense mechanisms,
the anxiety, and the impulse may be represented in thought or
deed by their symbolic representations or as themselves. The
"conflict" thus described in mental or behavioral terms is synonymous with "compromise formation" in structural terms. For
example, a child may be found to behave clumsily or ineptly
even though he is without physical impediments. In the course
of treatment or evaluation it is found that he is afraid (becomes
anxious) when behaving competently. Further exploration reveals that he is afraid that his competence will reveal a wish to
best or depreciate an already denigrated father. The compromise formation consists of ineptness as a defense against the
anxiety generated by the unconscious, repudiated wish to harm
his father. Another child may tell you that when he is around
any authority figure that represents his father, he dares not

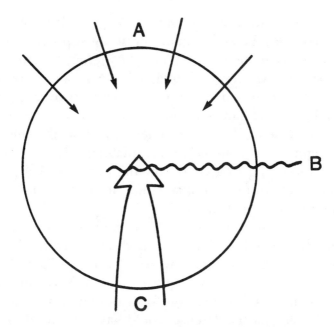

Figure 12-2. A schematic representation of the compromise formation. The defense or defenses (A) are developed to protect the patient from anxiety (B) which is generated by impending awareness of an unconscious impulse, wish or conviction (C).

become active because he fears that he will come into conflict with him and thus expresses the conflict or compromise formation in a relatively undisguised manner.

There are times when a single, neurotic symptom may express both the impulse and the defenses against it. The oft-used description of the hysterical, spastic paralysis of the arm and hand manifested by a clenched fist is an example of this: the paralysis is a symbol of the inhibition as it defends against the anxiety that would occur if the patient became aware of the wish to strike, symbolized by the clenched fist.

The process of interpretation begins as the therapist seeks to render the symptoms expressing the compromise formation as foreign bodies in the patient's psyche. The child, who uses passivity as an inhibiting defense, for example, cannot begin to question his passivity if it is accepted as an inevitable given in his life. As we have seen in earlier chapters, if a conflict is to be interpreted, the environment must not support, reward, or reify some component of it. When the therapist is satisfied that there is no environmental complicity in keeping the conflict alive, he can begin to interfere with the child's working defenses. A number of techniques can be employed to achieve this.

1. Describing a defense sometimes allows the child to see it in a light that reveals its limiting qualities.

2. Indicating to a child how the defensive behavior was inappropriate in one social situation or another may help the child interfere with its use.

3. Demonstrating the ineffectiveness of a defense in producing the desired result for the child can interfere with it. The child, described in chapter 9, who on learning of the therapist's illness, called at 10:30 at night because he was worried, was using the defenses of reaction formation and undoing. When he could see that the defenses could have produced the effect opposite to that of a good wish, he became anxious and was moved to scrutinize his behavior further.

4. Demonstrating the rigidity of a defense may help render it a less desirable option. If a child who reacts to *all* threatened expressions of his aggression with passivity, can be helped to see that in some circumstances his very passivity is the expression of a form of aggression, he can be shown the value of having a choice rather than an automatic response.

5. Refusal to take complimentarity to a defense can be effective in interfering with it. Billy, described in chapter 3, longing to be treated in special ways, maneuvered the therapist with his helplessness. When the therapist refused to take complimentarity to his assumed helplessness, he was not only applying the principle of abstinence, he was also interfering with Billy's defense.

6. There are times when a defense can be destructive or dangerous, and the therapist has no choice but to *prohibit* its expression. For example, some children become terrified of having to passively suffer some hurt or injury and will become hyperactive or aggressive. The aggression may have to be cur-

tailed by the therapist, and parents and teachers may have to be told that if the child cannot control himself they must take measures to control him.

As the therapist begins to interfere with defenses, and the child becomes aware of the anxiety against which the defenses were directed, it must be once more ascertained that the therapeutic alliance has developed no serious breaches. A feeling of friendliness and oneness with the child should continue to be nurtured, even if the description and revelations of the defenses may have painful components. New words or phrases may have to become part of the dialogue, and care may have to be taken to prevent the techniques used to interfere with defenses from sounding like scoldings or accusations. In this context, the therapist can contemplate the idea of "dosing" an intervention.

Imagine that a child of eight or nine becomes silly and starts to clown whenever sad or angry feelings about the loss of his mother come close to awareness. The therapist, noting that the child becomes the clown at times of stress, feels that he needs to interfere with this defense. He could say the following things to the child.

1. There are times when you play the clown and make it impossible to talk about important things.
2. There are times when you play the clown and I know you really don't feel like one.
3. I knew a boy once who clowned around when he was afraid of something.
4. Boys sometimes clown around for a good reason that only they know about.
5. All kids clown around. Sometimes though it's not just to have fun. It's for other reasons. What do you think?

All of these declarations are accurate, and any one of them may be used, but in any given circumstance some will be more productive than others, and still others may be counterproductive altogether. What determines the productivity of each? The reader will have noticed that each statement is less direct than the one before it and each a bit more distant from a direct description of the behavior of the boy. Each is a different dose of the same medicine. Determining the dosage will depend on variables like the length of time that the child has been in therapy; the number of times that the problem has been addressed; the response of the child to earlier interventions; the state of the therapeutic alliance at the time and an estimate of the freight it will bear; the child's general psychological toughness; and the physical state of the child at the time of the intervention. When in doubt, the therapist can use the lighter dose, and work his way up to a more direct statement.

As the therapist interferes with defenses, the child will frequently begin to show that anxiety is reaching awareness. This can be shown by a direct expression of fear and repugnance, or by the child's expressed wish to avoid subjects that touch on the conflict. In other instances the child will describe or play out fantasies of catastrophies or danger. In still other instances the anxiety or the conflict will be acted out or lived out.

> Marcie was almost six and had been in treatment for about a year for her impulsive and sometimes destructive behavior. In the course of evaluating the family situation, the therapist learned that Marcie's mother and father had been having marital difficulties for several years, and were contemplating divorce. Both had had affairs, but were convinced that they had successfully hidden their conflicts as well as their affairs from Marcie. At this time in the treatment, it had become clear that Marcie had used a number of defenses to avoid awareness of the parent's quarrels, and to maintain the conspiracy of silence with them. As the defenses of denial, reaction formation, and projection began to dissolve, Marcie began to express a fear that her house would burn, that there would be an auto accident when her mother brought her to sessions, and various other calamities would happen. The therapist had seen evidence that Marcie was anxious about recognizing her anger at her parents, and at how they

had jeopardized the security of her world. The therapist told her that he noticed that frightening things like fires and auto accidents came to her mind when she was no longer able to avoid seeing her parents fight, and would no longer pretend that things were always "nicely, nicely" at home. (There had been long conversations about her "nicely, nicely" pretend games.) The therapist said to her that she sometimes seemed to wish that she didn't have to see some of her own feelings and some of the feelings of her mom and dad. Some days after this session, Marcie's mother called the therapist, and was deeply disturbed as she told about Marcie having tried to blind the puppy the family had recently acquired for her. She told the therapist that she had heard the puppy squeal and had arrived in Marcie's room in time to see Marcie poking at the animal's eyes with a long hat pin. The therapist saw Marcie as soon as he could, and convinced the child that he was interested in understanding and not condemning or punishing her. Marcie revealed that it was not only destructiveness and anger that she was expressing with her action. Marcie said that she was trying to protect the puppy because he became very frightened when big dogs came into their yard, and he saw them fight. She thought that if he could not *see*, he would not be frightened. It was not difficult to convince Marcie that blindness was too high a price to pay to avoid fear. Marcie argued, however, that if her puppy were blind she would have to take care of him forever.

Although an extreme example in a seriously disturbed child, Marcie's behavior illustrates acting out in a transparent way. Her actions were understandable in terms of the conflicts with which she struggled. The adaptive compromise had been disturbed by the therapist's interference with her mechanisms of defense. Anxiety had resulted, and she was trying to master it through action and displacement.

When defenses lose their competence to diminish or vanquish anxiety, the therapist must begin to address the "scary feelings" and "worries" that begin to assault the child and be ready to recognize certain behaviors as attempts to carry conflicts into action in efforts to master the anxiety. Sometimes, for the protection of the child and that which surrounds him, the therapist may be well advised to alert parents and teachers that disturbing issues are being confronted and more vigilance may be required. The danger, of course, is that sometimes this would only generate more contagious anxiety in a family or school system that may be already overburdened. Also, there are some environments that seem unable to avoid the tendency to make prophesies come true. The therapist, therefore, here as in other segments of the therapy, needs to rely on clinical judgment in providing containment for the acting out. Fortunately for us in child therapy, acting out is less frequently dangerous than it is in adults and adolescents, and when there is an element of danger, there have been warning signs before the child entered therapy. But there are times when acting out in destructive or self-destructive fashion may appear *de novo*.

The therapist has a powerful tool in tackling the task of inducing the child to express conflicts in verbal terms that can be conceptualized and examined in therapeutic sessions. He can confidently assure the child that the consulting room is one place in the world where conflicts and wishes can be expressed without condemnation or negative social consequences. If the therapist has been able, up to this point, to avoid actions or communications that influenced the child's social environment, this reassurance is naturally more convincing. If in previous encounters the therapist has revealed information that caused consequences outside of the session, the situation may yet be salvaged by a discussion of the conditions that forced the therapist's hand earlier and about whether or not those conditions would be likely to recur. If successful, the "safe haven" of the therapeutic hour can be offered as the place to which the child's pain and turbulence can be brought. If the child's fragile trust has been irreparably compromised, as in rare instances it can be, the therapist should consider the invariably painful possibility of transferring him to another therapist.

Having come to this point in the process of interpretation (having interfered with the defenses and acknowledged and named the anxiety against which they were directed), the therapist will begin to see the impulse or the conviction that the child dreads begin to be expressed in the therapy. Often the therapist will have known about it from inferences made earlier in therapy. At other times our old ally, the attitude of inquiry may have to be called upon again to discover what "painted devil"* conjures dread in the child.

> Paul was a ten-year-old boy who had suffered years of physical abuse before being removed from his home. A sister, six years older than he, was suspected to have been sexually abused and lived in a separate foster home. Paul had always felt his sister had had it better than he. He was referred for treatment because he had become a tyrant and a bully in school and with his playmates. His imagined enemies were legion and he attacked them physically and verbally. To him his schoolmates and playmates were "fags" and "queers" and he vented his rage on them whenever and however he could. As treatment progressed and the therapist could show him that his bluster and bullying was in the service of keeping from being scared, Paul began to direct most of his attacks to the therapist. During one session he refused to sit on a chair near a window that had been his customary place during much of the treatment. When asked about this, he first avoided answering and then half jokingly, but with some anxiety said that he was afraid that someone hiding behind the window drapes would "shove a knife or something" in his back. After many more sessions of deciphering and making connections between fears and wishes, the

---

*"It is the eye of childhood that fears a painted devil." W. Shakespeare, *Lady Macbeth*, Act II, Scene 2.

therapist could tell him that he had acted like he was
the tough guy and everyone else was "the fag" because
he was so afraid that he might find out that he wanted
to be used by his father like his sister had been so that
he could get a better deal from Dad, as he imagined
she had gotten.

The association of being stabbed in the back was of course
not the only clue that Paul had given about this fantasy of
offering himself as a sexual object in a wish to win his father's
benevolence. The therapist had made inferences to himself
about Paul's wish, but the point of this example is that he had
not talked about these inferences until he could describe to Paul
how the defenses could be *understood* as measures to ward off
the anxiety that his impulses or wishes occasioned. With adults
the form that the interpretation takes may vary. At times the
defenses are mentioned first. At other times the anxiety the
patient feels may begin the description of the compromise formation. If impulses, anxiety, and defenses are included in the
description of the compromise formation, the adult patient
rearranges the order in which these components appeared in
the clinical process. With children, my impression is that the
interpretation is better utilized if each component of the compromise formation is described in the order in which it appeared in the clinical process, and linked to the setting in which
it occurred. The behaviors that represented each element of
the conflict and the affects that accompanied the behavior
should also be included when they are known. The therapist
can then recall the life situations in which they occurred and
review them. An interpretation to a child may appear, therefore, like one of the examples below.

> "We didn't know what you were scared of when
> you first came to see me. We figured out that having
> to count up to a thousand before you went to school
> was a way of trying to get rid of the scary feelings.
> Now we know that you were scared because you were
> furious at your teacher when she didn't treat you spe-
> cial."

In this example the anxiety was described first, then the obsessive defenses and finally the impulses. The second example might be:

"Remember how we first found out that every time you got mad at your sister you became frightened when you went to bed at night. That's the reason you stayed up and watched horror movies; to avoid bed and to try to give yourself a reason for being afraid."

In this case the impulse was described and its concomitant anxiety. The defenses which were understood and interfered with later were the last to be described.

Although it is usually only after there has been interference with the defenses that the anxiety and the impulses of a compromise formation are available to the child for conscious scrutiny, the derivatives or the symbols of any of the three components may have been present in thinking or behavior from the beginning of therapy. By placing them in the context of time and action, the therapist provides clarity and specificity for the child, and this permits the child to make maximum use of the intervention.

A word of caution is indicated at this point. Clinical processes have their own pace. These sometimes seem abysmally slow to a parent or a clinician. Due to impatience or sometimes due to lack of experience, a therapist will feel that if he has evidence for or surmises that a child should feel a certain impulse, conviction, or affect he may "interpret" it before the defenses have been addressed. Even when the timing is accurate and the defenses have been worked with, it is not unusual to see the child institute a new set of defenses to cope with the anxiety mobilized by the interpretation. Patience is essential in these instances, and if the process has to begin again, the therapist can take heart in the knowledge that even if the child did not master the content of the conflict, he learned from the process.

Equal caution should be exercised to insure that impulses or affects are not seduced or stimulated by the therapist. When an affect or impulse is suggested, there is no way of knowing if the therapeutic work unearthed it or if it was, from the child's point of view, justifiable reaction. In preparing the child for therapy, for example, a therapist will be in a position to make more accurate observations if he says "feelings or thoughts that embarrass you may come to your mind. It would be best if we could understand them together rather than just feel bad about them." This is preferable to "if you get mad at me, you should tell me about it, even if it embarrasses you." Unless the child has already had some perception of disturbing, angry thoughts, and has been able to see how he defends himself against awareness and expression of them, the latter statement may act as a seduction of anger rather than a revelation of it.

At this point a question arises that has been one of the most difficult for teachers of psychotherapy to answer. *When* does the therapist make the complete interpretation? Thus far "how to interpret" has answered this question in part. After the defenses have been interfered with, and the second-string substitute defenses have been patiently disposed of, and the affects that this interference occasions in the child have been named, we are ready to address the wishes or convictions that were the prime movers of the conflict. Any of us who have relied on this criterion know that there are times when it guides us well and other times when our interventions are ignored or shouted down by the child. It is very tempting to fall back on stock responses, such as "use your clinical judgment" or "rely on intuitive signals," but a couple of suggestions may add a bit to these stock answers.

In the context of the overall flow of the clinical process, the therapist will note that when the child is struggling with persistent anxiety or a recurring troubling thought, he will signal this by returning repeatedly to a comment or a pattern of play that signifies the anxiety or thought content. For example, if a child pretends that a car is an ambulance in one session, a fire truck racing to extinguish a blaze in the next, and a police car rushing to save a victim in the next hour, the therapist can assume the child is playing out a rescue fantasy or alerting him to a perception of danger. It may take a while to see a theme in play or in associations, but by the time a repetitive theme is detected, an intervention is called for. Repetition of clinical material is therefore one indicator for interpretive action.

Another clinical cue that seems valid in a variety of clinical situations is the child's actual physical posture and activity in relationship to the therapist. Two examples of this are typical. The first occurs when a child while performing an act or making a statement, darts several quick, intense glances at the therapist. Anxiety or expectation are clearly communicated by the glances, and the therapist can be sure that the child is expecting a response.

The second example usually occurs when the therapist starts to make a comment. As he begins to speak, the therapist can literally see the child withdraw his attention from his play or perusal of the physical surroundings, and rivet it on the therapist. This can happen suddenly or gradually while the therapist is speaking. Either way the little one's attention becomes fixed, his gaze is unwavering, with eyes alert and expectant, the expression is solemn, and the little body seems to fill the therapist's entire field of vision. At this moment both the therapist and patient are ready to exchange something of great conceptual importance. It is that instant of time that Winnicott (1971) called the "sacred moment" (pp. 4–5) and is of great significance even for the very young patient. Neither of the clinical cues mentioned here are foolproof, of course, nor are they exhibited by every child, but they are frequent enough and clear enough to be recognizable when they appear. If they do not appear, the therapist can be fairly certain that as the dialogue deepens the child will teach him the signs and signals that indicate that he is ready for further exploration, or for a clarification or an interpretation to be made.

Tami, the child mentioned in chapter 11, who had lost her mother, played out a dollhouse scene in which the child denied that the mother was gone. She mentioned the doll mother repeatedly and pointedly, occasionally glancing at the therapist.

Therapist: "I know now why you want to pretend that your mother is still alive."
Tami: Rising from her play on the floor and staring fixedly and solemnly at the therapist.
Therapist: "You want to pretend that your mother is still alive because you're afraid that it will hurt you too much to say that she's dead."
Tami: Still looking intently at the therapist. "I want her to stay alive."
Therapist: With heartfelt sadness. "I know you do."
Tami: "When I go up there (pointing to heaven) I'm going to miss you."

The intense, direct stare of Tami suggested to the therapist that he could proceed to interfere with her denial.

WORKING THROUGH

Children who are being treated in psychoanalytically oriented psychotherapy, like adults and children engaged in psychoanalysis must have the time and life space to work through an intervention in order for it to be effective. Working through is a concept Freud introduced (Freud, 1914) based on clinical observations made while analyzing his patients. It consists of a number of operations that the patient undertakes on his own after he has cognitively understood and affectively resonated to an intervention made by his therapist. The patient begins to work through an interpretation by seeking to apply or extend the theme of the intervention to situations in his daily life. As Anna Freud points out (Sandler, Kennedy, and Tyson, 1980) in undertaking this, the patient also consolidates the various segments of the interpretation which took place over weeks and months. At the same time these segments of interpretation, which were first perceived by the patient as a thought imposed from the outside, begin to be integrated into their inner perception of themselves. It is as if they were saying, "This is *me* we're talking about." Gradually, as the extension of meaning, consolidation, and integration of the interpretation takes place the patient masters the anxiety of the conflict to which the intervention was directed. When the anxiety is mastered, new choices of the way impulses, wishes, convictions, or fears are managed become available to the patient. Thus, the old ways no longer need to be repudiated, abhorred, or struggled against. They simply become indifferent or ineffective as coercive forces in determining behaviors or affects. When the working through process can be viewed, it is the most convincing evidence available that interpretation is the specific agent of change in conflict reducing psychotherapy.

The process of working through can take place either in relationship to the therapist in the treatment hours following the interpretation, or it may be lived out by the child in his daily life with parents, friends, and teachers. Frequently, it occurs in both settings and the extratherapeutic events are reported by the child or the adults in the environment.

Typically, at the beginning of the working through period, the child will repeat the behavior or experience the affects that characterized the conflicts prior to the interpretation. *After* the episode he will remember the interpretation. As the working through process continues, he will begin to recall the interpretation, and will modify the behavior or buffer the affects even as they occur. As more time passes, awareness of the interpretation, which has become the child's own now rather than being experienced as the external voice of the therapist, anticipates behavior or affects and helps to free the child from their grip.

Randy, of chapter 11 and the "world come before me" feelings, misbehaved in school because he was convinced that his teacher disliked and depreciated him when she attended to other students. As he began to work through his hunger for exclusive attention, he needed to be reminded repeatedly by the therapist after misbehaving that he had acted as if he had been purposely offended. Gradually, he himself would report that he had forgotten his vulnerability until after he had become angry. One day he proudly reported that he stopped his own expression of anger even as he experienced it by telling himself that the teacher "had to help the dumber kids." After he and the therapist struggled with this new defense he was able to anticipate his anger when his demands for attention were frustrated, and finally the demand itself began to disappear and the conflict became incapable of disturbing him.

The process of working through provides the patient with an experience that no other form of therapy can offer. In working through, the regulation of behavior and affects no longer needs to come from outside the patient. It can now come from within and serve the patient in addressing new challenges in growth and development.

Once more let me mention here that with some children after an interpretation has made it possible to work through a conflict, it may be necessary to reestablish or strengthen the therapeutic alliance before the next conflict may be tackled. While this may be true with adults too, it has seemed to me that it needs to be done more frequently with children. It is almost as if the child cannot make the abstractions necessary to convince himself that the principles involved in solving one problem will be used in addressing the next one.

ASSESSING THE EFFICACY OF AN INTERPRETATION

The therapist needs to know, of course, whether the interpretations that are made have had a beneficial effect or not. This is not only for the benefit of the child and to gauge the progress of treatment. It is also to help the therapist maintain optimism and enthusiasm in cases that can sometimes be tedious and draining. There are times when the child is so open and communicative that there is little trouble in seeing the effects of an intervention. Many other times, however, evaluation of the accuracy and efficacy of an interpretation must be based on subsequent clinical signs.

1. Evidence of attempts to work through a conflict, of course, confirms that an interpretation was on target.

2. Diminution of anxiety as reflected in the child's play, associations, or daily habits such as sleeping or eating patterns, indicates that the interpretation was at least on the right track.

3. Revelation of a deeper conflict, which was hidden by the conflict most recently resolved, indicates that an interpretation was effective.

> When Randy, mentioned above, could see that he was misinterpreting his teacher's interest in other children as depreciation he could begin to explore his pain and anger at his parents, whom he felt preferred his sister to him. The whole compromise formation which involved his teacher thus could be considered only the defensive component of a deeper conflict in which the cast of characters involved his parents.

This new conflict then takes its place in the cycles spoken of earlier in the chapter, or may drop out of the cycle completely thus shortening its duration and complexity.

4. The disappearance of symptoms *may* be a sign that an interpretation has shifted the forces acting on a youngster. This sign must be addressed cautiously because people may give up symptoms for a number of reasons that have little to do with the interpretation. They may do so because attention begins to be paid to them and not their symptoms, or because the symptom no longer produces the unconsciously desired psychologic effect. They may give up a symptom because they have been deconditioned, or knowledge acquired elsewhere has helped them master the conflict the symptom represented. Sometimes children give up their symptoms because they are fond of their therapist and empathic with him. It is when the child demonstrates that the interpretation offered in the therapy was actively used to master an unwelcomed symptom that this sign can be used with confidence.

5. An interpretation can sometimes be confirmed by a new activity that the child undertakes, or by a burst of enthusiasm for an activity already in his repertoire.

> When Howie, age eight, began treatment, he was

apathetic about all of the activities organized by his
family or his school. As his competitiveness and fear
of not being the best in everything that he did began
to show itself, the therapist could demonstrate to him
that he deprived himself of enjoyable family activities
for fear of not being as competent at everything as his
older brother. That year he became an enthusiastic
weekend skier, a sport enjoyed by his whole family.

This criterion frequently confirms Freud's (1914) point
that much of what is bound in conflict would be of use in daily
life if free (p. 152).

In addition to these criteria, there are other signs that may
signal the therapist that an interpretation has found its mark.
The child's comfort during the hour, exuberance, more expressive freedom, humor, and the therapist's own sense of en-
joyment of transactions with the child are valid clues.

WHEN NOT TO INTERPRET

As mentioned before, there are times when we find ourselves attempting to interpret anything that comes into the
hour. Usually when I have found this in myself or in supervisory
work, there is a countertransference operating, or some other
state, such as fatigue or chagrin that is eroding therapeutic
sensitivity. Sometimes this has to do with feeling a sense of
urgency in relieving a child's symptoms or rendering a service
to the child's parents or his school system. Sometimes it comes
from frustration at not understanding the clinical material.
Whenever this tendency appears, scrutiny of the therapist's attitudes is indicated.

This tendency to interpret too much is frequently accompanied by a feeling of working very hard. In these instances the
therapist needs to review the therapeutic process as well as his
own states. While constant work and vigilance may be indicated
in therapy, the work should usually be accompanied by a feeling
of relative comfort. Sometimes scrutiny reveals that the problem
arises from an error in therapeutic planning. For example, the

therapist may find that he is trying to treat a child in an outpatient setting when day treatment or inpatient treatment are
more indicated. At another time the therapist might find that
perhaps one or both parents needed more therapeutic attention. Bombardments with interpretations do little to alleviate
impasses such as these.

When conversely, the therapist finds that interpretive flur-
ries serve to counter some unwelcome attitude or state in himself, some self-analysis is in order. If, for example, I find myself
fighting boredom with a flurry of interventions, I can usually
trace my boredom to concern about not understanding some
aspect of the material the child brings to the hour. If, on the
other hand, I find myself becoming sleepy during the hour, I
can usually trace my somnolence to irritation toward the child
that I feel is unjustified. I have on occasion found myself reacting to both states with bursts of interpretive activity that were
more in the service of my concerns than those of the child.

In addition to these examples of therapeutic hyperactivity
due to a mistake in treatment planning or to some internal
malaise in the therapist, there are instances when *as a rule of
thumb* interpretations should not be made.

1. By and large, the child's positive feelings for the therapist should be accepted as expectable unless they clearly cause
conflict, embarrassment, or inhibition in the child. Then it is
the conflict, embarrassment, or inhibition that is the focus of
the comment and not the affection.

2. When the child is suffering great pain or intense affects,
interpretations are best delayed.

> Greg was a nine-year-old boy whose treatment was
> largely involved with his anger and resentment of his
> father. During the treatment his father died suddenly
> of a myocardial infarction. Greg was devastated. In his
> next session, following the father's funeral, his grief
> showed itself first in tears, and then as he sat stony-
> faced, and stared into space without saying anything
> else. The well-intentioned, but misguided therapist
> told him that his father's death had had such a pro-

found effect on him because he thought he had caused it with his anger. In supervision, the therapist revealed that he didn't know what to say to the child about the father's death. His supervisor asked what he would have said had the child not been in therapy. The therapist then saw that his own anxiety, which he tried to master with interpretive vigor, had interfered with a more natural, compassionate reaction to the child.

The process of psychotherapy counts on an element of human relatedness as an ingredient, but psychotherapy cannot be substituted for the ability to relate. In moments of great pain, the little patient needs someone to care about his pain, not to interpret.

3. My own conviction is that conflicts regarding a stage of development that the child is just entering should be left uninterpreted, unless the child specifically asks for advice about them, or is clearly troubled by them. I'm sure a number of excellent therapists would argue convincingly against this statement, stating that the act of relieving a child's conflicts or current stresses helps the child to develop confidence in the process, and frees energy for the more arduous work of addressing more fixed conflicts. While accepting these points, I feel that to interpret to the child, who is in the midst of trying out his own solutions to a developmental conflict, may interfere with his own creativity. To be able to solve a developmental problem creatively provides the child with confidence and a precious quantity of self-esteem. If the child can acquire it unaided, all the better. Should the developmental conflicts bring the child to a solution that is maladaptive and relatively fixed, the therapist can intervene at that time.

In the course of a treatment the child therapist may find that certain social or intellectual skills which the child should have developed were arrested or distorted by earlier conflicts. Reeducation or teaching is required rather than interpretation to remediate these problems. Generally, the therapist should work to address the conflicts that produced the deficit rather than try to provide remediation for the deficit. When the conflict is resolved, either the parents, the school system, or a special education effort will usually bring the child up to developmental potential. To attempt to remediate while a conflict still exists may place the child in a position to fail again. Many of the children we treat have already had too much experience in failure.

In summary then, the middle phase of therapy is a time of recognizing and analyzing unconscious, repetitive themes and trends that coerce the child, diminish his choices, and impede development. As these are scrutinized, child and therapist find the essentially human, understandable reason for their repetitive quality, and these reasons are summarized by the therapist in terms that are understandable and specific for the unique and resonant little human being that stands before him. In this phase, as in the other phases, not everything the child says or does is accepted or excused. But nothing that he says or does is willingly excluded from the therapy or from understanding. When understanding comes, the need to excuse disappears.

CHAPTER 13

Termination of Treatment

Therapeutic termination of a child's psychotherapy is a victory for child and therapist that comes with delicate tones of regret mixed with the flush of achievement. Both have come to recognize that the child can use the hours in more productive ways. He can be getting on with the priceless process of living with actual rather than fantasied gratifications; with a sense of pride in accomplishment and development accompanied by inner convictions of his own worth even as he enjoys the recognition of others; with a feeling of exuberance about his actual existence that renders daydreaming a pleasant, optional interlude rather than a necessary refuge from unhappiness.

This refers to those therapeutic terminations that are, unfortunately, too infrequent in actual practice. In fact, it appears that whether one practices in an institution or a private practice, whether one is in training or has completed one's formal education, unilateral decisions to terminate treatment made either by the therapist or by the patient far outnumber genuine shared decisions that treatment is no longer necessary. Novick, Benson, and Rembar (1981) present evidence that a figure of 85 percent comes closer to reflecting the true percentage of unilateral terminations than the lower range of from 28 percent that Ross and Lacey (1961) cite to the 71 percent given by Tuckman and Lavel (1959). These figures demand that some space be devoted here to this type of termination. Management and therapeutic posture in both premature and therapeutic terminations will be addressed.

PREMATURE TERMINATIONS

Simplistically, the causes of a premature termination are to be found in a motive or an error of the therapist, in the wish or resistance of a child or his family, or in circumstances that are outside of the therapy. I label this a simplistic concept because more often there are subtle interplays of feedback loops between patient, therapist, and environment that contribute to cycles of causality causing termination rather than one direct, sufficient cause.

A nine-year-old boy, who had been labeled hyperactive for years, had been in treatment about six months. The treatment was abruptly terminated by the child's mother ostensibly because he was not improving. As the therapist discussed the case with a senior colleague in an effort to understand what had led to the sudden interruption, evidence began to emerge that the mother, a psychologist, married to a pediatrician had competitive and angry feelings toward males in general and physicians in particular. (Her father had been a physician.) She had virtually demanded that the therapist confine himself to administering medication for hyperactivity and leave psychological matters aside. He had refused to do so and an impasse was created that was resolved by termination of therapy. Had the inquiry stopped here, the explanation for the termination would have been clear, simple, linear, and wrong. The therapist felt that there was more to be explored, and his discussion revealed plenty of competitive feelings of his own toward psychologists, and the child's mother was no exception. The child had become an "old pro" at playing off the mother psychologist against the quietly stubborn and denigrating father physician. It was an easy step to use the same maneuvers to play off the therapist against the mother. The father could maintain his posture of sitting back, and deriding all three of the combatants, and the result was a more complicated impasse than had been first perceived.

This is an example of how a number of conditions conspired to create the ultimate cause of the nontherapeutic termination. The interplay of these conditions defies our efforts to compartmentalize a cause into one category or the other. Further subtlety of the causes of termination is described as Novick (1982) calls attention to the possibility that a termination may be made unilaterally by therapist or patient, and then forced on the other members of the team so that it appears to be a mutual decision when in reality it represents compliance or collusion. Despite these caveats, an attempt to classify the causes may help organize therapeutic thinking in cases of unilateral terminations.

TERMINATIONS INITIATED BY THE THERAPIST

The first ones to be considered are those situations in which a therapist-in-training must terminate because he is graduating or leaving the area. There are a number of complications that plague these terminations. Because he was in training, the therapist may have been relatively inexperienced, and the pace of progress may have been slower than usual. (In fairness to young therapists, it must be said here that this is certainly not a given. There are many therapists in training who are doing work which compares favorably with that of seasoned colleagues.) Due to the pace the child may, therefore, be on his second or even third transfer. The impatience or hurt of the child and his family and the guilt of the therapist in these cases may complicate the termination markedly.

In training centers it is not infrequent to see a higher percentage of the population from less affluent socioeconomic groups. In some instances these groups come to us with the burden of social problems as well as the chronic problem of poverty. When a transfer is necessary, it is more difficult to place a child with another therapist if the family is beset by multiple problems, and cannot afford the fees of therapists in private practice. Here the therapist's frustration in finding a replacement for his patient renders the termination period more difficult. I do not know of a training institution that has been completely successful in solving this problem for their patient population. In some places there is an unspoken policy that after a child has terminated treatment with a person in training, who must move on, a staff or faculty therapist assumes the responsibility for further treatment of the child. In other places, the case is reviewed in a termination conference, and if the child has suffered unduly from separations in the course of his life prior to treatment, special efforts are made to place him in treatment with a staff member who is thought to be less likely to move than a person in training.

Whatever the institutional policies there are considerations that the departing therapist should address in managing the termination. Ideally, the child and the family should have known how long the therapist was going to be in his present position. If this were not possible for some reason, or if the therapist has the impression the child did not recall or was not able to conceptualize the time that the therapist was due to leave, the child should be told of the impending departure enough ahead of time to permit him to react and to grieve. How much time is "enough time?" In many instances most people have found six to eight weeks to be adequate time. I would suggest, however, that this figure be used only when there are no clinical cues to suggest another period. With close scrutiny of the clinical material the therapist may find that the child has a particular way by which he organizes his orientation to time that does not rely on a calendar. Sometimes he thinks of time in relationship to recurring events in his life. "When school is out," or "right after my birthday," or "when summer comes" is more meaningful cognitively and affectively than a date and month. At other times the therapist knows the child is capable of understanding the concept of months and weeks, but any period of more than a month or so loses its significance to the child. The "end of June" may have to be reified with "when you finish the third grade." With children younger than seven or eight it may be useful to have a calendar in which the days can be counted and marked.

Sandler, Kennedy, and Tyson (1980) suggest that whenever possible children in analysis should be transferred from a less experienced therapist to one more experienced (p. 32). They also suggest that the transfer or termination is best made during a natural break like a vacation or a trip that child or therapist must take.

Anna Freud (1970), according to these same authors, offers the suggestion that the therapist be ready to consider a termination rather than a transfer to another therapist. The reason for this is that frequently we underestimate the gains that the child has made, and the amount of work that the child can, with the help of the environment, do on his own. Certainly, when the therapist has ascertained that the child and those who surround him are sensitive to psychological dysfunction and responsible in their wishes to alleviate it, he can suggest that an interruption be tried, and then offer the child and family the names of people they can contact if they feel a resumption of therapy is indicated.

A possible countertransference, of which the terminating therapist should be aware, is signaled when he considers the available therapists in his clinic or community, and finds that he deems none suitable to continue treatment with his patient. This one may be too directive, the other may be too passive, and still another may be too "analytic." To be sure, there may be some settings where there are no competent therapists for the case being transferred, but in so concluding the child's therapist must be sure that he is not looking for an ideal that can never be met. He must have scrutinized carefully that his caring investment in the child has not imperceptibly changed into a parental possessiveness that is unconsciously saying, "no one can be as good a parent to this child as I am." A therapist that terminates for reasons of his own is particularly vulnerable to countertransference reactions. He may feel guilt about leaving the child (especially if the child has been difficult to treat), and may be compensating with undue feelings of responsibility. If the therapist has been in training the child patient may have been among the first children he has treated, and therefore occupies a special place in his caseload. The therapist may through inexperience be harboring an unconscious illusion that therapy was to have made the child "perfect," and feel an unspoken compulsion to make the illusion a reality. When the therapist is leaving the community, he is then also leaving behind friends, teachers, and even a phase of his life. His own grief may make him so vulnerable to the child's grief that he seeks an ideal object to replace him. Finally, I would mention that some of our willingness to care for other human beings who are helpless comes from the sublimation of identifications with a parental image formed at a time in our life when we thought them to be omnipotent and omniscient. If the situation we are in is stressful enough to cause regression, we may unconsciously operate as if only an omniscient and omnipotent therapist can replace us.

PREMATURE TERMINATIONS CAUSED BY CONDITIONS IN THE CHILD

One of the most frequent reasons for premature terminations initiated by the child is his unwillingness or inability to tolerate interference with his defenses. In older children this may manifest itself in acting out or acting up to the extent that treatment must be discontinued. In younger children the child directs his persuasive powers toward parents and therapist, and is sometimes successful. With older children who act out or act up, the therapist can be put in a position to be helpless. As the child approaches adolescence, acting out can become dangerous, and when this happens the therapist is obliged to decide if the treatment should continue with the child in an environment equipped to protect the child from physical or social harm, or if the best course is to interrupt the psychotherapy in favor of another mode of intervention.

With the younger child the therapist may wish to weigh the possibility that affording the child an interruption when an impasse has truly been reached, may allow the child to return to treatment with his own motivation restored, and above all the security that the therapist will not ask the child to tolerate more pain than he can bear. This, of course, must be weighed against the severity of the child's problems, the symptoms, and the urgency of treatment.

A second, but relatively infrequent reason for discontinuing treatment originates with the child. This is the instance in which psychological decompensation occurs.

Myra had started treatment when she was twelve because she had become forgetful, somewhat slovenly in her schoolwork, and occasionally silly or inane with her peers and at home. After an initial period of several weeks of apparent improvement, she began to show further slow deterioration of her personal habits and hygiene, schoolwork, and relatedness. Despite the therapist's increased efforts and availability, the downhill course continued. When finally the therapist began to suspect an organic process, he requested a neurological consultation. This revealed that the child was suffering from subacute sclerosing panencephalitis. The feasible and well-documented psychodynamic reasons that were formulated during the diagnostic evaluation did not exclude or prevent the slow virus from devastating her brain. In this case the therapist discontinued the formal therapy, but stayed in regular contact with the family and with Myra until she died.

Todd, a fourteen-year-old boy was in treatment because he appeared depressed and withdrawn, and had begun to behave irritably at home and in school. About six weeks after he had begun treatment, he left home late one evening without telling anyone, and was found the next day wandering along a highway miles away. When his therapist could see him, he learned that Todd was on his way to a town (which was actually in the direction opposite to the one in which he was headed) to buy a gun to "defend myself against the people who are putting too much pressure on me." More inquiry revealed that Todd was developing a dangerous delusional system and felt he was in harm's way from every direction. Treatment had to be interrupted to refer him for inpatient care for a period of time.

In both of these situations there had been either a misdiagnosis to begin with or a disease process that manifested itself after the treatment had begun. The treatment, as it was being conducted, had to be interrupted for more appropriate measures to be taken. In Todd's case the therapist acknowledged feeling guilty and defensive. The important point, however, is that the therapist did not permit his guilt and feeling of vulnerability to interfere with prompt acknowledgment that the treatment plan he was using was not an appropriate one. In cases of more subtle manifestations of the pathology, a therapist's unwillingness to acknowledge this for defensive reasons can delay appropriate treatment, and even allow dangerous situations to develop.

An obvious but nonetheless important principle that child therapists must carry with them in all therapeutic endeavors is that they are involved with a developing organism in whom both health and pathological changes occur with astonishing rapidity. A therapist cannot commit himself so firmly to preserving treatment that he is unresponsive to changes in the child.

There are times when what the child needs cannot be supplied by the therapist, and although the child is suffering from psychopathology, this cannot be addressed until more basic needs are met.

In the third month of treatment for school refusal,

seven-year-old Paul's father was killed in an accident. The family, which had numerous problems even before the father's death, now began to disintegrate. The mother had to take her family to live with her own mother, who was also helping to care for two of her other daughters and their families. The chaos in the maternal grandmother's home was incredible. Paul did not know from one day to the next whether or not he would be sleeping in the same bed or eating at the same table. Therapy hours were frequently missed, and the therapist felt that continuity was all but destroyed. At this point the therapist stopped attempting to reduce conflict through insight with Paul, and began to support his coping and adaptive efforts whenever he could. He also began working directly with the Department of Welfare and with Paul's mother to improve Paul's living conditions. It took the better part of a year with several agencies working together before Paul was provided with what the therapist could not provide—a stable, predictable living environment. It was then that the child had the serenity to turn his gaze inward and look at his anxiety, conflict, and psychological pain. At this time the therapist reviewed the situation to see if after having been so active in changing Paul's life in reality, he could return to being a person with whom Paul could discuss painful issues without fearing social consequences.

In this instance the therapist interrupted the process by which he attempted to make himself an ideal recipient of transferences. He did not, however, interrupt his availability as a useful, real person to Paul. Interruption of treatment (or a treatment modality) is not synonymous with interrupting the relationship.

TERMINATIONS DUE TO ENVIRONMENTAL CIRCUMSTANCES

Young families move more often than older, more settled families, and since our patient population comes from younger families, the need to terminate treatment due to a family move is not infrequent. The management of this situation varies with the stage of treatment at the time the move is contemplated, of course. The one rule of thumb that I would offer here is that the therapist address the question of the move *actively*, and not passively accept as inevitable the conditions of the move, as proposed by the family.

The therapist should meet with the child's parents to hear the reason for the move, and how the need for the move is perceived by both of them. He should learn how much the child knows about the move, and not be surprised to find later in talking to the child that the child knows a great deal more than the parents assumed. The inevitability of the proposed move and the ways the parents propose to carry out the move should be weighed and examined in the context of the stage of treatment and the possible importance of the timing of the termination. The therapist may wish to agree with the parent's proposed termination date, or ask them to consider delaying it, or perhaps make it earlier. If, for example, the family must move on September 1st, and the therapist or the child were to have planned a vacation in July, the therapist may deem it wise to suggest that the termination date be set on the last session in June, rather than see the child for several sessions in August after a month's interruption. If an additional month or two is thought to be essential to a therapeutic gain, it is perfectly legitimate to ask the family to consider postponing a proposed relocation for that period. If a problem was sufficiently important to be treated, it is sufficiently important to be considered when the family is organizing their plans. To fail to do so may prejudice the decision to procure further help for the child in his new location, should he need it.

Other parental reasons for terminating may present a more difficult management problem. There are times when parental guilt, resistance to a change they may have to make, an unconscious wish they harbor for or against the child, may be the underlying cause which seeks a manifest reason in such issues as the cost of treatment being too high, or that they see no improvement in the child, and they may even fear that he is getting worse. The therapist should try to avoid an adversary posture in these instances. Most often direct argument does little good, no matter how convincing the therapist may be. It sometimes becomes virtually impossible to maintain a working relationship with the parents at this time because they may have regressed to an adolescent adaptive mode, and seek to free themselves from the relationship with the therapist through strife and rebellion. If it is at all possible, the therapist can take the position that whether to terminate the child's treatment or not is, of course, up to them, but they may wish to meet a couple of times with the therapist to make sure that they have thought the issue through as thoroughly as possible. If the therapist is successful in getting the parents to meet with him or with a colleague, a good bet is that the child will be allowed to continue.

A particular variation of resistance to treatment are those instances in which parents and school personnel unconsciously collude for one reason or another to make coming to the treatment hours difficult for the child. In these cases the therapist must review his management of the case to see if through negligence or insensitivity he may have ignored some concern the school might have. If the therapist has any reason to believe that he has been less than circumspect in appreciating the school's wish to be included in managing the child's difficulties, he would do well to contact them with the permission of the child and parents. Even if he feels that he has included the school as much as possible, a call or visit with the teacher may salvage the situation.

Other environmental reasons that are responsible for premature termination of child cases are the reduction of child services, the closure of clinics where children are treated, and other examples of our culture's unwillingness to make the commitment it takes to support the welfare of those we profess to love so much. The only thing that can be suggested about this unfortunate state of affairs is to be prepared for it.

In all of these situations of premature terminations there are a number of measures the therapist can take to minimize

the possible adverse effects of the termination, and to solidify
the benefits that the child may have already received from the
treatment. Before all else, the therapist should remember that
more psychotherapy is a distinct possibility in the future for
these youngsters. Some of them may have to wait until they are
young adults to procure it on their own, but at whatever age
that they may make another treatment endeavor, the management of the current termination can influence their willingness
to try again. To try to leave children and parents optimistic that
there is help to be found in psychotherapy if they feel they
need it in the future, is no mean accomplishment.

In those cases in which a new therapist must be found, the
terminating therapist can be helpful in offering suggestions
about who is available and competent in his place or in the new
locale if the family is moving. If it is the therapist who is moving,
it is sometimes helpful to introduce the child to the person who
will be the new therapist. Besides allaying some of the child's
anxiety about a transfer, his seeing his present therapist relate
in a cordial and collegial manner to his new therapist offers
him a sense of comfort and a shared positive predisposition.
Even if the termination is accompanied by negative and hostile
feelings on the part of the child and family, an active attempt
to demonstrate that the therapist would maintain a benevolent
and helpful attitude in any future encounter would be valuable
to the family. Sadness, guilt, irritation, and even petulance may
plague the therapist in a premature termination. To acknowledge these feelings is necessary; to indulge them is regrettable.

THERAPEUTIC TERMINATIONS

Despite the sobering and disappointing statistics on the
frequency of nontherapeutic terminations, the therapist con-
ducts each child's therapy with the hope that there will be a
therapeutic ending to the relationship with the child. And if
this comes to pass, there are some techniques devised to max-
imize and consolidate the benefits of the treatment. It is useful
here, however, to recall the admonition of Anna Freud, quoted

by Sandler, et al. (1980), when she said that the analyst often foresees some of the dangers and difficulties of the child's next developmental phase. "If the aim of child analysis is to promote normal development, then the aim is fulfilled when the previously held up development proceeds again. Otherwise an analyst would not want to terminate analysis with any child" (p. 243). Wallace (1983) in describing termination of psychotherapy with adults, also touches on this in saying, "you will never be involved in a totally satisfactory one" (p. 314). There are so many benevolent, but unrealistic wishes involved in wanting a "perfect" termination that a whole chapter could be devoted to this segment alone. Despite our unconscious wishes to immunize the child against conflict forever, the desire that our psychotherapeutic tools be universally and unequivocally effective, and that we be omnipotent in erasing all pathology, past and future, there are times when we can be convinced that therapist and patient have achieved enough to permit the child to take over his own regulation and development again. As in the case of interpretation, the question of *when* to terminate becomes central.

The cues indicating that it is time to think of termination come from two main sources, the therapist and the child. Surely, there will be reports from parents and teachers that are to be considered, but it behooves the therapist to recall that the environment often wants the child to be good, while the therapist is attempting to judge if he is well. Also, the child may have improved greatly in interpersonal transactions, and yet still suffer from painful affective states or frightening subjective convictions that he will express to no one but his therapist.

One of the most pleasant indicators that termination is approaching is the therapist's observation that he is beginning to be more fond of the child (or becoming fond of the child if he did not particularly like him at the start of treatment). To be certain that this is not simply a shift in the subjective state of the therapist, he should scrutinize this fondness to see if he can discern what has become appealing about his patient. If treatment has indeed led to a therapeutic termination, the therapist can see this increase in fondness is predicated on a number of new qualities in the child.

1. The child has become more interesting to the therapist. This is because the sphere of the child's own interest has expanded. He is no longer so preoccupied with his anxiety or the avoidance of it that he ignores the rest of the world.
2. The therapist feels better liked than before because having resolved ambivalences the child's affection springs more spontaneously from attachment rather than loneliness or fear.
3. The therapist feels less need to support. This is because the child is more secure since his trust has not been betrayed and he has been respected.
4. The therapist feels less responsible for "carrying" the relationship because the child is more spontaneous. Neither trust nor affection have been demanded of him, but have been earned by the therapist. The spontaneity has grown from the child's initiative and the therapist's availability.
5. The therapist has come to feel special to the child. The child shows his respect for intimacy and eschews promiscuity. Therapist and child have shared intimate moments productively and with dignity.

These are but a few of the qualities by which a child, freed from internal oppression, lets us know that he has reestablished his ability to relate productively to others. Sometimes other qualities like these appear, and can be traced to treatment. At other times, only one or two of these traits strike us.

Another reaction of the therapist that can be a harbinger of termination is his expectation that he will discuss a problem with the child, rather than have to demonstrate that a problem exists. This indicates that defenses have become fluid, and the therapist is involved in mopping-up operations rather than assaulting the bunkers behind which problems are entrenched.

Finally, when the therapist awaits the child's hour with the pleasant, expectant feeling tone that he experiences when expecting a friend, rather than the feeling of having to mobilize his resources to confront a problem, the therapy is beginning to end.

It is a poignant quality of child therapeutic practice that as the child begins to be a bright spot in our caseload, we must think of giving him up so that he may be enjoyed by others.

As the therapist notes these internal reactions, the child begins to evidence observable traits.

1. The child begins to show a definite and recognizable sense of self. When this was absent or muted at the start of therapy and begins to appear, the contrast is remarkable. At the beginning of treatment when the child said "I," the therapist was not quite sure if the child were expressing his own attitude or wish or reflecting that of someone else. The child with a firm sense of self leaves us no doubt about who is speaking when he says "I."

2. The ability to contemplate a variety of ways to respond or adapt to the demands of the environment may be termed *plasticity*. In the place of rigid, repetitive modes of responding to environmental demands which touched on the child's vulnerabilities, the therapist can see plasticity begin to afford the child options and alternatives.

3. When freedom from symptoms can be linked to evidence of the working through process, it is a reliable sign that termination can be contemplated. Without evidence of working through, the disappearance of symptoms is not a reliable sign that there has been a change in internal organization. Children, like adults sometimes exhibit a return of some symptoms during the termination period. The return of the symptoms in this period, however, is with concomitant insight and much less fear. The cycles of reactions and adaptation to symptoms reviewed in chapter 12 are much more brief, sometimes taking place in one session. These too are accompanied by insight.

4. Age appropriateness begins to be a clear commitment that the child makes when he is ready to terminate. He begins to relate to peers of his age, play games that are appropriate for his age, and seeks entertainment that is age appropriate. It is not that the child is afraid or ashamed to regress. In fact,

regression is available to him for the sake of fun or when relating to younger children or in the service of treatment. But now the child *utilizes* regression, and is not the victim of it.

5. As the treatment nears its end, the therapist can indulge in some laziness because the child will often undertake to associate, observe, and conclude something about himself on his own. One can see in overt or disguised form the child identifying with the process of psychotherapy. This identification may have started as a defensive or competitive attempt to reach a conclusion before the therapist. Now it becomes a talent for the child. This identification is different from identifying with a trait of the therapist, and is more like that described by Kris (1956) in his paper on the vicissitudes of insight (p. 453).

6. Children, who saw all of their ills coming from the hostility or insensitivity of the environment, begin to lose interest in grievance collecting as their treatment progresses. This is not only due to a reduction of conflict. It is also because as anxiety decreases they invest the environment with more positive expectations of pleasure. The environment usually responds.

7. While there may be a mild recrudescence of transferences during the terminal phase of treatment, the child becomes aware that "old feelings" or "old thoughts" are disturbing his serenity when they occur, and can often reevoke the insights he used to resolve conflict as well as the method by which he could reestablish harmony with his world.

8. As illustrated by the case of Howie (chapter 12) who began to enjoy skiing with his family after resolving his competitive conflicts, children often show a new interest in topics and activities. Their "love affair with the world" increases or is reborn.

These are but some of the more frequent ways by which the time for termination announces itself. Since each child is unique, the therapist ultimately needs to count on his ability to understand the individual child and the significance of his communications to perceive the message that he wishes to stop.

Having decided that termination is indicated, the therapist must now turn to the process of terminating. This topic must be introduced with what Glover (1955) said about the termination process in adult psychoanalysis. He maintained that the analysis went on until the very last moment of the very last hour (p. 164). The psychotherapy of the child continues throughout the termination phase. Time out for leave taking, indulging that from which the child had previously abstained, "unbending," self-revelation of the therapist, and other departures from neutrality, inquiry, understanding, and interpretation by the therapist when indulged without understanding the significance of the activity may undo some of the benefits the child has won from the treatment process. Of course, the therapist has been a "real person" to the child, and of course there will be some pain in leaving him. But if in order to make up for this loss, the therapist creates "palship time," or loving periods which can be looked back upon as the child strolls down memory lane, he may miss some important opportunities for insights that may be available due to the process of separating. This does not mean that the termination phase must be characterized by stiffness or rigidity, but only that it must be guided by the same disciplined scrutiny that obtained in the earlier parts of the treatment. This may be a more difficult task in this phase, because the therapist has come to be fond of the child, is experiencing his own sadness or grief at the contemplated separation, and may long to be remembered fondly by the little patient.

When a treatment has progressed satisfactorily, the termination phase will have arrived of its own accord. The recognition that it will occasion the end of regular meetings may be introduced by the therapist or by the child. The child may do this directly and simply by stating that he wishes to come to treatment no more. Or he may indicate this indirectly in his play, stories, or interest in people who leave a safe haven to strike out on their own, for example. Another indirect way that the child communicates readiness or the sense that it is time to terminate is by telling you of the number of activities in which he wishes to participate in his school or neighborhood, and for which he has insufficient time. When the therapist is satisfied that these communications are not a new resistance, he can assume that the child is announcing a legitimate wish to stop treatment.

Tami, the child referred to in chapters 11 and 12, gives us excellent examples of a child who is motivated by resistance in suggesting a termination date, and later expresses a more well-founded and genuine desire to end treatment.

> After one year and two months of treatment, Tami began to express some anger that she had felt toward her depressed mother before the mother's death. This frightened her, and she said that she wanted to stop coming to treatment hours so that she could go to school in September. Although two of the three most prominent symptoms she manifested (hyperactivity and repeated "accidents" in which she hurt herself) had disappeared, the third symptom, isolation and distance from other family members, remained. The following occurred in a session in the first week of September.
>
> Tami: "I just want to come five more times (holding up her hand to indicate 5). That's all, five more times. Then I can go to 'everyday work school.' " (This as opposed to 'not everyday play school' as she called nursery school.)
> Therapist: "Well, maybe we can talk more about this, because it seems to me that there are still some worries that still buzz around in your head once in awhile."
> Tami: "Nope. Nope. I don't got no worries—just five more times."
>
> The rest of the hour was relatively neutral, superficial play that revealed little. (The therapist confined himself to commenting on how hard she worked to stay away from anything that showed her worries.)
>
> The next session, later that week, Tami began by holding up her right hand and announcing that she would come to see the therapist five more times. The

therapist noted that they still needed to think and talk about her progress and her worries.

In the treatment hour of the following week, Tami once more announced that she was going to come to her treatment sessions five more times. Following this announcement, she got down her hands and knees and in a seemingly purposeless manner began crawling over the carpeted floor. She finally found a place in the orlon rug that had been burned and melted into a sharp, jagged fault in the texture. Tami knew this spot on the rug because she had pricked her heel on it once before when she had been barefoot during her hour. Attempts had been made to repair it, which were apparently only partially successful, because when she found the spot again she jammed her hand on it, causing a small puncture wound. With a sad and serious face, she went to the therapist's side and held her injured right hand up for him to see. He told her that the hand that she used to tell him only five more times now told him that she was hurting herself at the thought of not seeing the therapist anymore, like she had hurt herself when she couldn't see her mother anymore. She stopped insisting that she terminate, and work began again.

About six months later Tami's grandmother called to say that the withdrawal and resistances to loving interchanges had all but disappeared. She wondered if Tami could miss a session so that she could take her on a trip to visit relatives in a distant city. On their return, the grandmother reported that Tami seemed her old self again. She was loving and expressive, and sought her grandmother out for all kinds of affectionate interchanges. In her very next session, Tami announced that she wanted to stop treatment, and that she wanted to come just five more times. The therapist asked that her progress and her worries be reviewed, and this was done for several sessions. In the course of the discussions Tami frankly acknowledged she would miss her doctor, but made very realistic provisions for exchanging phone numbers, and procedures by which she could call him. When she started the "five more session countdown," she proceeded in subsequent sessions to announce four, three, two, and finally one. In the last session, she showed her therapist a scrape on her hand, and said that she had fallen down. This was reviewed and discussed by both Tami and the therapist in the context of what had happened when her Mommy died and when she had jabbed herself on the rug.

In these two examples we can contrast the conflicted, ambivalent quality of the first defensive announcement of a wish to terminate, with the more comfortably decisive announcement of the second time. Also, the therapist was aware of the improvement that had occurred from communication from her family, and that her wish to stop occurred after engaging in pleasurable experiences rather than as a refuge from frightening thoughts.

There are other instances in which the therapist may present the idea of termination to the child. If possible this should be presented as an issue to be explored rather than as an edict.

Karl had been in treatment close to two years. He was a ten-year-old when he had started, and had progressed well through fifth and sixth grade. He had done well in his therapy, and was deeply involved in the academic and social activities of his seventh grade class. Music lessons and the school band rounded out a very busy schedule. During an hour in which he was telling about his activities with relish, he said that he really wanted to attend a karate class but could not due to his schedule.

Therapist: "I guess if you really want to learn karate you're going to have to give up one of your other activities."

Karl: "Yeah, but what? They really need me on the school paper, and I'm just getting into the good part in photography. And I really like the band."
Therapist: "Anything else that might go?"
Karl: "Well, if I could stop coming here, but would you let me stop?" (Parental coercion had been a central issue that we struggled with in his therapy.)
Therapist: "Have I ever forced you to do anything?"
Karl: "Noooo! But . . . could I stop?"
Therapist: "Do you think we've done enough to understand your problems?"

There followed a review of Karl's functioning at home and at school, and in the next session they were able again to address his tendency to seduce his mother and father into making decisions for him and then feeling coerced, as he was on the verge of doing with the decision about his termination. A date, about two months in the future, was set and termination proceeded once more, working through patterns that had already been explored and that reappeared in this termination phase, briefly, in diluted form.

Following the introduction of a termination date, the therapist is in an optimal position to view how the child now handles relationships, anticipated separations, anxiety, and the array of problems with which he came into treatment.

There are times when parents rather than the child will introduce the notion of terminating treatment. They may have sensed from their child that it is time, or they may simply be tired of paying for psychotherapy. This latter becomes more probable when the child's symptoms have disappeared, or when he is no longer making a nuisance of himself. With the child's knowledge, the therapist should hear the parents out, even if termination talk is premature. If it is not premature, the therapist and parents can devise ways to involve the child in the decision to avoid a situation in which the child has remained passive or feels that the decision has been thrust upon him. In any case, the therapist should avoid the trap of dismissing out of hand the possibility of terminating because neither he nor his patient raised it.

Once the termination date is set, an evaluation is in order regarding whether or not developmental lags due to earlier conflicts have been reduced. If they have not, the therapist may wish to prescribe ways in which these deficiencies can be remediated. An explanation to the parents may be necessary about the need to first reduce the conflict, and then rehabilitate functions through remedial techniques.

As the actual termination date draws near, the therapist may indicate to the child's caretakers, as well as the child, how he can be reached in the future should they wish to contact him. If the therapist is going to leave the area, the parents should probably be given the name of a colleague or a clinic for future reference.

This termination phase should serve to demonstrate to child, parents, and therapist:

1. that the child is regretful, and maybe even sad to leave the therapist, but not depressed;
2. that he is grateful but not obliged or dependent on the therapist for his well-being;
3. that new situations may make him apprehensive, but not immobilized with anxiety;
4. that the parents can accept the child for what he is and not only for the promise of what they want him to become;
5. that the therapist who had become a part of the family system is no longer necessary in order for them to relate to each other productively;
6. that both parents and child understand that although psychotherapy cannot immunize people against future ills, it leaves them in a much better position to resolve their own new conflicts by virtue of the skills they developed in reducing old ones, and should this fail, to recognize which problems are beyond their competency to manage alone.

If the child brings to the treatment situation the experience of having been a child in a family, the therapist brings to it the experience of being a parent or aspiring to be one. In this lies the *natural* component as opposed to the artificiality of the therapeutic process and perhaps one of its pitfalls. It has been mentioned by a number of authors that therapists are sometimes reluctant to give up their patients, and a number of reasons have been given for this tendency.

One reason that is sometimes not clearly recognized is the one mentioned earlier, which was addressed by Anna Freud in describing the therapist's wish to immunize the child against all future conflict. I will close the chapter by citing a father's description of a poignant moment spent with his three-year-old daughter. It touches on the depth of the wish to protect our little ones from "all future harm," and may reveal where the tendency to "hang on" too long originates, at least in some therapists.

> "It was a magnificent spring day and Cathy and I were going to have the better part of it to ourselves because her mother and grandmother were going to be otherwise engaged. Cathy and I were looking for something very special to do. Something just for us. We finally decided that a visit to the Zoo would fit the bill. On the drive there Cathy's attention had moved from contemplating the whole universe to describing the wondrous things she expected to see. As she told me of these expectations, she mentioned that on that day she particularly wanted to pet the tiger. I told her that tigers couldn't be petted because it would be dangerous to do so. She said, 'But I will go aw, aw tiger, and then it will know I like it.' I told her that tigers did not understand being petted, and they were so powerful that they could hurt people without meaning to. Cathy repeated more emphatically that she would say 'Aw, aw tiger' lovingly and accompanied this with gentle pats on my hand to illustrate her benevolence. She was sure that the tiger would understand and welcome her gentleness. I was moved by her conviction

that her love could overcome any aggression, but persisted in my efforts to convince her that tigers had different social standards than we.

At the Zoo Cathy's desire to make direct contact with the animals was rekindled. Once more during one of our rests, we discussed how ethologically effective 'aw, aw' would be in allaying a tiger's fear or reducing its aggression. After awhile, Cathy, more despairing of my lack of vision than convinced by my arguments, asked to see the green alligators. At that time the Irish Rovers had popularized a song about a unicorn in which there was a line about 'green alligators and long neck geese.' When she went to the reptile building, she was disappointed that the alligators were laying there tranquilly rather than dancing to the lively rhythm of the Irish Rovers' song. Her attention, therefore, turned to the small windows behind which were various snakes. In one there was a snake on a branch that was difficult to see. As I was pointing it out to her, she put her hand on the glass, asking, 'Is that it?' Whether the snake struck at her hand or not, I don't know, but a quick movement brought its head into contact with the glass, and Cathy blanched. With an expression of some fear, but mostly regret and hurt, she asked, 'Why did it do that?' She did not add, 'I meant it no harm,' but I knew she thought it.

Perhaps it was my involvement in her experience or the closeness I felt for my daughter in those hours that accounted for the intensity of what I felt next. Whatever the reason, I was at that moment overwhelmed with my own feelings of regret that a moment's sadness should mar her wonder. In addition, I experienced enormous protectiveness and a wish that I could buffer her from every future disappointment and hurt when she offered her love and experienced aggression or callousness in return. As I held and comforted her on a convenient bench, I realized with some sadness that I could not buffer her from the future. All I could do was to offer the best of my being in the present for her use in the future, and hope that the strength she developed would see her through."

Part V

Clinical Management of Especially Complex Cases

Introduction

While participating in seminars or supervising beginning psychotherapists, certain clinical problems or situations arise repeatedly. In the process of addressing these issues, the clinician begins to develop a style of treatment, or comes to rely on a particular solution as being especially effective. So one reason for this section is to offer some suggestions for clinical management and understanding of especially complex cases that to my knowledge have not been suggested elsewhere. In addition, certain principles of treatment described and recommended by others earlier seem to be easily forgotten. Yet, they are both important and effective when recalled. Some principles of treatment that seem to carry this vulnerability will be reiterated in this section.

The three clinical situations addressed in this section will not be dealt with exhaustively, but only in a way that will permit discussion of the concepts that are being presented. Although limited in focus, I hope that the concepts will be therapeutically useful to the reader when integrated with what is already known about the topics being discussed.

CHAPTER 14

Some Historical and Therapeutic Ideas on Child Abuse and Sexual Abuse

SOME HISTORICAL PERSPECTIVES

After Kempe, Silverman, Steele, Droegemueller, and Silver presented their findings on "The Battered Child Syndrome" (1962), the lay and medical world reacted with a measure of shock and chagrin. In retrospect, this reaction could be considered at best uninformed, and to some degree hypocritical. We can return to the issue of hypocrisy later.

Following the expression of disbelief at the finding that 10 to 15 percent of children under five who come to the emergency room with a physical injury are abused or neglected, our society began looking for culprits. The cries for punishment of the abusing parents and the absence of empathy, understanding, and, above all, curiosity about them made one think that our prime objective at that time was to punish the guilty rather than protect the innocent.

Society has probably not yet been able to fully appreciate the impact of contributions made by Brandt Steele and Carl Pollock (1968) and others who sought to understand the forces at work in the abusing parent. Quite apart from the important, discrete discoveries made by these investigators, the findings were used to demonstrate that causal understanding of the phenomena leading to child abuse brought compassion and a reasoned approach to prevention rather than only retribution toward the abusing parent; retribution that sometimes pained the little victim as much as the abuse that had already occurred. Their findings, presented in the context of understanding individual and public reaction to child abuse, helped to move the attitudes of a nation from outrage and guilt toward postures of inquiry, protection, and prevention.

To return to the issue of hypocrisy, one must say first that even a cursory glance at history makes society's reaction of disbelief, amazement, and outrage incomprehensible. Can we forget that under Mosaic Law a child that cursed or struck his mother or father could be put to death (Lynn, 1974)? Greek fathers could reject their children at birth and condemn them to death by exposure. In the center of Rome, there is a cliff called the Rupe Tarpea where children could be hurled to their deaths if there was a chance that they would become a burden to their family or to the state.

In the less remote past, the good citizens of the Renaissance followed Saint Paul's injunction, "Let your women keep silent in church." But by the end of the sixteenth century, church music had become very demanding and complex. Sopranos with powerful, adult voices were needed, and since women were to be silent, the choirs and theaters of the world turned to their male children to supply this need by castrating them before puberty. Lest we think that occurred only in the remote past, we can recall that Alessandro Moreschi, the last of the well-known "castrati" or "evirati," retired as director of music of the Sistine Chapel in 1913, and died in 1922 (*Encyclopedia Brittanica*, 1974, Vol. 16).

Turning to our Anglo-Saxon heritage, that left us the Magna Charta and the concept of fair play, we find that its law contemplated that fathers had the power of life and death over their children until the child's lips had touched either milk or honey. In addition, a father under this law until the thirteenth century could sell a child into slavery if he could demonstrate his need to do so.

It would be difficult to imagine that Charles Dickens' efforts merely provided us with poignant and amusing tales to be remembered at Christmastime. Surely someone must have seen that he was attempting to call the world's attention to the plight of children during the Industrial Revolution; a plight he knew all too well, even though he had not seen all the workhouses of London, the textile mills of Manchester, nor the collieries of Pennsylvania.

If these examples are too remote or too esoteric, one must wonder why the medical world did not respond to the revelations of Ambroise Tardieu (1868), Professor of Medical Jurisprudence at the Sorbonne, and of Balestrini (1888) in Italy whose autopsy tables revealed that newborns were left to die by being exposed to the elements, or murdered by the adults unto whom they had been entrusted, by nature or the law, to nurture and protect. And one must wonder too why the efforts of John Caffey (1946), who, by observing an experiment in nature, demonstrated that the combination of subdural hematomas and long-bone fractures were a result of trauma rather than exotic systemic disease.

Indeed, it would seem that Western civilization would have preferred to forget that it had treated its children like lifeless possessions of the environment, and that it made little provision for their care other than the institution of the structure called the family. When this unit became inefficient or broke down, there was little that society offered to protect its young. The reaction of outrage was, at least in part, a mass disclaimer of responsibility and an externalization of guilt in the direction of people who we would like to believe are unlike us. We would have liked to pretend that maiming, torturing, and the murder of children occurred only when adults in their environment were primitive and brutes. Once more then, we must recognize that a side benefit of inestimable value that emerged from the work of Caffey, Kempe, Steele, Pollock, Gill, and other investigators, was the gentle and compassionate insistence that child abuse was part of the human condition as we knew it, and not a monstrous anomaly or an atavistic throwback to some horrendous past state of primitive man. All of this must be remembered, not to flagellate ourselves with guilt, for guilt is a relatively useless human experience. It must be remembered, as George Santayana once stated and a once relatively obscure Viennese neurologist demonstrated, "Those who cannot remember the past are doomed to relive it" (1905, p. 82).

THE CLINICAL PROCESS

In order to organize our clinical thinking around the treatment of abused children, some early findings need to be reviewed with the model on parenting presented in chapter 8 (Figure 8-2), and earlier papers (Coppolillo, 1975, 1978) elaborated to accommodate more recent concepts. The clinical findings that have guided us so well can be summarized as follows.

1. Virtually all adults who abuse or neglect their children were physically or psychologically abused themselves as children (Steele and Pollock, 1968).

2. The abusing parent is often an isolated person, who neither seeks nor can readily accept help from others. They are distant and uninvolved even with members of their own families (Steele and Pollock, 1968).

3. Role reversal exists in the families of abused children, in that the abusing parents often look to the child for gratification, and are unable to appreciate the immaturity of their infants (Kaufman, 1962; Morris and Gould, 1963; Galdston, 1965).

4. Child abuse is more likely to occur in single-parent families, and while it appears to occur more frequently in lower socioeconomic groups, it can and does occur in every strata of society (Gill, 1970).

5. In the introjects of the abusing parents there is an imbalance with a predominance of the identifications being with a harsh, depriving, and punitive image of the mother. The gratifying nurturant images are all but submerged by these

more frustrating ones. As a result, in the abusing situations, the parent frequently appears righteous, demanding, and authoritarian (Steele and Pollock, 1968).

In attempting to revise our model of the parenting process, we would cite the works of Benedek (1938, 1952, 1956a, b, and 1959), and underline that the quality of a person's parenting ability is directly related to their experience of having been cared for by a parent. When it is their turn to parent, for better or worse, they unconsciously relive their own experiences and bring to the nursery, often without awareness, a prepared script of how things will go. In addition to the actual experiences, a parent has also developed to some measure an image of what an ideal parent should be, and this too contributes to the ambience in which he or she and the child will interact.

We have already described the process by which the expectant father, in the latter stages of his wife's pregnancy and during the child's infancy, develops parenting, supportive attitudes toward the mother and becomes a hovering protector and supplier (see chapter 4).

Central in this context is the fact that as the father makes this shift in his relationship to the mother, and as he prepares to parent his own child, his own experiences in being cared for as a child are as important in determining his success as those of the mother. That the past experiences of the father are crucial in permitting him to be successful is further documented when we realize that "motherly" qualities in men do not receive unqualified social support. Since this phase of a man's life does involve reinvestment in identifications with his mother, there are indeed some men who are made anxious by the shift, and resort to maladaptive measures.

The model presented in chapter 6 (Figure 6-2) must therefore be elaborated to include the history of the father, as he developed in his family of origin, and of course the clinician must, in cases of child abuse pay special attention while collecting the family history, to the images and memories the father has of his early experiences with his parents. (See Figure 14-1.)

As was proposed elsewhere, these images and percepts of

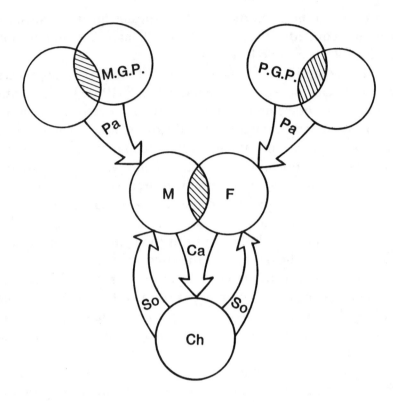

Figure 14-1. As mother and father unite (M-F) to create and care
(Ca) for their child, they are supported by the child's competence to
be soothed (So) and by reliving the experiences of being successfully
parented (Pa) by their own parents (MGP, PGP).

the family system offer support to the parent as they engage
in the demanding process of parenting the child. Mother is
sustained by reliving the gratification of being mothered, by
living up to an ideal of motherliness, by the mothering functions
of her mate, and by the intensely gratifying feedback and identifications with the child. The father in his turn is replenished
and bolstered by the reliving of his experiences with his parents,
by identifications gleaned from his oneness with his wife, the
pleasure in successfully supporting her, and from the identifications and actual nurturance of his offspring. In cases of

abuse and neglect the clinician cannot help but be amazed to see how few mental images there are of a sustaining family structure in the abusive parent. Memories of transactions with their own parents are pained and unrewarding. The ability to achieve intimacy and pleasurable exchanges with the mate is almost nonexistent. Most striking of all is the absence of appreciation, tenderness, or tolerance for the child's immaturity or helplessness. I believe it is the latter blind spot, and not only role reversal that permits the abusive parent to make remarks like "When this kid cries, you can see the hate in his eyes," when talking about a three-month-old son. Or, ascribe intentionality to a two-month-old daughter as a mother says, "She waited until I changed clothes and then threw up all over my only good dress."

Without the mental images of a supportive family structure, the parent cannot meet the incessant demands of the needy infant, and must find a retreat; some flee. Others cannot flee, and take refuge in alcohol, drugs, or illness. Still others cannot find refuge, and attempt to provide a structure for their interaction with their child by elaborating or accepting rigid rules rationalized by misusing principles of religion, discipline, or even pseudoscientific principles. These jury-rigged structures do not adequately protect the child or parent, however, and we can see cases of abuse in which the child was "disciplined," was punished for a sin or was being prevented from becoming "spoiled." As an example of this we recently saw an unbelievably poorly conceived idea publicly justifying parents taking sexual license with their children, as one proponent stated, because it prevented frigidity and isolation in the child's later life.

When parents cannot take refuge from the demands of their children in any of the above ways and are bereft of the support needed to cope, further disintegration of the family is likely to occur with one form of child abuse or another occurring. It is into this disintegrated family system that the therapist is drawn by the hurt child. The care needed is immense, and some special measures are in order.

The observations and suggestions that follow pertain to both sexual and physical abuse of the child. They are similar in the aspect that is described. This is not to say that they are not different in many other ways, and, in fact, it is obvious that the therapist must individualize his treatment to suit the child in any case.

One of the first issues that must be considered is the function of the child psychotherapist as he is brought into the case. If he is asked to evaluate the psychological state of the child, and this evaluation is going to be used in the legal process with its inevitable social consequences, the therapist must judge if this role will interfere with his ability to treat the child psychotherapeutically later. Of course, the age of the child and the measures taken to insure his safety will be important determinants in this judgment, but the therapist must be especially vigilant about the possibility that serving in one role has not disqualified him from the other.

In terms of assessing the need for therapy, the age at which the abuse occurred and the time that has lapsed between the abuse and the time of the evaluation needs to be considered. The nature of the relationships that the child has had in this interval can help or hinder therapy. Generally, I believe a period of three to six months in a stable, nonthreatening environment is helpful before beginning treatment. If the environment in which the child has lived was sufficiently comfortable to allow the child to express sadness, fear, regret, or anger, this too is an aid to treatment. Given these conditions, I believe that most children of two-and-a-half or three years and older, who have been abused, benefit from therapy. If the child has been abused at an age of less than two-and-a-half or three, a diagnostic evaluation when the child is three or three-and-a-half is indicated. The fact that the youngster is a "good," compliant child does not reduce the need for an evaluation. There are many children who are good not from a sense of well-being, but out of fear and at tremendous expense to themselves and their developmental potential.

If treatment is indicated, it should be determined if the

child's caretakers will be willing and ready to bring him to his therapeutic hours, and be involved in his treatment, quite as though they were his natural parents. The scars of abuse do not disappear easily, and there are times when these children are not easy to care for. This is especially true if the treatment reactivates old patterns of reactions in the child. It is well to remember here that about 35 percent of abused children are reabused when placed in foster homes.

The therapist, who will treat the abused child, may find that he needs a support system of his own to cope with some of the intense reactions he may have to the child's history or his provocations. At times, the therapist needs actual, direct help in dealing with the legal system, the social welfare system, or the schools. At other times, colleagues with whom a case or cases of abuse can be discussed will go far to help the therapist maintain equanimity during the treatment.

In order to offer a specific suggestion regarding the psychotherapy of battered and sexually abused children and adolescents, a brief review of the pathology is in order. Some of the information has already been presented in chapter 4 on the role of the father in the family. It is presented again not only because of its importance but because of the need to examine it from the point of view of treatment implications. In organizing the significance of the clinical picture, the therapist may find it useful to separate the traumata that the child has suffered into two groups: those that have resulted from actual commission of the abuse, and those that have resulted from the omissions that permitted the abuse to occur. The active traumata include, of course, the physical damage to the child resulting from the violence or the sexual assault, the child's psychological reaction to these, which may include fear, guilt, repugnance at the thought of future sexual activity, counterphobic promiscuity or violence, and hostility toward all adults who cannot be avoided or manipulated. These symptoms or sequelae will be managed as indicated and the therapist can be certain that the psychological reactions will manifest themselves in transferences to him or others in the child's environment. A special problem regarding the results of the active abuse arises in the situation in which there has been permanent disfigurement or destruction of a function, or an injury that will require a long period of time to repair. In these instances the therapist will have to contemplate the possibility that the child will experience a revival of fear, anger, or bitterness in a future developmental phase.

Deanna was a sixteen-year-old girl who was referred to a therapist because she had become depressed and reclusive. She had been abused by her mother when she was four by being hit in the face with a hot iron after having soiled herself. The resulting scar had been rendered almost invisible by excellent surgical care, and Deanna had had a course of psychotherapy with good results, starting about six months after she had been abused. She had lived in the home of a cousin of her mother after it was deemed that the mother was too unstable to care for her. About a year after the abuse, the mother committed suicide. Her father's whereabouts were unknown, and the cousin adopted Deanna when she was about six years old. She appeared to have made an excellent adjustment socially in her adoptive family until the onset of her depression and isolation. In the course of reevaluating her, the therapist discovered that with adolescence the nearly invisible scar had become an obsession with her, and she was certain that she was repugnant and unlovable. With adolescence came a new edition of the guilt and rage she had felt as an oedipal-age child when she was abused.

As with Deanna, children who have been sexually abused may show a new edition of symptoms when they reach adolescence or young adulthood. Perhaps a new comprehension of what happened introduces a new configuration of the conflict that must be worked through again.

Less attention has been paid to those symptoms that are

the results of omissions in the child's development than those that are the results of the act of abuse. The omission that I feel urged to address here is that of the child having failed to experience nonsexualized or nonaggressive affection. By this I mean the kind of affection that is offered the child with little or no overt demand or advantage for the adult other than the joy of experiencing the feeling. I would call this tenderness. We may tend to romanticize this affect or not accord it the immense value it has in development. It is a component of the child's self-esteem; it provides the child with a motive for complying with unwelcome parental demands; and is one of the factors that help children resolve conflicts in ways that will insure that their supply of tenderness is not interrupted. Perhaps the most important aspect of the tenderness in the context that we are considering here is that tenderness blunts, buffers, or neutralizes whatever aggressive or sexual impulses adults may experience toward their children. When abuse occurs, we are safe in assuming that parental tenderness was at least inconsistent, and too often altogether absent. Evidence of the void that this deficit leaves in the personality can be found in the treatment of late adolescent and young adult women who had been sexually abused by their fathers or adult caretakers. Their relationships and transactions with men are often characterized by a striking absence of any conviction that they can be liked or loved on their own merit. They must be useful to be acceptable or even tolerated. Being sexually *useful* (not desirable) is a frequent theme in their character structure. This is coupled with an absence of initiative in gratifying their own sexual desires or even wishes to be supported, sought after, or wanted.

Even after the therapy has addressed and resolved issues of anger at the abusive parent, resentment at the nonabusive parent for not protecting them, guilt at the secret pleasure of being selected, and other direct sequelae of the abuse, the therapist must still reckon with the possibility that his patient does not contemplate the possibility of being cared for or loved by someone for simply existing. If the patient has experienced tenderness at some time in his life and subsequent events caused him to despair of ever reexperiencing it, the inhibition of these expectations can be treated as a conflict. The patient's reluctance or inability to seek unqualified affection may be treated as the defenses, and the conviction of being left dissatisfied as an equivalent of the anxiety they feel with the longing to be loved. If, however, the patient seems to have never enjoyed unqualified love or tenderness, it is not conflict reduction that is required, but a direct, gratifying, educational experience. In these instances I do not believe the therapist is the one who can provide these experiences. The therapist has been the person who was the recipient of transferences. He has struggled with the patient to resolve conflicts and bolster the stable logic of the ego as it mastered the turbulence of past wounds. He cannot risk losing the gains made in these areas in an attempt to provide an experience that the patient can and should acquire with another person, preferably of his own choosing.

In working with the younger child, the therapist may be able to indicate to the caretakers what the child needs. A much more difficult task is undertaken when treating adolescents or young adults. Occasionally and under special circumstances, speaking with the patient's boyfriend, or fiancé, or spouse without revealing confidences may be helpful. At other times all that is left the therapist is an educative description of what every human being alive has a right to expect as they interact with others in the world; a measure of love, respect, and admiration with no strings attached. As the patient then seeks these responses from the therapist, he can with gentle encouragement point the patient toward the world at large.

A recent publication by Adele Mayer (1983) offers an exhaustive overview of the problem of incest, and practical, varied, and innovative concepts of treatment of this syndrome whose incidence and prevalence we only just begin to appreciate.

CHAPTER 15

The Profoundly Disorganized Child

When a child is profoundly disturbed and disorganized, the pain to the family and difficulty in treating him is increased exponentially. It is a situation that requires special patience, flexibility, and creativity for any therapist, no matter how experienced he is. In this chapter two issues will be raised for consideration. These are some suggestions about working in the therapeutic milieu, and the centrality of the child's ability to develop a workable relationship to the therapist. By this latter I do not mean the usual working alliance, but something far more fundamental. I refer now to the child's gaining or regaining the ability to distinguish himself from others, and in making this distinction recognize the difference in percepts and convictions about the therapist that come from within himself as opposed to those that come from some actual perception of the therapist.

WORKING IN THE MILIEU

As far back as the Temple of Aeschulapius there were places where people with emotional problems or mental illnesses could repair to protect themselves from the demands of the world. Later asylums were developed to protect society from the insane and only as people such as Chiarrugi, Pinel, and Rush began to be heard was the focus shifted back to healing

351

the sick within their walls. While the focus on treatment for the sick has remained a consistent aspiration of most institutions since their reformation, it was not until the twentieth century that the concept of the therapeutic milieu began to be formulated. The idea begins to be articulated in Aichorn's (1935) descriptions of his treatment of adolescent delinquents. Bettelheim and Sylvester (1949) were the first to use the phrase "milieu therapy," and described the concept with clinical examples. Prior to their descriptions, the therapeutic milieu was the holding environment in which there was concern about support and safety for the patient while he was being treated with various modalities. Bettelheim described an important departure from this concept when he described the milieu as the therapeutic agent. Since his and Sylvester's original description, there have been a number of elaborations and descriptions of refinements of a milieu in which psychodynamic principles are translated into principles of relationships, procedures, architecture, and policies that surround the child daily and guide his therapist (Bettelheim 1950, 1955, 1967; Bettelheim and Sanders, 1979; Redl, 1959; Rinsley, 1968; Harrison, MacDermott, and Chethik, 1969; Szurek, Berlin, and Boatman, 1971; and Noshpitz, 1984).

At this time it must be said that there have been so many modifications and grafts onto the idea of a milieu of approaches other than the psychodynamic model of treatment that a therapeutic milieu means essentially an environment in which people are treated for their psychiatric ills by any technique. Unfortunately, there are milieus that are so designated only because children are housed there and no treatment philosophy other than kindness and protection is offered. Others have a treatment orientation that is incompatible with a psychodynamic, exploratory, conflict-reducing psychotherapy. In this chapter the topic will be the psychodynamic treatment of severely disturbed children in a treatment milieu as Bettelheim described it. In order for this form of treatment to be effective the milieu must have a treatment philosophy that aims at revealing unconscious impediments to the child's integration and development, and the therapist must be capable of interacting in a way that is synergistic and not antagonistic to the milieu's therapeutic thrust. These are some of the principles that will be reviewed in this section of the chapter.

It must be acknowledged immediately that finding a therapeutic milieu in which a therapist can participate in a child's treatment is no easy matter. Despite the relatively modest cost of the tuition at the Orthogenic School where Bettelheim did his original work (Bettelheim and Sanders, 1979), there are many families who cannot afford even a minimal amount. Public institutions that could offer treatment at a lower cost are frequently bombarded with demands for housing children from the court, welfare departments, and health care facilities, and are stretched beyond their capacity to offer the kind of staff to patient ratio that is required for successful treatment. They become so burdened by paperwork and providing relief for environmental problems that they cannot take the time to understand the internal forces working on the child. Other private facilities, needing to be "cost effective" often find that the fees they must charge for inpatient care are prohibitive for the majority of the population. Insurance coverage may be available, but in some cases will cover costs for a month or three months and then cease. Adapting to these conditions, a number of institutions are available for short-term care, but leave the community without places or provisions for treating children who need a prolonged period in a therapeutic milieu. The therapist who treats such a child may therefore encounter a good deal of difficulty in finding a place where he can treat his patient.

There are those who maintain that long-term treatment milieus are no longer necessary given the gains made in treatment modalities other than the psychoanalytically oriented ones. I cannot subscribe to these views. I have personally seen children who have been in dire need of a long-term treatment facility, and it was reasonable to assume would have benefited from it. Not having had one available they continued to travel the road to chronic hospitalization, or worse became a part of first the minor and then the major league prison system. Perhaps because they are not immediately troublesome to society, once in these systems, these youngsters are quickly forgotten and do not act as reminders that expedient measures do not get the job done. To compound this, therapists cannot advertise their successes. In deference to confidentiality and the dignity of patients, people who have been saved from having to spend their lives in an institution cannot be asked to describe their recovery. Any who have treated a child in a therapeutic milieu, and have witnessed the working through leading to recovery, attest with profound conviction to its utility. This, while a clinical observation rather than a scientific demonstration, is nonetheless a convincing experience.

The responsible therapist recognizes immediately that a decision to place the child in a therapeutic milieu is a weighty matter. Noshpitz (1984) reviews the complexity of the ethical and economic issues involved. When, however, one comes to the determination that a therapeutic milieu is essential, there seems to be no substitute for it.

The criteria for deciding to place a child in a therapeutic environment are not predicated on categories or classifications but on diagnosis. There are some psychotic children that can be treated while remaining at home or attending a day treatment center. Conversely, others that would be classified as neurotic or suffering from character disorders may need milieu therapy. A diagnosis is needed which contemplates the state of the child's personality, and the capacity of the surrounding environment to protect the child and itself from possible harm.

By and large children need a therapeutic milieu when they suffer from disintegration of their personality structure to the point that they cannot learn from the reality they encounter and remain idiosyncratic and unpredictable in their perception of and responses to external reality. In addition, children, who may be destructive to themselves or others, and children who have entered into an otherwise irreversible, maladaptive pattern of interaction with their environment require it.

As was mentioned earlier, the first task of the therapist must be to find a place that will accept the child. The therapist must then determine if the milieu philosophy is harmonious with the form of treatment he deems necessary for his patient. If, for example, it is determined that the child must come to understand unconscious convictions and impulses that keep him from interacting productively with those that surround him, the milieu must be able to tolerate, understand, and describe the defenses that he uses to avoid the anxiety of relatedness or of revealing unconscious mentation. In these instances a milieu whose philosophy is to modify the behavior through negative or positive reenforcement without exploring it would not be indicated (Bettelheim and Sanders, 1979). Once these issues are decided the therapist can prepare to become part of the team.

The therapist must now be ready to assume a role that has some very different aspects from those of being an individual therapist. In individual psychotherapy, he was the kingpin of the therapy, and now he is but one person in the therapeutic team. While in individual psychotherapy he could be reasonably sure that he would be the person around whom the child would organize most of his insights, he must now be ready, at times, to see the child pick another person on the milieu team as the important relationship around which fantasies and convictions are lived out and understood. Observations and descriptions of behaviors that lead to insights may now have to come from members of the milieu team, other than the therapist, and the therapist must be ready to consider clinical formulations and insights that they have developed. There will be times when mistakes in formulation or technique, which are almost inevitable in the treatment of children, can no longer be contained in the privacy of the consultating room, but must be examined freely by the members of the treatment team. These are not easy adjustments to make.

From the point of view of interpersonal relationships with members of the therapeutic milieu staff, the therapist will come to recognize that virtually no aspect of the relationships are insulated from affecting the child's treatment. A like or a dislike, an alliance or an antagonism, a bit of jealousy or a competitive feeling can all be perceived by the child, or can alter the way the child is treated.

Warren B, a twenty-eight-year-old physician, was the therapist of a seven-year-old psychotic boy in a therapeutic milieu who had expressed a number of his delusions through somatic complaints. Warren, a handsome young bachelor, had casually dated a staff careworker before he had become the boy's therapist. He had since begun another relationship with a young woman not part of the therapeutic milieu. He was irritated one morning to find that his patient had been sent to the pediatric clinic without his knowledge for examination of a complaint by the careworker he had dated. The matter came to a discussion in the staff meeting when the patient's teacher reported that the child had disrupted the class by chanting repeatedly that "Warren is mad at Dori (the caseworker)." Warren acknowledged being miffed at Dori for bypassing him, and after some painful self-revelation, Dori acknowledged that she had had thoughts about the milieu being rid of Warren. The unresolved and unspoken tension between Dori and Warren interfered with the unity of the child's treatment.

Even without these personal, individualized breaks in the milieu's integrity, there is a need for the staff to constantly explore what is going on throughout the milieu, and not focus only on the patients. The reaction of a teacher whose pupil is taken out of class in order to go to his therapy hour; the feelings of the parent's therapist when the patient's home visit is canceled and he must bear the heat of the parents' reaction; and the therapist's conviction that a description of his patient's misbehavior is a covert commentary on his competence are all examples of issues that must be addressed and resolved if the milieu is to be effective in fostering reintegration of the patients that are part of it.

In recent years the varieties and refinements of psychoactive medications have increased. Indeed there are medications that can reduce anxiety and alleviate depression to significant degrees. With some caveats these medications can be used to facilitate milieu therapy. The first issue that must be considered is the attitude with which the medication is being given. If the aim of the relationship is to get the child to take the pill, the philosophy is contradictory to the orientation of milieu treatment. If the aim of giving the pill is to make it possible or easier for the child to relate, medicating can be made compatible with the philosophy of a therapeutic milieu as we use the term. If the latter situation is the case, the child should be aware of the criteria involved in setting the dosage and in deciding when to use and when to discontinue the medicine. Whenever possible the child should be allowed to participate in discussions regarding medication management.

The person who prescribes the medicine and dosage should be part of the milieu, and be aware of all that is occurring in the environment. We physicians are especially vulnerable to taking refuge in medical mystique when the heat is on us and sometimes acting as if all medical decisions are precise and inviolable. The prescriber must be ready to hear feedback from the environment about how the child is reacting to medication, physiologically, behaviorally, and psychologically. For medicine to be prescribed from an unreachable perspective can interfere with treatment.

> Joey was five years old when he was rescued by the Child Protective Team from an environment that was on the way to destroying him, and was placed in a therapeutic milieu. Unfortunately, damage had already been extensive. Head injuries from abuse were thought to be the cause for forty to fifty *petit mal* seizures per day, and neglect as well as misuse were thought to be the causes of his psychotic disorganization. Medication for his seizures was prescribed, and they decreased in frequency dramatically. After about eight months of treatment, falls and accidents began to increase and since they were thought to be the result

of an increase in seizure activity, his medication was increased. This time the seizures did not diminish. The physician prescribing the medication, not a member of the milieu team, insisted that increased doses be tried for a longer period. When the milieu staff attempted to tell him that these later accidents had a different pattern from the ones they had seen earlier, he dismissed their wish to discuss the issue as being "imagination," and launched into a complex explanation of brain electrophysiology. When finally a physician of the treatment milieu team could persuade him to listen, and the staff could discuss Joey's functioning in the milieu, it could be demonstrated that Joey's "accidents" occurred in two contexts. One was on the days when his mother was allowed to visit, and the other was when a careworker to whom he was becoming attached was away for more than a couple of hours. As human vigilance increased, the dosage of the medication was lowered, and as his longings and fears were acknowledged, Joey's "seizures" were reduced to zero.

In the milieu the therapist may find that as he tries to adjust to the new role, he will lean over backward to avoid being authoritarian and a one man show. Certainly, these aims are laudable because being authoritarian does not pay off in the long run, and the rest of the milieu team did not sign on only to applaud. But even as one attempts to avoid being authoritarian and exhibitionistic about one's knowledge, one must not shirk the responsibility to be *authoritative*. Often the therapist is the one person among the people on the milieu that is most extensively trained. With the training comes knowledge and wisdom that can be used by the team. How does one make this knowledge available in a useful and palatable manner? I think in most instances this can be accomplished by asking oneself a question. Is what I am about to say for the purpose of improving the efficacy of the *milieu as a whole*, or will it serve only to enhance my position in it or that of my patient? As Bettelheim

(1955) and Bettelheim and Sanders (1979) have demonstrated and articulated, it is in the effort of milieu to achieve integrity that a potent thrust is given to the integration of the child. Thus, wisdom that is shared gives this thrust to milieu integrity, while knowledge that is imposed often disrupts it.

One last comment must go to the issue of confidentiality. The therapist must often walk a narrow line between participating in the free discussion so necessary to the milieu and maintaining a patient's confidentiality. At times this is literally impossible, and the issue to be discussed is sufficiently compelling to warrant telling the child that it will be discussed. If the therapist has any sense that the child has given the therapist "confidential information" to separate him from the rest of the team, it is important to explore this with the child. If the child is not using confidentiality as a wedge, the therapist should preferably reach an agreement with him as to what will be communicated. If agreement cannot be reached, the therapist can inform the child what must be communicated to the milieu and why. In many instances, however, the implications or significance of what the child tells you is more important than the details of the behavior that revealed it.

> Chris was a seven-year-old boy who had lived in a chaotic environment for the first four years of his life. His father was violent, his mother promiscuous, and Chris witnessed these tendencies in both parents many times. When he was four, his father murdered his mother and was sent to jail. Chris was placed in a number of foster homes, but his behavioral and psychological disintegration forced the welfare department to place him in a therapeutic environment when he was six. While in treatment it was discovered that he was convinced that he had killed his mother and father by his voyeurism and his rage. In one session he attempted to swear his therapist to secrecy, and then told him, with anxiety rather than pleasure that he had looked up a careworker's dress and saw her "underwear." He then began to avoid her and when

he could not avoid contact with her, he would mis-behave. This puzzled her since she had originally been one of Chris's favorites. The therapist found it was enough to explain that Chris had thought that his curiosity and voyeurism were lethal and now that he was drawn to them by pleasurable rather than hostile motives, he was frightened. This permitted the milieu group to find ways to show Chris that looking could be pleasurable and candid and not just hostile and clandestine. The act remained secret, the dynamics could be revealed.

A therapist who would treat a child in an effective therapeutic milieu must be ready to contemplate these and other considerations. A therapeutic milieu is a sophisticated treatment modality, and not a place to help keep the child "on ice" until it is time for his treatment hour.

OBJECT RELATEDNESS AND TREATMENT OF THE PSYCHOTIC CHILD

Childhood psychosis is invariably accompanied by serious disturbances in the capacity to relate to other human beings. Early infantile autism and childhood schizophrenia are virtually synonymous with nonrelatedness or massive distortions of relatedness. The pathogenesis of this condition remains a subject of inquiry, debate, and even controversy. It has still to be determined whether a child abandons the organizing influence of distinguishing himself from objects due to pathology in stimulus-processing abilities, or because to relate to an object means more psychic unpredictability and pain than he can bear. Yet to the clinician there can be no doubt that distortions in relatedness not only contribute to the pathology, they also pose a formidable problem in doing psychotherapy. When one recalls that the whole system of Aristotelian logic as well as the ability to organize notions of what constitutes a real, outside world as opposed to internally generated percepts and fantasies, is based on the ability to distinguish subject from object, we can appreciate the disorganization that results from losing or never having developed this ability.

When children who have for a period of time possessed the ability to distinguish "I" from "they" or "it," and then lose this faculty through regression, a number of clinical consequences ensue. The lines between that which is imagined and that which is perceived become blurred. Stimuli that come from the outside world must compete for attention with those that are internally generated, and the corrective influence of information from the world of reality on subjective convictions is inconsistent or nonexistent. In these circumstances the child does not experience reality subtly distorted by transference, he experiences his subjective states as concrete, unquestionable reality. Unable to be distracted from thoughts and sensations that originate from within, we will often see these children give bizarre meaning to internal perceptions that others not so burdened, are scarcely aware of. Enteroceptive sensations thus become "deterioration of their organs," or proprioception becomes evidence for having been "invaded by evil spirits." Standing next to these grotesque images of self-perception are images of the external world that may be equally as frightening, threatening, or repugnant. This state of affairs is frighteningly well demonstrated by the essay of an eleven-year-old child.

> Betsy was an eleven-year-old girl who was referred for an outpatient evaluation by a sensitive and worried teacher who reported that Betsy was becoming increasingly more withdrawn over the past six months, and her English compositions had become horrifyingly similar in their themes and imagery. Her developmental history was unremarkable except for intellectual precocity and a rather marked achievement orientation in school. She had been an excellent scholar. Her family history, however, had been filled with pain. When Betsy was four, a younger sister was born. Following this birth, her mother started to decompensate, and began a hospital course from which she never recovered. She was diagnosed as suffering

from paranoid schizophrenia, and after some three months of intensive psychotherapy at a local hospital was moved to a state hospital about sixty miles from their home for long-term care. Relatives and hired help provided care for the children. Betsy's father remained concerned and caring for his wife as well as his children. He visited his wife frequently and whenever her condition permitted, took the children to visit their mother. The mother's overall hospital course was one of deterioration, both psychologically and physically. When Betsy was ten, her mother died of congestive heart failure, obesity, and an ill-defined neurological disease.

Betsy was said to have reacted rather blandly to her mother's death. After her mother's funeral, a woman whose husband had died in the same hospital as Betsy's mother and who had met and come to know the father when they both visited their spouses, came to visit the family to offer condolences and help. The relationship between Betsy's father and the widow deepened, and about eight or nine months after her mother's death, Betsy had a new stepmother. All reports indicated that although Betsy showed little warmth for her stepmother, there was no overt friction between them. It was about six months after this marriage that Betsy's teacher noticed withdrawal and the bizarre ideation expressed in her writing. During the diagnostic evaluation the teacher sent to the clinic an essay that she said was typical of the ones Betsy had been writing.

"OLD MAN MASHER"*

Long ago, in a village, lived Old Man Masher. They called him Old Man Masher because he had the horrible reputation of mashing other people.

This is how it worked. Anytime anyone came to

*This story was taken from (Coppolillo, 1965a).

his bone-fenced house he would tell them to come in. Then he would take them down to dingy dark cellar, where he kept his gigantic potato masher. Then he would merely chop off their heads and shove them under his potato masher. When they were done being mashed they made the best hash you ever tasted. Or at least he thought so.

If anyone tried to run away he'd simply chase them around with his devil's pitchfork until he caught them. He had got the pitchfork from Santa Clause last Christmas.

One day a little beggar girl came to his house. She was pretty scrawny, but he decided to use her anyway. And her head was pretty hollow so he knew it would make a splendid cooky jar.

Another day a square came to his house. Old Man Masher decided to use him for a chair because he was so square. So he did.

Old Man Masher was always seen waring a different color of eyes to match the hair ribbon he happened to be waring on his beautiful green hair. He kept all his eyes in a drawer, which he called his own "Private Eye Drawer." The next day a soldier, which was coming home from the war, came to his frightening house. So Old Man Masher took him down to the cellar. Just as he was about to chop the soldier's head off. He fell through the trap door which he used for disposal of the head that were slightly cracked. So that was the end of Old Man Masher. But it was very unfortunate because after that the soldier took Old Man Mashers place and it happened all over again.

As is evident from the child's writing, she viewed the world as a danger-filled, bizarre place in which people are captured, exploited, and killed. Relationships are ambivalent and blessings are laced with evil (the devil's pitchfork that was received from Santa Claus). Cannibalism and mutilation are expressed without defense or disguise, and black humor is based on clang or concrete associations (mash = hash; chair = square; and private eye drawer). Affects are either blunted, not expressed, or bizarre (he *merely* chopped off their heads). All of these elements combine to give a picture of madness. But it is the preoccupation with the body and its distortion and dissolution that attest to the self-preoccupation of the young patient.

One may ask, how does the diagnostician know that this essay was the result of the child's psychosis and not her talent. Of course, there was talent and intelligence in the expressions of madness. But madness there was, and this could be documented by the findings of the rest of the evaluation, and because the child was unable to write or describe events in any other way. When Franz Kafka turned away from writing *Metamorphosis* or Conrad Aiken from writing *Silent Snow, Secret Snow*, two of the most powerful descriptions of psychosis ever written, they could write a perfectly coherent letter to a friend or the gas company if needed; Betsy could not. Her outer world had been fused and merged with inner fears, bizarre sensations, terror, or repugnance and above all confusion. This inability to distinguish inner terror from reality was the massive obstacle that anyone approaching her therapeutically would have to overcome.

In the remainder of the chapter, a ten-month segment of the treatment of a seven-year-old will be described in some detail* This is for the purpose of documenting the process by which child and therapist worked to penetrate the barrier which separated him from a threatening world of human relationships.

Kenny was seven years old when he was referred by his pediatrician for encopresis of six months' duration. During the diagnostic workup we learned that the pediatrician had thought to refer Kenny as long as a year before because he had also suffered from intractable asthma since the age of two. He was born

*The clinical material of this case is reprinted from the *Journal of the American Academy of Child Psychiatry* (Coppolillo, 1969).

to parents who had had stormy and unhappy prior marriages and were well on the way to demolishing the one in which they were currently involved. In the three and one half years that he lived with both parents he witnessed many scenes of both verbal and physical violence and rage. For example, when Kenny was about three the father became enraged during a quarrel and shouted that he was going to kill both the mother and Ken. He then forced his wife and the child to sit in the living room for about three hours while he brandished a gun and ruminated on whether or not he should shoot them. When Kenny was three and one half, his younger brother was born. Shortly after the birth the mother and father were separated. The mother returned to the Midwest and had a brief psychotic episode for which she was hospitalized. Several months after the hospitalization, there began a series of painful surgical procedures for an osteomyelitis of her maxilla, caused by an abscessed tooth. Both the mother and Kenny believe this to have been caused by a blow on the face she had received in a quarrel with the father long before their separation.

During the diagnostic interviews, the mother was functioning at a borderline psychotic level. She found it virtually impossible to give us any history regarding the boy, so taken was she with recounting the suffering she had endured at the hands of her ex-husband.

Kenny appeared at first glance to be a friendly, articulate youngster with great intellectual potential. He looked alert, lively, related very well, and it was difficult to understand how a boy with such serious symptoms and such a chaotic history could appear so intact. Shortly, however, some rather ominous signs began to appear. During one of the diagnostic interviews Kenny began to construct some simple structures from tinker toys, commenting that no matter what he attempted to construct, it always came out a gun. He demonstrated this by starting several projects and interrupting each one to point out how it resembled a cannon or a rifle. At times this was accompanied by such obvious discomfort and chagrin that he seemed to be reacting as if there were a real gun on the table. Occasionally, he would begin to speak in a bizarre mechanical voice that gave one the eerie feeling that one was listening to a Chatty Cathy doll. This intonation was not simple immaturity but had rather a dissonant quality which some authors have described in reference to adult schizophrenic patients (Spoerri, 1966). During the third interview, Kenny began playing with dominoes on the floor. He erected a square structure, which he called his home. Building it higher he announced that his was a very special home since it had a special fire alarm system. Whenever a fire broke out that became too dangerous, this home had a shaker in each of the bricks which caused it to shake itself apart and smother the flames. He demonstrated this by shaking the bottom of the structure and causing it to topple. He then sat looking at the dominoes for a long time, sadly lost in thought.

Finally, during the first month of his treatment, Kenny demonstrated an amazing capacity to drift off, even in the midst of a transaction, leaving the therapist feeling as if he had been abandoned and had practically become nonexistent. These observations led us to consider the diagnosis of borderline psychosis. Psychological testing confirmed our impression, indicating that whenever aggressive impulses tended to emerge his synthetic, adaptive, and integrative ego functions would be seriously impeded by the eruption of primary process forms of mentation as well as by the withdrawal of his investment in object relationships. The testing further revealed that Kenny's full scale IQ was around 140 and that he had learned to use cognitive functioning to great advantage both intrapsychically and interpersonally. We debated the possibility of hospitalizing Kenny, finally deciding that he had some assets that would make outpatient treatment possible. We began, therefore, to see him twice weekly in analytically oriented psychotherapy. From March, when his treatment started, until August, the therapist could offer Ken little that was useful other than consistency, patience, and some supportive advice. Although his play was often transparent and clearly revealed both his longing for and intolerance of relationships, as well as his terror of aggression and his loneliness, he seemed totally incapable of communicating these feelings directly about himself or permitting himself to acknowledge that he experienced them. Inquiries about his loneliness or isolation elicited either a blank stare or a withdrawal into banal, repetitive play. Occasionally, he would respond by telling some inconsequential story in his bizarre voice. In August, the therapist suggested that since Ken had found it difficult to say some of the things that he felt, and since pictures reflect what people feel inside, we might be able to understand some of his problems if he could draw pictures which we could discuss. The associations to his pictures which reveal the course of this phase of treatment are as follows:

Immediately after the therapist's suggestion that Kenny might draw, the resistances once more made themselves felt in that it took him the whole hour to color the whole picture. At the end of the hour he announced that time was up, and he wanted to leave. The therapist convinced him that they could take a few more minutes to talk about the drawing. (See Figure 15-1).

Figure 15-1 (August 10): Drawn silently. The blue background was meticulously colored in. The spaceship is blue, dark red, and violet. The planets and satellites are dark brown and green.

Figure 15-1

Therapist: "What is that?"
Kenny: "A spaceship going through space."
Therapist: "Where is it going?"
Kenny: "Nowhere. Just going on and on (bizarre voice)."

Therapist: "Might it land on one of those planets?"
Kenny: "No. No one can land there, they're too hot."
Therapist: "That must be frightening."
Kenny: "No. It's very quiet there. That's a space communication station" (pointing to the figure with the antennae on the lower right-hand corner).
Therapist: "Oh. Then the spaceship can talk to someone."
Kenny: "No. It's burned out."

Noteworthy in this picture was the somber blue background, that each body is unrelated to any other body, and the absence of anything that suggests human form.

Between August 10 and November 15 Kenny drew several pictures which were identical to the first one. Each time the therapist would point out how Ken saw everything separate and distant and never close and friendly. Gradually, the idea that he must feel pretty lonely was added to the statement. Finally, the therapist suggested that there must be something rather frightening about closeness if Ken felt that it was so important to keep everything apart. Kenny made no verbal responses to this, but during the period from August to November there were some attempts to show positive feeling toward the therapist, which were followed almost immediately by withdrawal and superficiality.

Figure 15-2 (November 15): Kenny produced this drawing which had a markedly different quality from the previous ones. There is no background color. The sun, the trail of the satellite, and the meteoric dust are in brilliant yellow. The rest is in blue. He began to tell about the drawing spontaneously.

Kenny (pointing to the two central figures): "This is a spaceship that is going to orbit around the sun. It passes this satellite, see."

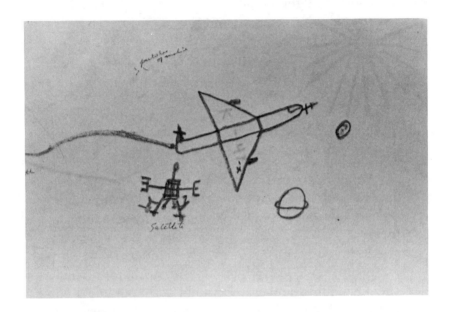

Figure 15-2

Therapist: "What do they say to each other?"
Kenny (pause): "Nah. They don't talk (pause). They came from the same place once (pointing to the line behind the satellite and the line behind the spaceship). They could talk to people once, but now they're going a different way."
Therapist: "I wonder what those dots are. Is that snow?"
Kenny (slightly disgusted): "Nah. There's no snow in space. No rain either. There isn't any water at all. That's meteoric dust. If it hits the ship it could hurt."
Therapist (attempting to recover): "Oh, I see. It's still dangerous if you get too close to anything."

In this drawing the awareness that two bodies were

once related is clear. Furthermore, the first reference to anything resembling the human form is made in drawing the satellite.

Figure 15-3 (December 6): Ken worked silently for a long time on this drawing. The colors in this drawing are brighter reds, blues, and greens. When

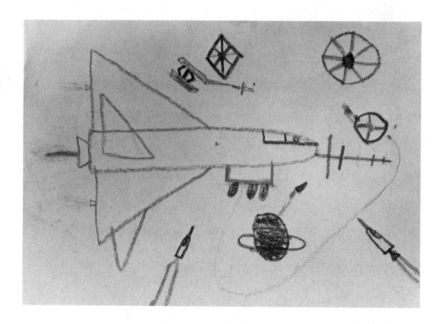

Figure 15-3

he finished the therapist asked questions and he answered with the briefest possible answers. He volunteered nothing during this session. He stated that the big spaceship in the center was sending missiles to the space stations (i.e., the wheellike structures, the diamond-shaped one, and the two-hull structures above the big spaceship). There was nothing more he could tell, either about the ship or the stations. When asked about the blue planet with a ring, he answered that that was the Diamond Ring Planet. He could say no more about it than this, however. It occurred to the therapist that the Diamond Ring Planet appeared in almost every one of Ken's space drawings, but little could be elicited about it. The little figure leaving the space station, which has roughly human form, left it because it was getting too hot. When the therapist suggested that the missiles the spaceship was sending to the space platform looked like bombs, Ken fell silent and withdrew.

Figure 15-4 (December 10): This drawing, also in lively colors, showed much more interaction between the various components. The main spaceship was identified as belonging to the "United States Space Force." There are two well-defined heads in the cockpit of the main spaceship. At the extreme right of the picture he described "an old space station" in purple and below it a space detecting station in blue with a red light. To the left of this he placed a complex space station. A ship left from there. Below the main spaceship two spaceships seemed to be bound together. Ken said that a ship was being built in space.

Therapist: "What's happened there, Ken?" (pointing to the main spaceship).
Kenny: "Oh, they're just blasting."
Therapist: "What are they blasting?"
Kenny: "Just asteroids. To clear them out of the way. They could get in the way and cause a crash (pointing

Figure 15-4

to the middle structure). They're building a ship in space (pointing to the three structures on the right). There's a space station and an old space station and a detecting station."

Therapist: "What does it detect?"

Kenny: "Nothing."
Therapist: "Maybe all that blasting has something to do with some feelings you have of wanting to blast something or someone."
Kenny (tentatively): "No" (falls silent).

Encouraged and perhaps seduced by the increased interaction in the picture, plus the appearance of two human heads in the spaceship, the therapist again interpreted aggression. In retrospect this was premature, and did not address the defenses with sufficient attention. The child had already given the therapist a clue that he was not ready to face his aggression by withdrawing and falling silent in the last session. The effect of the premature interpretation is evident in the next drawing produced in the next session.

Figure 15-5 (December 14): Once more he drew detached and unrelated bodies. Only the red color was used, while the two bodies at the top of the picture are all in pencil. One is a box with the label T.N.T. on it and the other is the Diamond Ring Planet which has made a reappearance. Having committed himself to a course of action, the therapist felt it more appropriate to pursue rather than abandon the interpretation. It was suggested that Ken must have been frightened by what the therapist said last time and he felt once more that he had to keep everything apart. Gradually, over the next two sessions, during which there was no drawing, Ken acknowledged that he felt that terrible things can happen when people get angry—like when his father smashed his mother in the mouth and she had to have operations. This theme was repeated several times in the next four sessions.

Figure 15-6 (December 31): Kenny drew with more freedom than he had previously. The spaceship is violet, while the planet and the splashes of color are shades of yellow and orange. Both in his freedom and by having placed his own last name on the side of his

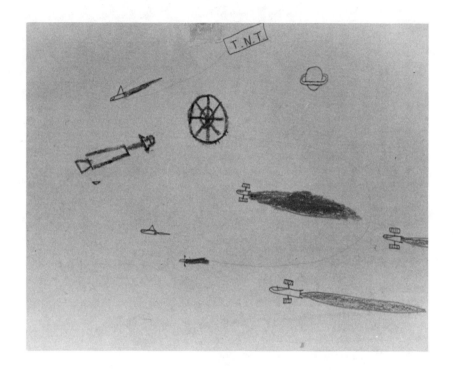

Figure 15-5

spaceship (which in the picture is blanked out for obvious reasons), Ken demonstrated his growing conviction that his drawings represented feelings and qualities
of his own about which he was concerned. After he
completed it he began spontaneously to tell the therapist about it. He first pointed to the orange splash in

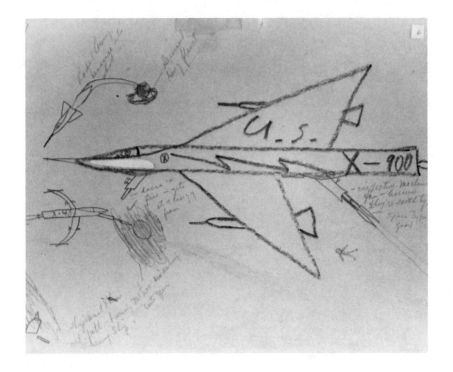

Figure 15-6

the lower left-hand corner and stated that a spaceship went through a meteor's path. He then said that the burning meteor had "smashed the enemy ship." He added that it had smashed into its front gun.

Kenny: "Here is another meteor (pointing to the yellow splash just below the main ship), it's smashing into the gun of this enemy ship. Then there's this rocket that's leaving the Diamond Ring Planet (pointing to the ringed planet above the main ship)."

Therapist: "What's happening?"

Kenny: "It's too hot on the Diamond Ring Planet. That ship is getting off."

Therapist: "But I wonder what's happening in general. What's going on between the main ship and the other ships?"

Kenny: "The main ship is flying through space, there are some enemy ships around because it is a war, but they're not fighting each other, just the meteors."

Therapist: "How come the main ship, with your name on it, has some parts which are in pencil?"

Kenny: "That's because those guns in front and in back don't fire. They don't work, they're earth guns and earth-type guns don't work in space. In space you need solar guns. And that man is exploring out there (pointing to a tiny figure below the spaceship), but he belongs to the spaceship where I am captain."

Therapist: "Those guns on your ship won't work. I wonder why they don't work both front and back."

Kenny: "I told you that they were earth guns. Oh (surprised). You mean like me?"

Therapist (smiling): "It's more important what you mean than what I mean."

Kenny: "I thought you meant my bowel block (his term for encopresis). That means that I don't work so good in back."

Therapist: "I guess sometimes boys feel helpless when something isn't working right, as if they can't fight back or like they have guns that don't work."

For the rest of the hour Kenny participated in exploring his feelings of impotence, fear, and hopelessness regarding expressions of anger. In the next month and a half he drew no pictures at all, but gradually began to develop the capacity to speak directly about his anger at his father who "had lots of money" but would give the family none. He reported that these were ideas that he had gotten directly from his mother and admitted when he was confronted that it was very difficult not to take sides in the situation and blame his father. Gradually, he was capable of expressing anger toward his mother too. This anger centered mostly on the fact that mother acted as if his "bowel block" were something over which Kenny had control. He recalled the many enemas his mother had given him when his bowel problem had first started with constipation and said that they were painful and unpleasant. He felt that she had given him these enemas because she was retaliating for both his constipation and his soiling. He also began to describe his resentment at mother's having begun to go out with men and leaving him and his brother in the care of the maternal grandmother.

Figure 15-7 (February 15): The two themes which had tentatively appeared in the former pictures became more pronounced. One was the presence of "enemy spaceships" and the other was his name on the central spaceship. The colors are a veritable orgy of red, violet, and yellow. There followed an animated description by Kenny on the chaotic, destructive space war which was taking place in the picture. The figure which had been drawn in a constricted mode in pencil in the former drawing now took a central position out in space actively engaging in the fighting and firing randomly fore and aft. The animation and glee with which Kenny described the scene was in marked contrast to all that had gone before and in direct proportion to violent splashes of color with which he drew. Following this session, there were long and direct discussions about his anger and his feelings of fear about expressing it. He did not draw for approximately a month, but frequently referred to the destructiveness

Figure 15-7

and the chaos in the picture when speaking of the
feelings that he had inside of him. Toward the end of
this month's discussions, Kenny had begun to recognize and clearly articulate his feelings of hopelessness
when he wished that his mother would attend only to
him and not indulge herself by going out with men

and leaving him in the care of the grandmother. The one exception to his abstinence from drawing was one picture of a PT boat that was engaged in active combat with enemy bombers and was carrying out its part of the fighting in a very successful and active way.

Toward mid-March, the first separation from Kenny took place when the therapist went on his first vacation since the beginning of therapy. Prior to the vacation, Kenny drew a picture of an airport scene.

Figure 15-8 (March 10): This picture is done completely in blue with the exception of headlights and taillights of the truck which are in red. In this picture he portrays clearly the airplane leaving, the control tower with its communication antennae, and the truck which is carrying airmail to the airmail post office. After the drawing was completed Kenny and the therapist discussed his uneasiness about being left. The therapist told him that the picture seemed to indicate that he would like to talk to the therapist and would like it if the therapist felt like talking to him too while he was on vacation. His response to this was: "Well, a guy gets used to coming here, you know." We related some of his present feelings to those he must have felt when he had to separate from his father as well as the constant fear of separation he had when thinking about his mother. On the therapist's return Kenny immediately produced another picture for him.

Figure 15-9 (March 18): Here Kenny quite consciously and directly announced that he was showing the therapist some of the feelings that he had had while the therapist was away. Again there was a chaotic kind of interaction in the picture. This time, however, each spaceship contained only one representation of the human figure, and in the picture were included some more earthlike shapes such as the twin-bladed helicopter at the upper center. The picture was drawn in somewhat muted shades of red, yellow, and brown.

Figure 15-8

The associations to this picture started a relatively prolonged discussion about the fears and sadness that
Kenny experienced in separation both with the therapist and with his mother and father. More importantly his techniques for trying to allay and alleviate
these fears came into direct focus. His associations fre-

Figure 15-9

quently took him to his "bowel block" and we were able to see that whenever mother was preoccupied with his bowel functions, she was forced to pay a great deal of attention to him. Another aspect of this came into clear relief when Kenny announced that he felt like a helpless little baby when mother gave him an enema.

He then pretended to cry in a high falsetto voice. When I commented that he was crying like a girl baby, he said that he knew that he had sometimes thought that it would be better to be a girl because men fight so much with women. There were no more drawings until mid-May when Kenny produced a drawing of a scene which he saw every time he visited the clinic.

Figure 15-10 (May 15): Kenny spontaneously began to comment about this picture as he was drawing it. He labeled the structure in the foreground the Prudential Building and the structure in the background the building that has the rotating light on it (the Palmolive Peet Building). He stated that he passed these buildings each time his mother drove him to the clinic. He then said that as the beacon rotated, it lighted up the antenna atop the Prudential Building. He drew in the observation tower with great care and then blacked in part of the windows. After some thought, he blacked in other windows that kept their shades drawn all the time and no one could ever look in. He then added the street lights and the stoplight which was on "full green." After a few moments of thought, he added red signs along the street level. He told the therapist that the street light was full green, but that there was a hill in front of the Prudential Building and that unless the red signs warned the traveler to slow down, they might get out of control. Many issues were discussed about this drawing. Some were those having to do with active communication rather than being a passive reflector, others had to do with feelings that certain secrets must be contained and never revealed, and still other issues had to do with the residual caution about letting himself slip into a relationship over which he had no control.

This was the last time that Kenny drew in his treatment. There was no consciously articulated decision that he would draw no more, but many times in the

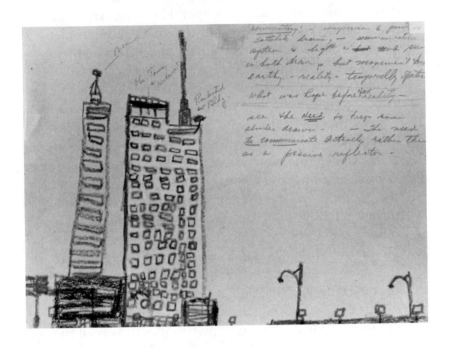

Figure 15-10

following hours, in attempting to describe affects or conflicts, the boy would simply refer back to pictures he had drawn as examples. The inhibition to express affects disappeared. Finally, as he developed increased capacity to describe inner feelings, even references to the drawing ceased to be necessary. On several occasions I discussed with him the steps he had taken in developing the capacity to put mental content into words. We tested out and became convinced that he was now capable of saying what he had previously only vaguely felt. It was evident that drawing had served its purpose and Ken could now use words. The therapist and he were separate but not isolated from each other and his words united them, and made it possible for the therapist to come to know Kenny. Kenny had broken the barrier of nonrelatedness and he could use his ability to relate to help organize his world and reduce his conflicts.

CHAPTER 16

The Child in the Multiple Problem Family: One Approach to Treatment

There is a problem in the practice of child psychotherapy which may be eroding some successful teaching and learning in the field. This is the problem that comes with the child who lives in an environment that is heir to so many problems that it cannot shield the child from them. Often, people in an environment such as this have had to develop a coping orientation that favors motor activity rather than verbal or conceptual modes of adaptation. The child frequently comes to the therapeutic situation with a mental set that values "doing" rather than exploring or conceiving. One of the most insidious aspects of this situation is that many of these families, unable to afford private care, will gravitate toward institutions that train young child therapists, and since these families are not ones that attract the attention of the most experienced therapists, they are assigned to those with the least experience.

When supervising or hearing of a young, dynamically trained therapist attempting to conduct treatment under these conditions, I cannot help but recall the old aphorism, "When all you have is a hammer, every problem begins to look like a nail." The therapist attempts to interact with the child verbally, or attempts to conceptualize the significance of some play with him, while the child reacts as if the therapist were communicating in some foreign tongue. Rarely is an adequate adaptation between the two possible and the treatment evolves toward endless, nonresolving play or toward sitting silently. If the child and therapist play, some benefits may result from the child's pleasure in the relationship, but there is little that is learned about conflict resolution or few insights that the child achieves. When it becomes an arid, silent series of meetings, the inevitable end of the relationship is covertly greeted with relief by both patient and therapist. At this point, however, there are a number of ill-effects that have resulted from the encounter, and that occur in such a subtle way that they are overlooked and therefore cannot be undone.

First and most important, the child did not receive the care that he needed, and in many instances no alternative plan was offered or requested. Second, the child and family lose whatever hope they had that any kind of psychological intervention could be of use to them. Finally, and from the point of view of the educational process, most insidiously, the young therapist in training begins to lose confidence in the therapeutic process and its discipline. A resultant attitude in the trainee that "you win some and you lose some," and implicitly that it makes little difference what you do in the course of a child's treatment, makes it more difficult for him to invest in and learn elegant principles of psychotherapy.

We developed an attempt to solve this problem in our clinic with a good degree of reward and success. It may be possible to adapt this approach to a private practice situation in some localities. In our clinic it consisted of designating a group of people who would meet for the purpose of reviewing cases of children who found themselves in situations in which there were multiple problems that would interfere with, or render psychotherapy impossible.*

*The members of the group were Mr. Larry Casorso, Denver Department of Social Services; Barkley Clark, M.D., Consultant, Denver Public Schools; John Dicke, Esq., Attorney-at-Law; Phil Madonna, M.S.W., Director of Child Social Work, Division of Child Psychiatry, University of Colorado; N. Nelson, M.D., Department of Pediatrics, University of Colorado; and W. Nicholson, M.S., Director of Psychological Services, Denver Juvenile Court. Each member of the group served with the support of their agency or as a volunteer.

As the group began to meet on a weekly basis, the mode in which it would operate began to evolve. It was decided that cases would be brought to the group from three sources. Each member could bring a case from his own practice to be discussed. Each agency that was represented by a member in the group could request through their member a consultation on one of their cases, and the child fellow or resident physician serving in the Division of Child Psychiatry could bring a situation to the group for consultation. The group would discuss the situation for as long as it took to provide a solution or group of solutions that the agency or the person responsible for the family could try to implement. Feedback to the group was encouraged in order to report if the measures were successful, or if they were not, what the therapist thought had derailed the effort. In the latter case corrective measures or new solutions would be proposed.

The single philosophical principle, which the group bore in mind, was that although the child had psychological problems which could not be ignored, psychotherapy alone was not the treatment of choice at the time we were reviewing the case. The child and family needed other forms of support and intervention to make psychotherapy possible, or to resolve problems that had a higher priority than the psychological difficulties.

As procedures were evolved and specific families and their problems discussed, it became clear that another valuable process was taking place. The group began to be aware of how their particular frames of reference influenced their communications and perceptions. Our attorney, for example, demonstrated to us how the action of a court, a guardian *ad litem*, or an attorney representing a family was mandated by law or the canon of ethics of his profession, and was not intended to interfere with our operation. Thus, a cooperative rather than an adversarial attitude could be assumed by our group. On one occasion when the rest of the group was committed to saving a psychologically disturbed sixteen-year-old from the clutches of the law, he persuaded us that a conviction in juvenile court, which could later be expunged from the boy's record, would render the boy eligible for services he could not otherwise obtain.

The welfare representatives were able to show us the extent and limitations of their available resources, and how our involvement and various ways of cooperating would increase their scope and effectiveness. In a word, the members of the team began to develop a therapeutic dialogue so that words and concepts meant the same thing to each of us. We were often able to synthesize goals and objectives in this manner, time was saved, and above all the creativity that went into solutions offered the family or agent responsible for the family was clearly increased.

A palpable benefit to educating the young therapist could be observed when a therapist-in-training brought a case to the group to be discussed. Often the case was presented tentatively, and sometimes defensively. Sometimes the presenter would communicate despair, and the notion that psychotherapy as a treatment modality was worthless. At other times it would seem that the therapist was communicating that he himself felt inept and worthless as a therapist. In either case the sincere acknowledgment by experienced members of the group that psychotherapy under the conditions being described was indeed impossible, not only for the young trainee, but for anyone else as well, almost invariably produced relief for the trainee, and renewed his interest in implementing measures to achieve more realistic goals. Expectations of that which psychotherapy could achieve were removed from the realm of magic, and the therapist was invited rather than driven to become interested in alternatives to psychotherapy. Frequently, the psychotherapists were drawn to one member of the team or the other as collaborators in the treatment of the family or patient and a new learning unit was spontaneously formed.

The Team's attorney (Mr. J.D.) requested that we review the situation of Sean, a fourteen-year-old boy, whom he had been asked to represent by the juvenile court. Sean had been accused of breaking into a federal building, stealing from it a number of hand guns and rifles and setting a fire in one of the rooms of the building. There was some evidence that he had also set fire to an apartment building near the federal building, although the evidence was not enough to warrant a formal charge. In the course of committing the acts at the federal building, Sean had left a trail and a series of clues that would inevitably lead any competent investigator to him.

The attorney had been able to have Sean freed on bail and placed in the custody of his family. In his capacity as Sean's lawyer he had interviewed Sean and his family several times in the office. It was after these interviews that he requested that our committee review the case and hear his concerns.

He first became uneasy when, in interviewing Sean's family, he noticed a blandness, and lack of concern that suggested that they had no appreciation of the severity of the accusations or the ominous significance of Sean's acts. He was also dismayed to learn that Sean was frequently left in the care of a brother only three or four years older than he for weeks and sometimes months at a time. This was because Sean's stepfather was a migrant farm worker, and when harvest or planting time came, Sean's mother would accompany her husband for however long his work took him afield.

In the course of learning about his young client's past, Mr. D. discovered that Sean's natural father had been sent to prison when Sean was about five years of age, and the mother had divorced him shortly after his conviction. Mr. D. felt that since the federal building that Sean had violated was a section of the Bureau of Prisons, there were more specific determinants in his behavior than simply delinquent tendencies.

Finally, Mr. D. described great frustration in his efforts to make meaningful contact with the boy intellectually or emotionally. He said that despite all of

his efforts to convince Sean of the seriousness of the
situation, and of his wish to be of help to him, he
remained unmoved, aloof and unresponsive. In fact,
after one of his interviews Sean left his office and sat
in the anteroom to wait until his parents came to take
him back home. When Mr. D. sought to dictate notes
on his interview with Sean, he found that the tape
recorder that he used had disappeared from his desk.
Since it had been on his desk only moments before,
he went to the waiting room and asked Sean and his
secretary if they had seen it. Sean, in a truculent and
agitated manner, jumped up and left the room saying
that his parents were probably waiting for him down-
stairs. After he left, the instrument was plainly in sight
between the seat cushion and the back of the chair he
had occupied. After a discussion of these issues and
other self-destructive and self-demeaning acts that
Sean had committed, the committee concurred with
Mr. D. that Sean was in immediate need of psychiatric
care whether he was found guilty or innocent. Several
of the clinicians at the staff meeting offered their
opinion that Sean was not only dangerous to others,
he was also potentially suicidal. With the court's approval we were able to arrange an evaluation for Sean
in our clinic even as he was being prepared for trial.
The evaluation found a thinly disguised depression in
an impulse ridden boy who had never adequately
grieved the loss of his natural father, and who had
suffered massive neglect for most of his life.

At the trial Mr. D. was able to obtain probation
for Sean on the condition that he be treated psychiatr-
ically. Sean spent several months on an inpatient unit,
and was then released with the understanding that he
would continue treatment as an outpatient. Against
the advice of his doctor and his lawyer, Sean's parents
decided to move with him to a nearby state where there
was work to be found. They resisted our efforts to find

a residential placement for him that would permit him to continue his treatment. Shortly after his move Sean attempted suicide.

Once more Mr. D. was consulted by the family, and once more the group addressed the problem. The representatives from the department of welfare and the juvenile court system found Sean a residential placement where he could receive both psychotherapy and adequate supervision. Mr. D. took the steps necessary to see that Sean's psychological well-being was not jeopardized by the instability and neediness of his family, while child psychiatry clinic staff provided the care and support necessary for Sean to make the transition to the treatment placement. After some months we received a report that Sean had improved, and was continuing to make use of his placement. We felt that we had been able to address Sean's multiple problems more efficiently and thoroughly because of the coordinating efforts of the group.

In our weekly efforts the team achieved some surprising insights. One of the first was to become aware of how profoundly disillusioned even seasoned professionals could become around a particular situation. This came most clearly to the fore when on a number of occasions a case was presented by a fellow or resident, and recognition of the case began to be registered on the faces of representatives of several agencies or disciplines around the table. The public school representative might say that they had discussed the child a few months before, had known about him for years, and that every effort to provide him with the education he needed had failed. The person from welfare told of the number of plans that his agency had made to help this family manage their children and their resources, while the person from juvenile justice said his agency had dealt with older children in the family. As the situation was discussed, everyone acknowledged that they or their agency had reached the place where they were only going through the motions of suggesting interventions because they felt that the family was refractory to every suggested improvement. By reviewing this situation openly, some optimism was revived, both because each member of the team was reluctant to burden other members with their own pessimism and because they experienced renewed optimism in the new alliances. When some gains were made, it fortified the group's conviction that concerted efforts were effective where individual efforts failed. If no gains were made, the group found value in reviewing the failure constructively rather than only experiencing frustration.

We were also a bit surprised by another awareness forced on us. So many times, in child care clinics we orchestrate a litany of complaints about the shortage of services in the welfare department, the rigidities of the juvenile justice system, and the lack of an individualized program in the public schools. To be sure, our team ran into problems such as these. But if there was a consistent impediment to working with deeply disorganized families, it was not among these deficits. What stood in the way most often was the resistance of therapists to bringing their cases to the multiple problem team. We perceived reluctance not only among the primary therapists, but also occasions of nonsupport or interference from supervisors and administrative personnel in the clinic. Sometimes we could detect among the therapists an understandable discomfort at the thought of exposing their feelings of failure or frustration that so frequently characterizes work with these families. But what was less understandable was that some therapists were reluctant because they thought it meant more work for them, and they could not see that it would help them become better psychiatrists.

It would be a distortion to say that the multiple problem clinic did not have its own problems that required more thought and work to solve. The preparation of cases in a way that will allow the greatest number of people to participate in creating helpful solutions has yet to be worked out. It is an expensive proposition to have eight or ten persons locked into an activity for an hour and a half or two every week. In our effort each individual and agency contributed the time without charge. Funding for a long-range project has not been developed.

Probably the most difficult problem we tackled was the ethical and legal problem of revealing to a group, confidential information about a family. Of course the family can sign a release of information, but that does not always resolve the issue. If, for example, in the course of a case presentation something was revealed that jeopardized services that the family was receiving from social services, the representative from welfare was put into the very difficult position of a conflict of interest between his agency and the family. Our attorney, as an officer of the juvenile court, could be torn in several directions in a number of situations. On one occasion he had to disqualify himself from discussion about a case because he was representing the parent of a child we were discussing in a legal action involving the department of welfare. Despite these problems it was the consensus of the members of the multiple problem team and the clinicians that utilized it that this component of the outpatient clinic made it possible to treat some children who would have otherwise been untreatable. It is for this reason that an effort in this direction deserves the time and attention required to solve the problems inherent in it, and refine its operation.

All in child care share something with our colleagues in the state hospital system and forensic psychiatry. Through no merit of our own, we have brought psychological services to segments of the population who might have never come into contact with it if the model of care delivery had remained limited to that of ambulatory care provided to those who came to seek it. Via the schools, welfare agencies, the juvenile justice system, and other child care agencies, children have been introduced to us who would have otherwise remained outside of our ken and care. While at times this has posed problems that taxed our imaginations, it has also provided us with opportunities to work toward a goal that should remain an eternal ideal for every society: The goal of assuring every child born that the society surrounding them has committed itself to doing all it can not only to keep them as free as possible from pain and threat, but also to guard for every child, his inviolable right to a sense of well-being, happiness, and dignity.

References

Achenbach, T. (1974). *Developmental Psychopathology.* New York: Ronald Press.

Adams, P. L. (1982), *A Primer of Child Psychotherapy,* 2nd ed. Boston: Little, Brown.

Aichorn, A. (1935), *Wayward Youth.* New York: Viking Press.

Aiken, C., (1947), Silent Snow, Secret Snow. In: *Great Tales of Terror and the Supernatural,* ed. H. Wise & P. Fraser. New York: *The Modern Library,* pp. 136–154.

"The Amazing Newborn." Film produced by the Dept. of Pediatrics Case Western Reserve. Distributed by Ross Laboratories.

American Psychiatric Association (1980), *Diagnostic and Statistical Manual III.* Washington, DC: The American Psychiatric Association.

Ashburner, J. V. (1968), Some problems of classification with particular reference to child psychiatry. *Austral. & New Zeal. J. Psychiat.,* 2:244-250.

Balestrini, R. (1888), *Aborto, Infanticidio ed Esposizione d'infante.* Torino: Bocca.

Beiser, H. (1979), Formal games in diagnosis and therapy. *J. Amer. Acad. Child Psychiat.,* 18:3–480.

Bellaman, H. (1940), *King's Row.* New York: Carrol and Graf, 1983.

Benedek, T. (1938), Adpatation to reality in early infancy. *Psychoanal. Quart.,* 7:200–215.

———— (1952), *Psychosexual Functions in Women.* New York: Ronald Press.

———— (1956a), Psychobiological aspects of mothering. *Amer. J. Orthopsychiat.,* 26:272–278.

—— (1956b), Toward the biology of the depressive constellation. *J. Amer. Psychoanal. Assn.*, 4:389–427.

—— (1959), Parenthood as a developmental phase. A contribution to libido theory. *J. Amer. Psycho-Anal. Assn.*, 7:389–417.

Berger, P. (1969), *A Rumor of Angels*. Garden City, NY: Doubleday.

Berman, E. (1973), *Scapegoat: The Impact of Death/Fear on an American Family*. Ann Arbor, MI: University of Michigan Press.

Bettelheim, B. (1948), Closed institutions for children? *Bull. Menn. Clin.*, 12:135–142.

—— (1950), *Love Is Not Enough. The Treatment of Emotionally Disturbed Children*. Glencoe, IL: Free Press.

—— (1955), *Truants From Life*. Glencoe, IL: Free Press.

—— (1967), *The Empty Fortress*. New York: Free Press.

—— (1974), *A Home For the Heart*. New York: Alfred A. Knopf.

—— Sanders, J. (1979), Milieu therapy: The orthogenic school model. In: *Basic Handbook of Child Psychiatry*, ed. J. Noshpitz. New York: Basic Books.

—— Sylvester, E. (1949), Milieu therapy: Indications and illustrations. *Psychoanal. Rev.*, 36:54–68.

Bibring, E. (1937), The theory of the therapeutic results of psychoanalysis. *Internat. J. Psycho-Anal.*, 18:170–189.

Brazelton, T. B. (1962), Observations of the neonate. *J. Amer. Acad. Child Psychiat.*, 1:38–58.

Caffey, J. (1946), Multiple fractures in the long bones of infants suffering from chronic subdural hematomas. *Amer. J. Roentgenol.*, 56:163–173.

Cain, A. & Cain, B. (1964), On replacing a child. *J. Amer. Acad. Child Psychiatr.*, 3:443–456.

Carek, D. (1979), Individual psychodynamically oriented therapy. In: *Basic Handbook of Child Psychiatry*, Vol. III, ed., J. Noshpitz & S. Harrison. New York: Basic Books.

Castaneda, C. (1972), *Journey to Ixtlan*. New York: Simon & Schuster.

Cath, H. S., Gurwitt, A. R., & Ross, J. M., Eds. (1982), *Father and Child: Developmental and Clinical Perspectives*. Boston: Little Brown.

Comte, A. (1966), *Introduction To Positive Philosophy*. Indianapolis, Bobbs-Merrill Co., Inc.

Conrad, Joseph (1914), *The Nigger of the Narcissus*, Preface. Garden City, NY: Doubleday & Company.

Coppolillo, H. (1965a), Conversion, hypochondriasis and somatization. *J. Arkansas Med. Soc.*, 62:67–71.

—— (1965b), The questioning and doubting parent. *J. Pedia.*, 67:371–380.

—— (1967), Maturational aspects of the transitional phenomena. *Internat. J. Psycho-Anal.*, 48:237–246.

—— (1969), A technical consideration in child analysis and child therapy. *J. Amer. Acad. Child Psychiat.*, 8:411–435.

—— (1975), Drug impediments to mothering behavior: *Addictive Diseases. An Internat. J.*, 2:201–208.

—— (1976), The transitional phenomenon revisited. *J. Amer. Acad. Child Psychiat.*, 15:36–48.

—— (1978), A conceptual model for the study of some abusing parents. In: *The Child in his Family*, ed. E. J. Anthony & C. Koupernik, New York: John Wiley, pp. 231–238.

Cushing, H. (1925), *The Life of Sir William Osler*. Oxford, England: Clarendon Press.

De Casper, A. J., & Fifer, M. (1980), Of human bonding. Newborns prefer their mother's voices. *Science*, 208:1174–1176.

Eissler, K. (1953), The effect of the structure of the ego on psychoanalytic technique. *J. Amer. Psychoanal. Assn.*, 1:104–143.

Encyclopedia Brittanica (1974), 15th ed. Vol. 16. Chicago: Encyclopedia Brittanica, pp. 789–790.

Erickson, E. (1963), *Childhood and Society*, rev. ed. New York: W. W. Norton.

—— (1964), *Childhood and Society*, 2nd rev. ed. New York: W. W. Norton & Co.

Fraiberg, S. (1959), *The Magic Years*. New York: Scribner.

—— (1965), A comparison of the analytic method in two stages of a child analysis. *J. of Amer. Acad. Child Psychiat.*, 4:387–400.

Freud, A. (1946a), *The Ego and the Mechanisms of Defense*. New York, International Universities Press.

—— (1946b), *The Psycho-Analytical Treatment of Children*. London: Imago.

—— (1970), Problems of termination in child analysis. In: *The Writings of Anna Freud*, Vol. 7. New York: International Universities Press, pp. 3–21.

Freud, S. (1900), The Interpretation of Dreams. *Standard Edition*, 4 & 5. London: Hogarth Press, 1958.

—— (1901), The Psychopathology of Everyday Life. *Standard Edition*, 6, London: Hogarth Press, 1958.

—— (1905), Jokes and Their Relation to the Unconscious, *Standard Edition*, 8. London: Hogarth Press, 1958.

—— (1909), Analysis of a phobia in a five-year-old boy. *Standard Edition*, 10:3–149. London: Hogarth Press, 1958.

—— (1911), Psycho-analytic notes on an autobiographical account of a case of paranoia. *Standard Edition*, 12:3–80. London: Hogarth Press, 1958.

—— (1912), The Dynamics of Transference. *Standard Edition*, 12. London: Hogarth Press, 1958.

—— (1914), Remembering, repeating and working through (Further recommendations on the technique of psycho-analysis). *Standard Edition*, 12:155–156. London: Hogarth Press.

—— (1915), The Unconscious. *Standard Edition*, 14. London: Hogarth Press, 1958.

—— (1917), A Metapsychological Supplement to the Theory of Dreams. *Standard Edition*, 14. London: Hogarth Press, 1958.

—— (1919), Lines of advance in psycho-analytic therapy. *Standard Edition*, 17:157–168. London: Hogarth Press.

—— (1924), Neurosis and psychosis. *Standard Edition*, 19:147–153. London: Hogarth Press.

Galdston, R. (1965), Observations on children who have been physically abused and their parents. *Amer. J. Psychiat.*, 122:440–443.

Gill, D. G. (1970), *Violence Against Children*. Cambridge, MA: Harvard University Press.

Glover, E. (1955), *The Technique of Psychoanalysis*. New York: International Universities Press.

Goodenough, F. L. (1926), *Measure of Intelligence in Drawing*. New York: World Book Company.

Graduate Medical Education National Advisory Committee to the Secretary of Health and Human Services, Summary Report of the, Vol. 1, September 30, 1980. U.S. Dept. of Health & Human Services DHHS Pub # (HRA) 81-651, Public Health Service Health Resources Admin.

Greenson, R. (1956), *The Technique and Practice of Psychoanalysis*, Vol. 1. New York: International Universities Press.

Greenspan, S. (1981), *The Clinical Interview of the Child*. New York: McGraw-Hill.

Group for Advancement of Psychiatry Committee on Child Psychiatry (1966), *Psychopathological Disorders in Childhood: Theoretical Considerations and a Proposed Classification*, Vol. 6, Report 62. New York: Group for the Advancement of Psychiatry.

Harlow, H. F., & Harlow, N. K. (1965), The affectional systems in the behavior of non-human primates. In: *Behavior of Nonhuman Primates: Modern Research Trends*, Vol. 2, ed. A. M. Schrier, H. F. Harlow, & F. Stollnitz. New York: Academic Press.

Harrison, S., MacDermott, J., & Chetnik, M. (1969), Residential treatment of children: The psychotherapist administrator. *J. Amer. Acad. Child Psychiat.*, 8:385–410.

Hartmann, H. (1939), *Ego Psychology and the Problem of Adaptation*. New York: International Universities Press, 1958.

—— Kris, E., & Loewenstein, R. M. (1946), Comments on the formation of psychic structure. *The Psychoanalytic Study of the Child*, 2:11–38. New York: International Universities Press.

Hobbs, N. (1975), *The Futures of Children*. San Francisco, Jossey-Bass Company.

Horton, P. C., & Coppolillo, H. P. (1972), Unconscious causality and the pyramid of science. *Arch. Gen. Psychiat.*, 26:512–517.

Inhelder, B., & Piaget, J. (1958), *The Growth of Logical Thinking from Childhood to Adolescence*. New York: Basic Books.

Josselyn, I. (1956), Cultural forces, motherliness and fatherliness. *Amer. J. Orthopsychiat.*, 26:264–271.

Kafka, F. (1946), *Metamorphosis*. New York: Schocken Books.

Kaplan, A. (1968), *Positivism: The International Encyclopedia of the Social Sciences*, Vol. 12. New York: Macmillan Co., pp. 389–395.

Katz, P. (1981), Psychotherapy with native adolescents. *Canad. J. Psychiat.*, 26:455–459.

———— Carrathers, H., & Forrest, T. (1979), Adolescent Salteaux-Ojibway girls: The adolescent process amidst a clash of cultures. In: *Female Adolescent Development*, ed. M. Sugor. New York: Brunner/Mazel.

Kaufman, I. Ed. (1962), Psychological implications of physical abuse of children. In: *Protecting the Battered Child*, Denver, CO: Children's Division, American Humane Association.

Kempe, C. H., Silverman, F. N., Steele, B. F., Droegemueller, W., & Silver, H. K. (1962), The battered child syndrome. *J. Amer. Med. Assn.*, 181:17–24.

Klaus, H., & Kennel, J. H. (1970), Mothers separated from their newborn infants. *Ped. Clinic Amer.*, 17:1015–1039.

Klein, M. (1932), *Psychoanalysis of the Child*. London: Hogarth Press and The Institute of Psycho-Analysis.

Kohut, H. (1966), Forms and transformations of narcissism. *J. Amer. Psychoanal. Assn.*, 14:2, 243–272.

Kris, E. (1956), On some vicissitudes of insight in psychoanalysis. *Internat. J. Psycho-Anal.*, 37:445–455.

Laing, R. D. (1965), *The Divided Self*. Baltimore: Penguin Books.

Lidz, T. (1968), *The Person*. New York: Basic Books.

———— (1976), *The Person*, rev. 2nd ed. New York: Basic Books.

Liebenberg, B. (1967), Expectant fathers. *Amer. J. Orthopsychiat.*, 37:358–359.

Lynn, D. B. (1974), *The Father: His Role in Child Development*. Monterey, CA: Brooks/Cole Publishers.

Macfarlane, A. (1975), Olfaction in the development of social preferences in the human neonate. In: *Parent-Infant Interaction. A Ciba Foundation Symposium*, 33 (new series). New York: Elsevier.

Mahler, M., Pine, F., & Bergman, A. (1975), *The Psychological Birth of the Human Infant*. New York: Basic Books.

May, J. G. (1979), Nosology and diagnosis. In: *The Basic Handbook of Child Psychiatry*, Vol. II, ed. J. Noshpitz. New York: Basic Books.

Mayer, A. (1983), *Incest*. Holmes Beach, FL: Learning Publications.

Micropedia. Perspective, *Encyclopedia Brittanica* (0000), Vol. vii, 15th ed. Chicago: Encyclopedia Brittanica Inc., pp. 893–894.

Miller, G. A., Galanter, E., & Pribram, K. (1960), *Plans and the Structure of Behaviors*. New York: Holt.

Morris, M., & Gould, R. W. (1963), Role reversal: A concept in dealing with the neglected/battered child syndrome. In: *The Neglected Battered-Child Syndrome*, R. Helfer & C. H. Kempe ed. New York: Child Welfare League of America.

Newman, C. J., & Schwam, J. S. (1979), The fatherless child. In: *Basic Handbook of Child Psychiatry*, Vol. 1, ed. J. Noshpitz. New York: Basic Books, pp. 357–372.

Nin, A. (1966), *The Diary of Anaïs Nin*, Vol. 1, 1931-1934. New York: Swallow Press & Harcourt Brace & World.

Noshpitz, J. (1979), *The Basic Handbook of Child Psychiatry*. New York: Basic Books.

———— (1984), Milieu therapy. In: *The Psychiatric Therapies*, T. B. Karasa, Chair. Washington, DC: American Psychiatric Association on Psychiatric Therapies.

Novick, J. (1982), Termination: Themes and issues. *Psychoanal. Inquiry*, 2:239–366.

———— Benson, R., & Rembar, J. (1981), Patterns of termination in an outpatient clinic for children and adolescents. *J. Amer. Acad. Child Psychiat.*, 20:834–844.

Prosen, H., Toews, J. & Martin, R. (1981), The life cycle of the family: Parental midlife crisis and adolescent rebellion. *Adoles. Psychiat.*, 10:170–179.

Prugh, D. G. (1973), Psychosocial disorders in children and adolescents: Theoretical considerations and an attempt at classification. In: *Joint Commission on Mental Health of Children, The Mental Health of Children: Services, Research and Manpower*. Report of Task Forces IV and V. New York: Harper & Row.

———— (1983), *The Psychosocial Aspects of Pediatrics*. Philadelphia: Lea & Febiger.

Rapaport, D. (1951), The autonomy of the ego. *Bull. Menn. Clinic*, 15:113–123.

———— (1958), The theory of ego autonomy. *Bull. Menn. Clinic*, 22:13–35.

Rausch, H., Barry, W., Hestel, R., & Swain, H. (1974), *Communication, Conflict and Marriage*. San Francisco: Jossey-Bass.

Redl, F. (1959), A strategy and technique of the life space interview. *Amer. J. Orthopsychiat.*, 29:1–18.

Rinsley, D. B. (1968), Theory and practice of intensive residential treatment of adolescents. *Psychiat. Quart.*, 92:611–638.

Ross, A. O. & Lacey, H. M. (1961), Characteristics of terminators and remainders in child guidance treatment. *J. Consult. Psychol.*, 25:420–424.

Rosen, V. (1969), Sign phenomena: An unconscious meaning. *Internat. J. Psycho-Anal.*, 50:197–207.

Sander, L. (1980), Investigation of the infant and its caregiving environment as a biological system. In: *The Course of Life*, Vol. 1, ed. S. Greenspan & G. Pollock. Washington, DC: U.S. Department of Health and Human Services.

———— (1983), Polarity, paradox and the organizing process in development. In: *Frontiers of Infant Psychiatry*, ed. J. Call, E. Galenson, & R. Tyson. New York: Basic Books.

Sandler, J., Kennedy, H., & Tyson, R. (1980), *The Technique of Child Psychoanalysis*. Cambridge, MA: Harvard University Press.

Santayana, G. (1905), *The Life of Reason. Vol. I Reason and Common Sense*. New York: Charles Scribner's Sons, 1954.

Silver, A. A. (1950), Diagnostic value of three drawing tests for children. *J. Pediat.*, 37:129–143.

Simmons, J. E. (1981), *Psychiatric Examination of Children*, 3rd ed. Philadelphia: Lea & Febiger.

Sorce, J., Emde, R., Campos, J., & Klinnert, M. (1985), Maternal emotional signalling: Its effect on the visual behavior of one year olds. *Development. Psychol.* 21:195–200.

Spence, M., & De Casper, A. J. (1982), Human foetuses perceive maternal speech. Paper presented to the International Conference on Infant Studies, Austin, Texas.

Sperling, E. (1979), The fate of the ego in analytic therapy. In: *Basic Handbook of Child Psychiatry*, Vol. III, ed. J. Noshpitz & S. Harrison. New York: Basic Books.

Spitz, R. (1945), Hospitalism. An inquiry into the genesis of psychiatric conditions in early childhood. *The Psychoanalytic Study of the Child*, 1:53-74. New York: International Universities Press.

———— (1957), *No and Yes, On the Genesis of Human Communication*. New York: International Universities Press.

———— (1959), *A Genetic Field Theory of Ego Formation*. New York: International Universities Press.

———— (1964), The derailment of dialogue: Stimulus overload, action cycles, and completion gradient. *J. Amer. Psychoanal. Assn.*, 12: 752–775.

Spoerri, T. H. (1966), Speaking voice of the schizophrenic patient. *Arch. Gen. Psychiat.*, 14:581–585.

Steele, B., & Pollock, C. (1968), Psychiatric study of abusing parents. In: *The Battered Child*, ed. R. Helfer, & C. H. Kempe, Chicago: University of Chicago Press.

Steinberg, J. & Simons, R. (1985), The role of psychological factors in the development and treatment of medical illness. In: *Understanding Human Behavior in Health and Illness*, 3rd ed., ed. R. Simons. Baltimore: Williams & Wilkins.

Sterba, R. (1934), The fate of the ego in analytic therapy. *Internat. J. Psycho-Anal.*, 15:117–126.

Stoller, R. (1975), *Sex and Gender*. New York: Jason Aronson.

Szurek, S. A., Berlin, I. N. & Boarman, M. J., Eds. (1971), Inpatient care for the psychotic child. In: *The Langley Porter Child Psychiatry Series*, Vol. 5. Palo Alto, CA: Science and Behavior Books.

Tardieu, A. (1868), *Étude Médico-Légale sur L'enfanticide*. Paris: J. B. Gailliere et Fils.

Thayer, W. S. (1919), Osler the teacher. *Johns Hopkins Hosp. Bull.*, 30:198–200.

Tuckman, J., & Lavel, M. (1959), Attrition in psychiatric clinics for children. *Pub. Health Rep.*, 74:309–315.

Wallace, E. (1983), *Dynamic Psychiatry in Theory and Practice*. Philadelphia: Lea & Febiger.

✓ Winnicott, D. W. (1949), Hate in the countertransference. *Internat. J. Psycho-Anal.*, 30:69–74.

—————— (1953), Transitional objects and transitional phenomena. *Internat. J. Psycho-Anal.*, 34:89–97.

—————— (1965), *The Maturational Process and the Facilitating Environment*. New York: International Universities Press.

—————— (1971), *Therapeutic Consultations in Child Psychiatry*. New York: Basic Books.

Zetzel, E. (1956), Current Concepts of Transference. *Internat. J. Psycho-Anal.*, 37:369–375.

NAME INDEX

SUBJECT INDEX